# PETRA
## AN UNBROKEN LEGACY

## LISA L. DORSEY

©2024 by Lisa Dorsey

Published by hope*books
2217 Matthews Township Pkwy
Suite D302
Matthews, NC 28105
www.hopebooks.com

hope*books is a division of hope*media

Printed in the United States of America

All rights reserved. Without limiting the rights under copyrights reserved above, no part of this publication may be scanned, uploaded, reproduced, distributed, or transmitted in any form or by any means whatsoever without express prior written permission from both the author and publisher of this book—except in the case of brief quotations embodied in critical articles and reviews.

Thank you for supporting the author's rights.

First paperback edition.

Paperback ISBN: 979-8-89185-057-6
Hardcover ISBN: 979-8-89185-058-3
Ebook ISBN: 979-8-89185-059-0
Library of Congress Number: 2024931115

Map designed by hope*books

Petra: An Unbroken Legacy

Lisa Dorsey has written an epic quest along the lines of National Treasure. Modern-day archaeologists dig up Petra's centuries-old secrets, hoping to find a letter from the apostle Paul to the first church in Arabia. This sweeping, dual timeline is full of adventure, danger, romance, and unwavering faith that builds on the unbroken legacy of trust in Jesus the Christ.

*Naomi Craig, Biblical Novelist,*
*Founder of Biblical Fiction Aficionados*

Are you looking to get lost in a terrific story? *Petra: An Unbroken Legacy*, by Lisa L. Dorsey, is a must-read. Prepare to be drawn into a heart-touching narrative filled with adventure and faith. Dorsey's vivid storytelling and rich characters bring to life a powerful message of hope and legacy. It's an awe-inspiring, unforgettable journey. A book you won't be able to put down!

*Krissy Nelson*
*Author, Speaker, Host*
*Krissy Nelson Ministries*

*Petra: An Unbroken Legacy* is a wonderful blend of ancient history and contemporary intrigue. In her debut novel, Lisa Dorsey has crafted a tale that seamlessly weaves the epic journeys of Saul as he encounters first-century Arabic Christians with the thrilling adventures of modern-day archaeologists. As the past and present collide, secrets buried for centuries come to light, offering an enriching tale of faith, discovery, and the enduring power of love.

*Kim Mosiman*
*Author: Reflections of Joy*

Petra is a must-read if you are looking for a thrilling literary experience. From the very first pages, the book immerses you in the story. Petra is akin to a captivating movie with imagery so vivid that you feel like you are right there with Issa, Kasim, and the Apostle Paul. It's rare to read a book that makes you feel like you are on set with the characters. I highly recommend Petra and suggest you prepare for an incredible adventure. It's a real treasure.

*Dr. Gwendolyn Matthews*
*Author, Speaker, Professor of*
*The International Institute For Spiritual Development*

# DEDICATION

To my husband, Charles, for your unwavering support, love, and prayers. For taking this journey with me, listening to me read each chapter to you for months on end. To my children, grandchildren, mom, sister, and family for believing in me and rooting for me from the beginning. And above all, to you, Jesus, for instructing me in the night season, Job 33:14-16. The gift of this novel, I dedicate back to You.

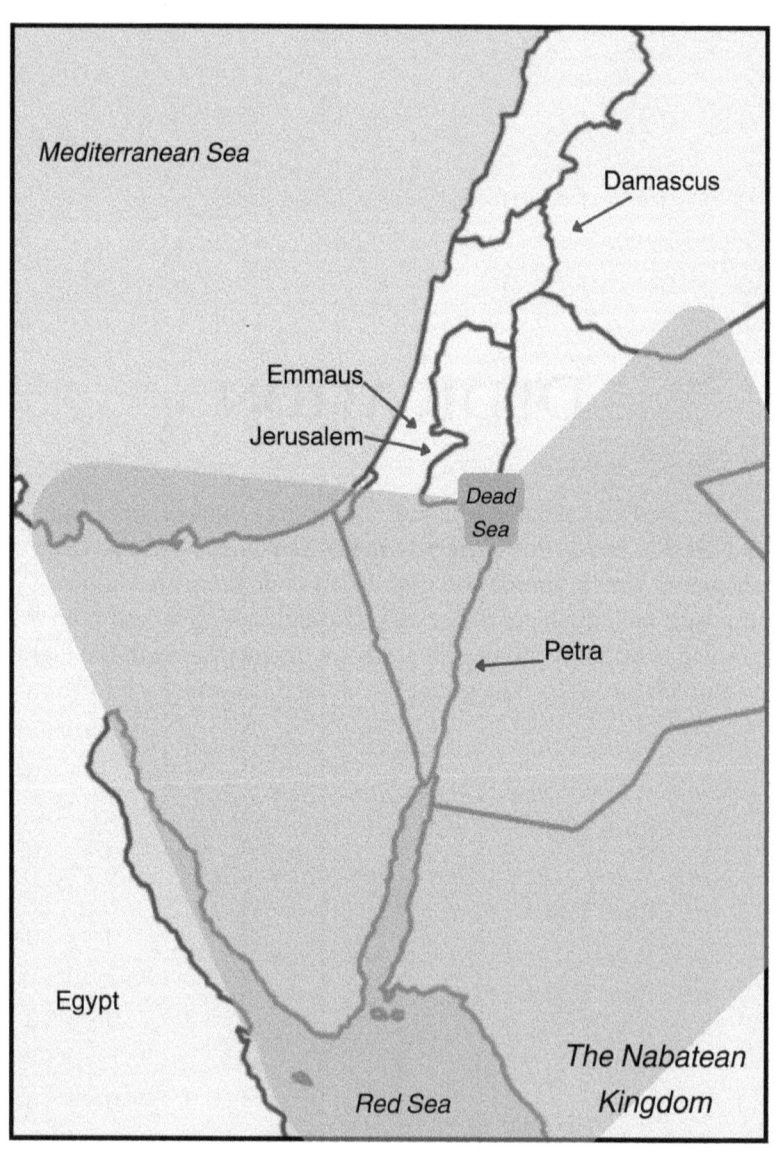

# Prelude

Get ready to dive into the heart of biblical stories. Imagine journeying alongside characters that resonate with your own experiences of love, disappointment, and hope.

With *Petra: An Unbroken Legacy*, you're not just reading a story; you're living it. While inspired by historical events, the narrative is a work of fiction, blending fact with creative storytelling. The narrative intersects with biblical events, providing a fictional yet insightful perspective on known biblical stories.

# CAST OF KEY CHARACTERS

**Abbie** She is the deceased wife of Dr. Kasim Fakmad Ma'an and the mother of Miriam.

**Abdi** He is a first-century Jewish proselyte of Arab descent and a close friend of Salim. He becomes a Christian after being filled with the Holy Spirit on the Day of Pentecost. (A reenactment of Acts 2).

**Akhab** He runs the Ma'an family's global import and export business and is a long-time family friend and a believer in Jesus Christ.

**Ananias** He is the disciple of Jesus who received a vision from the Lord to lay hands on Saul that he may receive his sight, be filled with the Holy Spirit, and be baptized. Acts 9:10-19.

**Anna** She is a first-century Jewish woman, the wife of Simeon, and an Innkeeper in Raqmu (Petra).

**Artemis** He is an official in the court of King Aretas IV.

**Benjamin** He is the son of Rabbi Joseph, who befriended Salim, the grandson of Kasim. He runs an Inn in first-century Jerusalem.

**Caiaphas** He is the High Priest in Jerusalem during the ministry of Jesus. Matthew 26:57-68; 27:1-2.

**Cleopas** He is a disciple of Jesus. He encountered Jesus on the road to Emmaus, after Jesus's resurrection. Luke 24:13-35.

**Dean Wright** He is the Dean of Veritas University in Santa Ana, California where Dr. Issa Stevens works as a professor of Archeology.

**Dr. Avraham** He is the lead archeologist at Tel Dan in Israel. (His character reenacts historical events. Dr. Avraham Biran was the lead archeologist for the 1993 Tel Dan or House of David inscription).

**Dr. Bashar** He is the Ma'an family physician.

**Dr. Dave Stevens** He is the deceased husband of Dr. Issa Stevens.

**Dr. Ibrahim** He is Fatima's father and of Muslim descent. He is like a second father to Dr. Issa Stevens, and later her mentor and colleague.

**Dr. Issa Stevens** She is the female protagonist, a world-renowned archeologist, and a leading authority in her field. She is the widow of Dave and the mother of Sky.

**Dr. Kasim Fakmad Ma'an** He is the male protagonist of the story, a descendant of the Patriarch Kasim of the Ma'an family of the first century.

**Ezra** He is a fellow Pharisee of Saul of Tarsus, who lives in Damascus. (In the biblical account, Saul stayed in the house of one called Judas. Acts 9:11).

**Fakmad Ahkmad Ma'an** He is the Patriarch of the Ma'an family in present-day Ma'an-Petra and the father of Dr. Kasim Fakmad Ma'an.

**Fasar** He is Dr. Kasim Fakmad Ma'an's cousin from his maternal side.

**Fasim** He is Dr. Kasim Fakmad Ma'an's uncle, the brother of his deceased mother.

**Fatima** She is the best friend of Dr. Issa Stevens since childhood. She is Muslim and the daughter of Dr. Ibrahim.

**Jabari** He is a first-century Egyptian merchant and business associate of Kasim.

**Jacob** He is a first-century leader at the Damascus synagogue, and also a believer of the Way (a disciple of Jesus).

**Jesus** He is God, the Word became flesh. He is Yeshua, the Messiah, the Anointed One, Jesus the Christ, the Son of God, the King of Kings and Lord of Lords.

**Joseph** He is a first-century traveling merchant who transports the letters written by Saul to his friends in Arabia.

**King Aretas IV** He is the King of the Nabateans, an Arab people, whose kingdom covers a vast area including South Palestine, most of Jordan, North Arabia, and Damascus from about 9 B.C. to 40 A.D.

**Miriam (Miri)** She is the daughter and only child of Dr. Kasim Fakmad Ma'an.

**Rabbi Joseph** He is a first-century Jewish rabbi of the Capernaum synagogue and a friend of Kasim. He is the father of Benjamin, who owns an Inn where Kasim stays during his merchant trips to Jerusalem.

**Rajah** She is the personal handmaiden to Miriam.

**Rebecca** She was betrothed to Saul of Tarsus but died before their marriage ceremony took place.

**Saba Kasim** He is a first-century Jewish proselyte. The Patriarch of the Ma'an family and the first Arab to convert to the Christian Faith.

**Salek** He is Dr. Kasim Fakmad Ma'an's Bedouin cousin and the head of the Bedouin elite fighters in Petra, Jordan.

**Salim** He is a first-century Jewish proselyte of Arab descent and the grandson of Kasim the Patriarch of the Ma'an family. He was present on the Day of Pentecost and was filled with the Holy Spirit. (A reenactment of Acts 2).

**Sam** He is a counselor at the Summer Archeology camp.

**Samir** He is an emissary at the Jordan consulate.

**Saul (Later called Paul)** He is a first-century Jewish Pharisee from Tarsus who persecuted the early church believers of the Way (believers in Jesus, the Christ, or Christians). He encountered Jesus on the road to Damascus and became an ardent believer and teacher of the Way. Acts 9:1-25; 2 Corinthians 11:32-33; Galatians 1:17.

**Shufa** He is a first-century caravan master who helped escort Saul to Arabia (Raqmu or Petra) near the end of his journey.

**Simeon** He is a first-century Jewish man, the husband of Anna, and an Innkeeper in Raqmu (Petra).

**Sky** She is the college-aged daughter of Dr. Issa and Dave Stevens.

**Sylvia** She is the friend of Dr. Issa Stevens from the Summer Archeology camp.

**Tirsa** She is a distant cousin to Dr. Kasim Fakmad Ma'an on his maternal side.

**Youssef** He is the brother of the Patriarch Kasim of the first century. He is a tentmaker and a friend of Saul of Tarsus.

# TABLE OF CONTENTS

Dedication ................................................................................. v

Prelude ................................................................................... vii

Cast of Key Characters ............................................................ ix

Prologue **New Beginnings** ....................................................... 1

Chapter 1   **Life is About to Change** ...................................... 11

Chapter 2   **The Damascus Experience** ................................. 15

Chapter 3   **Issa & Dave** .......................................................... 23

Chapter 4   **The Past Shapes the Future** ............................... 31

Chapter 5   **Encounters** ........................................................... 35

Chapter 6   **Summer Camp** .................................................... 43

Chapter 7   **Church Without Walls** ........................................ 51

Chapter 8   **Surprise, Surprise** ................................................ 57

Chapter 9   **Saul's Journey to Arabia** .................................... 69

Chapter 10  **The Ma'an Estate** ................................................ 77

Chapter 11  **Old Feelings Die Hard** ........................................ 87

Chapter 12  **Nothing But the Truth** ....................................... 97

Chapter 13  **The Legacy** ........................................................ 107

Chapter 14  **The Wadi Musa** ................................................ 115

Chapter 15  **Saul's Arrival in Arabia** .................................... 125

| Chapter 16 | **Guess Who's Coming to Dinner** | 137 |
| Chapter 17 | **All is Not as it Seems** | 147 |
| Chapter 18 | **Excavation Plans Interrupted** | 159 |
| Chapter 19 | **Issa's Trials** | 167 |
| Chapter 20 | **Getting Ready** | 179 |
| Chapter 21 | **Week of Celebration** | 189 |
| Chapter 22 | **Saul Preaches to the Gentiles** | 203 |
| Chapter 23 | **Change of Plans** | 213 |
| Chapter 24 | **The Gardens** | 227 |
| Chapter 25 | **Trouble in Arabia** | 237 |
| Chapter 26 | **Tirsa's Truth** | 249 |
| Chapter 27 | **Return to Arabia** | 255 |
| Chapter 28 | **Excavation Paradox** | 261 |
| Chapter 29 | **Epilogue** | 273 |

**ACKNOWLEDGMENTS** ... 279

**AUTHOR'S NOTE** ... 281

**ABOUT THE AUTHOR** ... 283

# Prologue
# New Beginnings

*A.D. 33, Jerusalem*
*~ Salim, The Journey ~*

"Forward!" I urged, anticipation coursing through my body as if the horizon held secrets poised to reshape our lives.

"Abdi, we can't be late," I said.

"Salim, I can only move as fast as this stubborn camel. We've been driving them hard all day."

"I know, my friend, but we're called to witness events told to come. This is what we've been waiting for!"

We needed to move with haste to make it to Jerusalem in time, but our travel from Raqmu had been taxing. While my grandfather's caravan traversed these parts often enough, I would never get used to it. The sun beat down like a relentless blacksmith's forge, a shimmering mirage of heat and light. The Arabian Desert sand found refuge in the folds of our tunics and clung to every inch of our skin.

As we were climbing a dune, the caravan master yelled, "It's a haboob on the horizon!"

Within the hour, the fast-approaching sandstorm turned the once bright sky into a dark nightmare. A chill ran down my spine. It was hard to see anything within a few feet. Abdi was close by. I could feel him fast on my heels.

"Salim." He groaned. "If I don't make it, please let my family know…"

"We will make it! We must!"

I turned to help Abdi and noticed he had collapsed. I was fumbling for the water jug when I heard the caravan master yelling, "Stay close, tie the camels together. We will wait out the storm here."

There was nowhere to take shelter. We were in the middle of the desert. I poured water down Abdi's throat—now thick with sand.

He croaked, "We'll be buried alive. They'll never find our bones in this desert."

I held him in my arms and prayed.

"Lord, you are the Creator of Heaven and Earth. You control the winds from the four corners of the Earth. Speak to the wind, and it will obey."

Within the same hour, the wind began to settle into little circles of dust in the sand.

"You see, my friend, our lives were spared for such a time as this," I said.

Instead of continuing on, our caravan set camp to allow men and animals rest. The dripping of water—from one stone vessel to the next— became a relentless drumbeat in my head as I pondered whether we would reach our destination in time.

We departed the following day before the sun could crest the horizon. The desert expanse was serene—mocking us as if it had not tried to swallow us alive the day before.

Abdi and I finally arrived in Jerusalem around the second hour. We secured lodgings at Old Benjamin's Inn despite the growing crowd of visiting Jews who came to celebrate the feast. Benjamin greeted us with a kiss to both cheeks.

"Shalom!" He roared, welcoming us in his embrace. "You made it just in time to celebrate the Feast of Pentecost."

Benjamin was certain Abdi and I would come, and for that, I was grateful. He was the son of a respected rabbi who came out of the Capernaum synagogue—about a five-day journey from Jerusalem. Benjamin had dealings with proselytes and God-fearers. I remember him telling me the story of how Jesus healed a Centurion's servant.

"Can you believe it? Jesus praised a Roman for having great faith," he said.

I was fortunate to have Benjamin as a friend. It was not easy being an Arab among Jews. My family had become proselytes—converts to Judaism. They were devout Jews who kept all the prescribed Judaic laws—including circumcision. It was my grandfather, Saba Kasim, a wealthy traveling merchant, who first heard of the stories of Abraham, Isaac, and Jacob.

Saba returned from one of his merchant trips with eyes ablaze and a broad smile, his voice carrying an air of wonder and excitement.

He announced, "I'm going to find a respectable rabbi who will teach me the ways of the Patriarchs."

On his next trip to Jerusalem, he met Benjamin's father, Rabbi Joseph. Joseph was more than willing to teach Saba the laws of God given to Moses. That's not all. Saba asked Joseph to circumcise his entire male kin. And I found myself included in that painful number.

My Saba did not anticipate that not only would he learn the Law, he would encounter the Giver of the Law, the One who came to fulfill it. He met Yeshua, the Messiah, the Anointed One, Jesus of Nazareth.

*~ Kasim, Road to Emmaus ~*

Cleopas and I walked on the road to Emmaus in silence. I had come to believe that Jesus was our long-awaited Messiah, thanks to Rabbi Joseph and my friend Cleopas. Now, Jesus was gone, crucified by the Romans at the request of the Jewish leaders. As I walked with Cleopas, I knew I was headed in the opposite direction of my home in Arabia, but I needed answers.

I took a moment to compose myself. My eyes were red and blurry, whether from the dust of the road or from the sadness I felt deep in my gut; it didn't matter. I knew nothing. I was too numb to feel, too lost in my thoughts to realize that someone had joined Cleopas and me on our journey.

I was overcome with grief. "How could they have killed Yeshua, the Messiah?"

Cleopas was more cautious. "Kasim, we must meet with the other believers so we may understand what happened. I feel there is more to this than we know."

The stranger who had joined us on our walk interrupted, "What are you discussing so intently?"

"You must be the only person in Jerusalem who hasn't heard the news." Cleopas looked at the man incredulously.

"What news?"

Cleopas began to explain everything to him.

"The things that happened to Jesus, the man from Nazareth. He was a prophet who performed powerful miracles and a mighty teacher in the eyes of God and the people. But our leading priests and religious leaders handed him over to be condemned to death by crucifixion. We had hoped he was the Messiah who came to rescue Israel. This all happened three days ago."

Cleopas told the stranger how Mary Magdalene and the other women of Jesus's followers were at his tomb early this morning. They returned to the disciples with tears in their eyes and laughter on their lips, explaining that Jesus's body was missing. The women reported they spoke with two angels who told them, "Jesus is alive!"

"Some of our men ran to see, and sure enough, his body was gone," I added.

The stranger's brow furrowed. "You foolish people! You find it so hard to believe all the prophets wrote in the Scripture. Wasn't it clearly predicted that the Messiah would suffer all these things before entering his glory?"

The stranger took us through the writings of Moses and all the prophets, explaining—from Scripture—the things concerning the Messiah. As we approached Emmaus, nearing the end of our journey, the stranger planned to continue on.

Cleopas and I begged him to stay the night since it was getting late.

The stranger followed Cleopas home. Fellow believers—who resided in the city—also gathered with us to break bread and receive news about Jesus. As we sat to eat, the stranger took the bread and blessed it. Then, he broke it and gave it to us. There was something familiar about what he did. Cleopas and I looked at each other. We gasped, and our eyes widened. At once, we recognized who it was among us.

Everyone spoke at once, "Master!"

At that moment, he disappeared.

*~ Salim, My Reverie ~*

I recall my Saba Kasim's stories of Jesus's teachings on love and salvation. He recounted the healings and miracles Jesus performed throughout the region. I recall him saying how kind Jesus was to beggars and lepers and how he admired and respected women. He told of Jesus's gentleness with children and how this was all so life-changing.

My Saba was there when the High Priest Caiaphas turned Jesus over to be crucified by the Romans. In fact, he was so distraught over the crucifixion that he lingered in Jerusalem for days and became an eyewitness to Jesus's resurrection while on the road to Emmaus.

I recall him saying, "Jesus instructed us to go to Jerusalem and wait for the promise of the Holy Spirit, whom He says will fill us with power from Heaven."

What that meant no one really knew, but there we found ourselves waiting in Jerusalem to receive the promise. If only Saba could have been there, but after his last trip, it proved to be too much for him.

"Salim, if I can't make this journey, you must go. You need to be an eyewitness to the events Jesus spoke of. It's our family legacy, our inheritance, to partake in the promises of our Lord Jesus. This will be carried down from generation to generation to be an unbroken legacy of the Ma'an family."

And indeed, it proved to be every bit as life-changing as Saba declared it would be.

## The Day of Pentecost
### ~ Salim, The Promise ~

Abdi and I were gathered in the square with Jews, Proselytes, and God-fearers from every nation waiting for the promise.

"Salim, I've never seen so many people gathered in one place," said Abdi.

"Yes, you have, every year at the pagan festivals and for the horse races."

"I mean, I haven't seen so many people who believe like we do in one place. This is amazing!"

Abdi appeared on the verge of leaping out of his sandals. Suddenly, a perplexed expression came over his face. "There's something in the air. Can you feel it?"

I held out my arms and could see the hairs standing on end. As the prayers were starting, we donned our prayer shawls when suddenly the wind lifted our himation, thrashing the tassels to and fro.

"Salim, what's happening?"

A resounding sound came from the heavens and swept in like a mighty rushing wind. The wind was so strong I almost lost my footing.

"Do you see what I see?" asked Abdi.

Abdi's eyes were dancing with delight. He had a smile as broad as the Golden Gate in Jerusalem. Then, I saw a fire resembling a divided tongue over his head. And when I looked into his eyes, I could see the reflection of fire hovering over my head, too!

"Abdi, I see it. I see it!"

## Prologue New Beginnings

I couldn't contain the feeling bubbling up within me. It felt like a fire began in the pit of my stomach and shot up through the core of my body, resting on top of my head.

We were all filled with the Holy Spirit that day, as Jesus promised. I heard Abdi speaking in an unknown language. I began to speak in an unknown language, too. I was amazed at the presence of God's Spirit among us. I heard visitors from Rome speaking in the exact dialect of our people. They were praising God and speaking of his wonderful works.

*What a day that was!*

*Ma'an, Jordan, Near Petra, 2019*
*~ Kasim, The Daunting Task ~*

I finished reading from the ancient scroll, with its withering parchment, that held the words of my ancestor Salim. My immediate family and some of our Bedouin kin were gathered around the hearth at my father's estate, as was our custom during Pentecost.

Our oral traditions were passed down for the first millennium. Despite our efforts, we haven't been able to find any written documents prior to the fourteenth century. After the Ottoman Empire took control of Arabia, my ancestors must have taken pen to paper to record the stories. It had become a tradition during the Feast of Pentecost to recollect the ancient stories, and the privilege was mine alone. After all, I was named after Salim's Saba Kasim, who was an eyewitness to Jesus's resurrection on the road to Emmaus.

While everyone was deep in their thoughts, I pondered my next assignment, a daunting task. It was my responsibility to find the lost scrolls that were given to my ancestors, letters written by Saul and given to the Christians in Arabia. Petra, to be precise. The ancient city of the Nabateans—Raqmu.

Saul was also known as Paul. Our oral tradition says that Saul had a difficult time because of his involvement with the persecution of believers. After meeting up with Barnabas, he went by his Roman name, Paul.

My ancestors told the story of how Paul visited Arabia shortly after his encounter with Jesus on the road to Damascus. In his zeal, and with his newfound faith, Paul taught the Arab Christians what he knew of Jesus—how he fulfilled all the prophecies of the coming Messiah.

In return, my ancestors taught Paul everything they knew about Jesus. They shared their experience of receiving the promise of the Holy Spirit on the Day of Pentecost. Paul even helped my ancestor Youssef make tents to earn his keep while in Arabia.

The stories say that Paul became like family and was saddened when it came time to leave. When he returned to Damascus, he wrote personal letters to Saba Kasim and Youssef and instructional letters to the Christian community in Arabia. Paul also had letters he wrote to other churches transcribed and sent to my ancestors.

The evidence is overwhelming, which means there must be a trail leading to the scrolls containing those letters. This is the proof I need to protect my family, to show their connection to the ancient families of Arabia. As tensions escalate in the Middle East and conflict unfolds throughout the region, our family's unbroken legacy is in jeopardy. Now is not the time to divulge our ancient secrets. Not yet, anyway. Not until we have the proof we need.

Just then, my phone vibrated. What I saw next chilled the blood in my veins.

The screen scrolled, "Breaking news, inside sources leak secret meetings held by the heads of State in key Arab countries."

I felt a deep pressure inside my chest, like someone was squeezing the life out of me. I stopped to catch my breath, holding my chest.

As the pain subsided, I continued to read, "In an unprecedented act of aggression, three major Arab nations have joined in declaring it an act of treason to worship Jesus Christ in any public venue."

Everyone's attention was riveted on me.

*I've exhausted my resources looking for those scrolls. My archeological skills have dulled, no longer matching my business acumen*, I chastised myself.

Then, it came to me. I abruptly stood, upending my coffee that now dripped on the ancient rug covering the marble floor. Miri was at my side in no time to clean up my mess. I turned my attention back to the matter at hand and, without preamble, said, "I know exactly what I need to do. It's time to take a trip to the States. I'm going to meet the renowned Dr. Issa Stevens."

A collective gasp filled the room. I gave everyone a wry smile and a raised eyebrow, but they knew I was up for the task.

## Chapter 1

# Life is About to Change

*Veritas University, Santa Ana, California*
*~ Dr. Issa Stevens, Introductions ~*

It was a warm sunny day, late spring of 2019, and my life was about to change. On my way to class, I silently reflected on my life. *I need a change. I need some excitement! I miss the dirt sifting through my hands and the touch of parchment on my fingertips.* Don't get me wrong, I love teaching. But ancient scrolls? Now, that's entirely another matter.

I had accepted a teaching position at Veritas University, a small, robust Christian school located in Santa Ana, California, because the commute was not too far. Besides, after the death of my husband, Dave, I needed time to grieve and put the pieces of my life back together. My daughter, Sky, was off to college halfway across the country. And well, all I had left was my work. Next to excavating and reading ancient scrolls, teaching was my passion. But restlessness seeped into my bones, a subtle discomfort that whispered an increasing sense of discontent. Dissatisfaction? Or maybe I was just tired of being alone.

I made it to class with little time to spare. My plan was to teach on the lost scrolls of the Apostle Paul, written to the Arab Christians, after he left Arabia to return to Damascus. Scholars have disputed the existence of such writings. However, having studied Paul and his missionary journeys, it made sense that he would leave written instructions for the believers in Arabia. These were the same people who traveled to Jerusalem on the

Day of Pentecost, who experienced the promise of our Lord Jesus, and who were filled with the Holy Spirit.

The excavations for the scrolls were an ongoing project that I would have loved to be a part of, but I was working hard at Veritas to earn my tenure.

Dean Wright interrupted my reflections, "There you are, Issa. I want to introduce you to our newest addition at Veritas, Miriam Fakmad. She's an international student whose interests align closely with yours in the area of ancient scrolls and excavations. Miriam, come and meet Dr. Issa Stevens."

*What a coincidence*, I thought.

"Hello Miriam, it's nice to meet you. I look forward to having you in my class."

Miriam's eyes glowed with excitement as I spoke. She looked to be about twenty, close in age to Sky. Miriam was tall with dark brown hair and eyes that seemed to change color depending on the angle of her face. At the moment, they looked hazel. Her smile was warm and had a dimple, a deep groove on the right side of her face, and a mole that accentuated her beauty. She looked like a model on the front cover of a fashion magazine.

I must have been staring because I heard a calm, commanding voice saying, "Hello, Dr. Stevens. It's a pleasure to meet you. I've heard good things about you and the work you're doing here at the university."

I thought to myself, *This girl speaks beyond her years. Why am I feeling intimidated by this college-aged girl who could be my daughter?*

I finally responded, "This semester, we're learning about ancient Middle Eastern scrolls and how to determine their authenticity."

"That's exactly where my interests lie. I'm glad I decided to enroll here."

"Then I look forward to seeing you next week," I replied. "My class meets on Wednesdays and Fridays."

Sure enough, Miriam showed up in class the following week and sat in the front row with her course books and materials—ready to learn. She asked so many questions my head began to swim.

"Yes, Miriam, how can I help you?"

"Dr. Stevens, if the lost scrolls of the Apostle Paul indeed do exist, isn't the most likely location of the scrolls in Petra?"

"Yes and no, Miriam."

I paused to gather my thoughts. I didn't want to give away too much information. First, I would need to consult with my long-time friend and colleague, Dr. Ibrahim. He was in the proposal phase of funding to find those exact scrolls.

Miriam interrupted my thoughts, "Where do you believe they might be?"

I leveled my voice to sound as genuine as possible.

"If the Arab Christians were in jeopardy, they would have fled to Egypt."

*Issa, Four Weeks into the Semester*

Four weeks into the semester, to my surprise, Dean Wright called me into his office to discuss an interesting opportunity for the school. And in his words, "A chance of a lifetime for you, Dr. Stevens."

Dean Wright sat behind his big mahogany desk with his hands clasped under his chin and a smug look on his face. His next words would change my life forever.

"Issa, I received a call from an important and well-known foundation in Jordan that deals with importing and exporting antiquities. They're looking to partner with the University on an excavation. They seek to unearth some ancient scrolls they believe were written by the Apostle Paul. This could be the find of the century! Not to mention a sizable donation to the university's Archeology department."

My heart quickened, and my thoughts scattered like startled birds. I hadn't been in the field since I lost my precious Dave nearly three years ago. I could no longer contain my excitement, and my curiosity got the best of me.

"So, what's the catch?"

Dean Wright's eyebrows shot up, and his face turned a few shades red.

"Well, Issa, the catch is they want you and only you to head up the project. The excavations begin in two weeks in Ma'an, Jordan. And this project is top priority, and top secret. You cannot share the news with anyone except to say you're going away on school business."

"But what about my classes?"

"I've already taken care of it."

"You assumed I'd say yes?"

"I know this is what you love to do, Issa! Besides, this is a chance of a lifetime and will all but guarantee your tenure. Just think what this will mean for the university!"

I gave him a crooked smile.

"I am excited, nervous, and anxious all at the same time, but two weeks?"

"Yes, the foundation we're partnering with has the bankroll to cover all the expenses, including your airfare and accommodations."

"Well, that's more than generous."

"Yes, Issa! They will have a member of their team—who's also an expert in ancient scrolls—fly out to meet you. He will debrief you in greater detail on the plane ride to Jordan."

## Chapter 2

## The Damascus Experience

*- A.D. 35, Saul -*

It was time for our midday prayers. The caravan stopped by a stand of trees. I dismounted from my camel and went to the shade. The sun was already high in the sky, and sweat trickled down my forehead. I put on my tallit, which I wore as a prayer shawl, and began my prayers reciting the ingrained words of the Shema 'Yisrael, "Hear O Israel, The Lord is our God, The Lord is One."

After prayers, I sat and partook of the noonday meal but desired to be alone. I was determined to remain focused on my mission in Damascus. The High Priest gave me the letters saying I needed to round up the followers of the Way and bring them back to Jerusalem to stand trial.

I did not enjoy the violence that often ensued, especially with the women and children. I kept telling myself had they not resisted, had they just denounced this Jesus they proclaimed to be Messiah, no one would have died.

I was not in the business of killing my countrymen. Rome was good enough for that. But these heretics were disrupting our way of life and soon would cause trouble between us and the Romans.

I mounted my camel as the caravan continued its journey. The heat was intense, and my eyes began to see ripples in the sand. I felt lightheaded and held on tight to the reins. The sun's rays began to disperse in every direction. A bright light shot from the center of the sun and beamed down upon me. The light was so intense, so piercing, that it was blinding. I was knocked off my camel. The weight and intensity of the atmosphere took my breath away.

That's when I heard his voice, "Saul, Saul, why are you persecuting me?"

I looked in every direction to see where the voice was coming from. I realized I couldn't see.

I cried out, "Who are you, Lord?"

The voice responded, "I am Jesus, whom you are persecuting."

I tried to get my bearings, but I couldn't move under the weight of this presence. My hands and legs were shaking violently, and I began to choke on my words.

My voice was barely audible, but finally, I managed to say, "Lord, what do you want me to do?"

"Go to Damascus, and you will be told what to do."

The light dissipated, but my sight had not returned.

I called out to the temple guards who accompanied me, "Did you hear what I heard?"

At first, I thought I was dreaming. Then I thought, *This must be a mirage.* But the two guards who came to help me from the ground were close by, and their fear was palpable. I could feel them trembling.

Simultaneously, they whispered, "I heard a voice but saw no one."

I tried to regain my composure as best I could.

I called out to the men again. "Help me up. The light has disrupted my vision. We must go straight to Damascus. Let the caravan master know we will ride ahead."

"Yes, Rabbi Saul, we will do as you say."

My men helped me to the side of the road and did as I bid them.

## The Damascus Experience

They, too, regained their composure, but fear seeped through their voices. I immediately donned my tallit and began to pray earnestly.

When the men returned, they helped me mount my camel, and we left for Damascus. The caravan master sent an additional two guards to accompany us. He knew who I was and feared reprimand from the High Priest if something were to happen to me under his escort. My camel was led by one of the temple guards, and we reached Damascus by sundown.

Arrangements were made for me to stay with Ezra—a fellow Pharisee. I didn't eat or drink for three days. I inquired of the Lord, "What should I do?" I, Saul, a Pharisee among Pharisees, was brought low, humbled, and humiliated.

I couldn't take care of my personal needs without the help of my guards. It had been two days, and still, I hadn't regained my sight. A prickling unease crawled beneath my skin, but I continued to pray to the voice that claimed to be Jesus.

The voice instructed me, "You will be told what to do."

Then, I heard a man speaking, but I had not heard the door open. It was as if I were in a dream, only I was awake. A vision, maybe?

I heard the man say, "I am Ananias. Jesus will send me to you tomorrow. I will lay my hands on you, and you will receive your sight."

Afterwards, there was complete silence. At that moment, I knew. From the depths of my soul, I knew. Jesus is the Anointed One sent from God. I fervently prayed until I could pray no more, and sleep fell upon me.

The next morning, I had my men prepare me to receive my guest.

Ezra spoke to me gently and said, "Saul, there is no one among the Pharisees named Ananias in Damascus."

I could tell by the sound of his voice he was perplexed. He thought I had gone mad. He probably attributed it to my Damascus Road experience and these past three days of fasting. Then, in perfect timing, there was a knock on the door.

As Ezra swung the door open, a man spoke.

"Shalom to this house. My name is Ananias. I have come to lay hands on Saul so that he may receive his sight. Take me to him."

When I heard their voices, I stood, making my way to the door using the furniture as a guide. Then Ananias entered the room, escorted by Ezra.

I immediately called out, "Lay your hands on me so that I may receive my sight."

Ananias placed his hands on my eyes, and at first, I felt warmth. I saw what looked like a blazing fire. Then, a burst of bright white light. It felt as if scales fell from my eyes. At that moment, I saw him. Ananias stood before me with his stark white beard and cloak covering his head.

Then he blew in my face and said, "Receive the Holy Spirit." We immediately went to the mikvah, where he baptized me.

Ananias and I supped together, and he told me all that the Lord had shown him in a vision.

When he was finished, I was filled with urgency. "Ananias, I must be allowed to speak at the synagogue. I must let them know that Jesus Christ is Lord."

"But Saul, both the religious leaders and the believers will see you as a threat."

"Go, tell them all you have seen and heard this day so they will receive me. I must preach Jesus!"

Ananias went to speak to the elders. When I arrived, the synagogue was filled with Jewish leaders and believers of the Way. The word spread quickly, so there were also Pharisees and Sadducees present. I recognized some faces from my earlier trips to Damascus and the Day of Atonement in Jerusalem.

Flanked by Ezra, Ananias, and my two guards, I entered the synagogue and immediately went to the platform to speak. No one dared stop me, a Pharisee sent with papers from the Sanhedrin court.

I started my speech with the typical greetings in the words of our beloved prophet Moses, "'Hear O Israel, The Lord is our God, the Lord is One.' These words have encapsulated the very essence of our faith—emphasizing the unity and oneness of God."

Everyone nodded their heads. I continued, emboldened to speak the truth of Jesus.

"Today, we come together to study Torah and seek wisdom and guidance from its eternal truths. Let's listen with open hearts and minds, engage in thoughtful discussions, and interpret to deepen our understanding of its teachings."

The tension was palpable in the room, but I knew what the Lord required of me. Ananias stood off to my right and Ezra to my left in support of me. A fellow believer on one side and a fellow Pharisee on the other. After all, they were both partakers in the miracle of regaining my sight.

"I, Saul, am compelled to share with you a profound truth that has been revealed to me through prayer and a heavenly sign."

The gasps were audible in the room, for the Jewish people had not received a sign from the Lord for nearly four hundred years. I proceeded with trepidation but knew it was now or never. I pressed on, and the words began to flow fluently off my tongue.

"Throughout the pages of our sacred Scripture, we find numerous prophecies that foretell the coming of the Messiah. These prophecies describe the characteristics and mission of the Messiah, and Jesus fulfills them in remarkable and unmistakable ways. I was sent by the High Priest to round up the believers of Jesus and bring them back to Jerusalem to stand trial. On the road to Damascus, I encountered this Jesus. A bright light appeared from Heaven, and I was thrown to the ground. Then a voice appeared to me saying, 'Saul, Saul, why are you persecuting me?' I replied, who are you, Lord? The voice responded, 'I am Jesus whom you are persecuting.'"

The same heaviness came upon me at that moment. I had to catch my breath. I felt like I was reliving the experience all over again.

I continued, but my voice was barely above a whisper. "Immediately, I was blinded and told to go to Damascus. Our brother Ananias was instructed by the Lord in a vision to lay hands on me that I might receive my sight. Then he blew in my face and said, 'Receive the Holy Spirit.' And here I am today looking over you, my fellow brothers."

My boldness picked up, and the strength returned to my voice.

"Open your hearts and minds as we search the Scripture. We cannot deny the overwhelming evidence that reveals Jesus is the Son of God. Our long-awaited Messiah."

Immediately, the room was thrown into chaos. Some were praising God, and others were shouting, "Blasphemy, blasphemy!"

Ezra and Ananias grabbed me by the arms, and we fled to avoid a riot. When we returned to Ezra's home, they tried to convince me to flee by night, but it was imperative that I stay.

I pleaded with Ananias and Ezra. "I need to learn more from the believers of the Way. I need to return to the synagogue to convince our fellow Jews that Jesus is the Son of God."

Later that day, I met with believers in the courtyard of Ananias's house. I shared with them my encounter with Jesus in more detail. At first, they were frightened of me.

I heard one believer whisper, "Isn't he the one who destroyed those in Jerusalem who believed in the name of Jesus? Isn't he here to bind us and take us to Jerusalem?"

I ignored the whispering and stood tall. "Fellow believers, I, Saul, am now a follower of the Way."

Chatter erupted throughout the courtyard.

"I preach Jesus, the Christ, the Son of God because I'm an eyewitness to the resurrected Christ. He has commanded that I preach to Gentiles, kings, and the children of Israel. Today, I will sit at your feet to learn of Christ from you."

Wide-eyed stares and open mouths greeted that statement. Jacob,

## The Damascus Experience

one of the synagogue leaders—also a believer of the Way—stroked his beard and proceeded to the makeshift platform. Jacob gave me a nod and a warm greeting before expounding on the Torah. He explained how Jesus fulfilled all the prophecies spoken of by the prophets.

"I, too, was an eyewitness to Jesus's resurrection. I waited in Jerusalem, as Jesus had instructed us, that we might receive the promise of the Holy Spirit."

As Jacob spoke about Jesus's resurrection, I remembered how upset the Sanhedrin were when they heard this rumor. Caiaphas dismissed it and told everyone, "That usurper's disciples have stolen the body."

I also heard the guards' reports of what happened at the tomb. Despite the discrepancies, I had dismissed it, too. Now, it all makes sense. Jesus truly rose from the dead!

When I went to the synagogue to preach Jesus the next day, the Pharisees and Sadducees were present as a united front. They stood there with all their phylacteries, leather boxes containing Torah writings strapped to their arms and foreheads, with piety pasted over their faces. *Lord, forgive me, is that what I looked like? How blind was I?* Seeing, I could not see. Hearing, I could not hear. I was blinded to the truth of the Messiah. As I moved toward the platform, I was met with resistance, and chaos erupted. Once again, Ezra and Ananias grabbed me by the arms, and we fled—this time to Ananias's home.

Later that evening, Ezra returned and reported that the Jews were plotting to kill me. I considered going to the Roman authorities but thought better of it. Ezra told us that the Jews were watching the gates day and night. During the third watch, Ananias and the other believers devised a plan to lower me down the city wall in a large basket.

"Ananias, there is no way this plan is going to work."

"Saul, there is no other plan, so it must work. Besides, Jesus said you will preach salvation to Gentiles and kings. So, it will work. However, I suggest you not go to Jerusalem. Head south instead, to Arabia!"

# Chapter 3

# Issa & Dave

*~ Issa, My Reverie, 2019 ~*

Restlessness consumed me. I longed to return to the field, my hands eager to sift through the soil in search of scrolls, each word a potential echo written from the hand of the Apostle Paul. But how was I supposed to get ready at such short notice? Two weeks to pack my life into bags—was everyone's sanity slipping?

My first priority was to reach out to Sky. Oh, how I missed her. What was I thinking when I let her go to college so far away? She's so much like her father. I doubt I would've been able to stop her anyway. After all, Yale was her father's alma mater.

Sky reminded me so much of Dave. She had her father's hazel eyes. And her smile, the way it lit up her face, makes her Dave's daughter.

Dave and I met during a summer excavation course at Yale. He was the perfect gentleman. He was smart, witty, handsome, and jovial. But what drew me most was his love for all things ancient, especially relating to the Bible. Soon after our graduation, we married. Dave got a teaching position at Harvard, and I became pregnant.

In those first few years, I stayed home with Sky. By her fifth birthday, I was back in the saddle and teaching at Harvard alongside Dave. Then, the unthinkable happened. During an excavation that Dave and I embarked on, Dave's life slipped away right before my eyes. Sky had just turned seventeen, and I was left continually replaying the events surrounding his death in my mind.

Sky and I mourned in different ways, which made us drift apart. I regret that she left for college with so much unsaid between us. But she seemed happier lately, and for that, I was grateful.

I, on the other hand, was lonely and without purpose. Dave was my everything. He was my rudder, my compass. Now, without him, I feel lost and without direction. *This trip will be good for me*, I thought. *Besides, Dave would want me to be happy, to move on, to consider remarrying*. But I wasn't so sure that would ever happen.

### *Issa, Tel Dan, Israel, 2017*

"Hurry, Dave, Dr. Avraham is waiting for us. We must be at the site before sunrise."

"Coming, my love. I can't seem to find my magnetometer."

"It should be in the closet to the right, sweetheart."

"Got it! Let's get going."

We reached the dig site at Tel Dan at 4:45 in the morning. Tel Dan is located in northern Israel in the upper Galilee region, known as the territory belonging to the tribe of Dan. The excavation was well underway, and we were joining for the first time. Dr. Avraham had called Dave two weeks ago to assist with the excavation when the rock findings suggested a dating of around the ninth century B.C. Dave had been so excited since his expertise was specific to the era of Israel's kings. A ninth-century B.C. find could represent relics from the reign of the house of King David.

Dave saw him first. "Dr. Avraham, it's a pleasure to meet you face to face. This is my wife, Dr. Issa Stevens."

"The renowned Drs. Stevens and Stevens. It's my pleasure to have the expertise of two of the finest archeological minds of our day."

"The pleasure is ours. We're aware that you could've called on a number of our associates in the field."

"Ah, yes, but none as lovely as your wife, Dr. Stevens."

*Finest archeological minds? He must be talking about Dave. Everything comes so hard for me. I have to study longer and harder than any of my peers. And my memory is like Jello.*

Dave interrupted my thoughts.

"Please call me Dave."

"Dr. Avraham, thank you for your kind words, and please call me Issa."

"I will do so in private, but in front of my staff, you are the renowned Drs. Dave and Issa Stevens."

Dr. Avraham seemed nice enough. Flirty, but more flattering than crude. Dave seemed to think nothing of it. So, I gave Dr. Avraham a warm smile. We put on our hard hats and followed him to a cavernous section where the rock formations were found. Dave was immediately drawn to the rock construction. I decided to do some detective work.

I was careful not to disturb the perimeter the team had already set up. Placing my hand on the wall, I traveled the length of it and began to notice a change in the grooves and structure of the rock. I made a mental note of it and continued my perusal of the area, observing the stability of the ground. I wrinkled my nose. The cave-like site smelled stale and musty, and the air was dry.

"Issa," Dave called. "Come see this stone."

As I walked toward Dave, my foot caught on a ridge in the ground, and I stumbled forward. One of the workers grabbed my arm and kept me upright until I could regain my balance.

"Issa, look at the ridges here in this stone and the smooth surfaces here. What do you make of it?" Dave looked at the stone quizzically.

"I noticed the same patterns in the rock surface about twenty meters along this rock, around that curve. I also nearly took a dive head first after tripping over a rock outcrop in the ground, about fifteen meters in the same direction."

"I wonder if the rock formation gave way due to age and then split and calcified? What type of readings did you get with the magnetometer? And do you have any aerial pictures?" asked Dave.

"I think we should also consider a LiDAR scan of the floor beneath us," I added.

Dr. Avraham started to say something when the ground began to rumble and sway. Dave grabbed my arm, and I grabbed the wall. The rumbling subsided quickly, but the ground continued to move back and forth.

"An earthquake?" Dave's face betrayed his nerves.

"I don't think so." Dr. Avraham shook his head. "I believe the Light Detection and Ranging scan is in order, immediately! The ground beneath us might be cavernous, and I don't want it to cave in on us."

Dave and I nodded simultaneously, and Dr. Avraham's assistant began evacuating most of the crew. Once the ancillary staff were safely out, Dr. Avraham barked orders to get the equipment needed to scan the cave floor.

He then turned his attention to Dave and me, "While we wait for the scan to arrive, I want to show you some interesting data we obtained with the use of an x-ray diffractometer. We were able to identify the minerals present in the rock and its phases."

"Have you obtained any data using x-ray fluorescence?" inquired Dave. "As you know, this data would be significant because it analyzes which elements and what quantity of elements are present within an object—thus creating a fingerprint for the artifact."

After Dave's pronouncement, it hit me like a ton of bricks!

"Exactly honey, uh, I mean Dave. This fingerprint is then compared to local and non-local material sources such as clay beds or rock features lending to a close approximation of the date of an object."

"Precisely, Dr. Stevens, that's why you are here. I'm depending on your skills in this area to confirm our approximate date range for this rock formation," said Dr. Avraham.

After several hours of data analyses and inspection of the rocks and artifacts found close to the site, Dave came up with an approximate dating of the mid-eighth century B.C. If his dating was accurate, this rock would have been in existence during the reign of the House of David.

"If we can further corroborate this data, this will be the discovery of a lifetime!" I said.

Dr. Avraham chuckled, and his eyes were bright with excitement.

"Yes indeed, Dr. Issa Stevens, yes indeed."

"Dr. Avraham." His assistant interrupted.

"The LiDAR scan has arrived and is set up. Should we proceed?"

Dave was so engrossed, gazing into a microscope, that I had to tap him on the shoulder.

"Honey, they're ready to commence with the scanning."

"If the scan can substantiate the data here, we should have enough information to call in the Israel Antiquities Authority." Dave looked proud and confident at his discovery.

"Yes, my thoughts exactly," replied Dr. Avraham.

We returned to the dig site to watch the scanning process. I decided to explore the ridge outcrop I previously stumbled across—literally.

After perusing the area, I asked, "Dr. Avraham, can I use this trowel to dig around the outcrop?"

"Yes, but do be careful."

Dave joined me and took over the dig. After thirty minutes of digging, we both looked at each other, staring in amazement, mouths agape.

Dave spoke first. "This find will provide the first historical evidence of King David from the Bible."

We heard a commotion by the scanning area, and Dr. Avraham began shouting and waving his arms. "There appears to be a monument directly below us!"

Dave yelled in return, "I believe we've found a starting point over here!"

After several hours of careful digging, Dave and the team unearthed what looked like a stela—a stone slab with an inscription. The inscription looked Aramaic, a language Dave and I knew well from our studies.

Dave called out, "Dr. Avraham, would you like to do the honors of translating the inscription?"

"Let's all grab a pen and pad and write our findings, then we can compare notes."

It felt like a sacred moment. The awe was palpable. You could feel it in the air.

"Issa, you go," said Dr. Avraham.

"Well, first, this is only a fragment, and we must continue the dig to see if we can find any additional fragments to piece together."

Both Dave and Dr. Avraham nodded their heads in agreement. I proceeded with my translation.

"The inscription starts with, 'under the divine guidance of the god Hadad, I vanquished thousands of Israelites and Judahite horseman and charioteers.'"

A sharp gasp escaped my lips, "This king claims to have defeated the King of Israel and the King of the House of David."

I pointed to the bottom corner of the stela and proceeded with my findings, "This broken fragment looks like King Jehoram's name."

They both nodded simultaneously.

"She's good," said Dr. Avraham.

"That she is," Dave responded with a smile.

Those were the last words I heard from my sweet Dave. After he spoke those endearing words, I saw him clutch his chest. His face became strained, and he started to sweat profusely. My world tilted. I knew the tell-tale signs. Dave was having a heart attack.

As if snapping out of a dream, I quickly stood, tears streaming down my face.

"Someone, call an ambulance! My husband is having a heart attack."

When I turned my attention back to Dave, Dr. Avraham and his assistant were performing CPR. I fell to my knees, buried my face in my hands, and wept uncontrollably. I prayed, and I prayed, and I prayed some more. Then, I begged God to save Dave.

When all seemed futile, I began to question God. "Why, Lord, why would you let this happen to me? How could you be so cruel?"

# Chapter 4

# The Past Shapes the Future

*~ Issa, My Childhood ~*

I hated every time we had to move. It meant going to a new school and trying to make new friends. No one wanted to be my friend. They found me fascinating because I had green eyes. Everything else about me they hated. I forced my legs to move at a faster pace. I didn't want to be late for school. It was my first week. I was eleven years old and starting the seventh grade. It didn't help that I had skipped a grade. Being smart in their eyes only made things worse. I was labeled a showoff and a nerd, among other things.

I walked past a group of boys and girls, who shot me a loathsome look, boring into me until my insides twisted uncomfortably. Then, the taunts started. I had become accustomed to it, immune even.

"There goes the Jewish girl with green eyes," announced one boy.

"Her mother is white, and her father is black, you know," said another.

"What a combination." One of the girls mocked. "No wonder she has no friends. No one likes Jews or Blacks around here."

I rounded the corner. When they were out of sight, I ran to the restroom. Only this time, I cried. I stood at the sink, staring in the mirror, noticing my red-rimmed eyes and the puffiness forming around them. Someone entered the restroom, but I didn't notice at first. I was too preoccupied with my own misery. I heard water running and saw a Middle-Eastern girl with my light complexion wearing a hijab that covered her hair. I guessed she was Muslim.

"I overheard those insensitive, entitled jerks out there. You should ignore them. I used to be the butt of their jokes until you came along," she said.

I stood speechless as this stranger tried to comfort me. Surprisingly, it was working.

"By the way, my name is Fatima."

Standing up straight, I dried my eyes with my sleeve and replied, "My name is Issa."

"Nice to meet you, Issa."

"Nice to meet you too, Fatima."

"We're actually in the same math class."

"Yes. I do recall seeing you."

"Well, I don't have many friends either because I'm Muslim. So we're in the same boat."

Fatima reached out her hand. "Friends?"

I lifted my hand and shook hers. "Friends."

I couldn't help but wonder if Fatima overheard the taunts hurled at me about my being Jewish. So I asked her, "Does it bother you that I'm Jewish?"

"No. Does it bother you that I'm Muslim?"

"No. Actually, I'm a Christian. My mother is of Jewish descent, but is a practicing Christian. My father is Afro-Caribbean and was born in the States. He is also a Christian."

After that, Fatima and I became best friends.

The fact that I was a devout Christian and she a devout Muslim didn't bother either of us. Her family all but adopted me. They didn't try

## The Past Shapes the Future

to convert me. Instead, they exposed me to their wonderful culture and heritage. I, on the other hand, made a conscious effort to show them the love of Christ so that they could come to know him through my deeds.

My parents didn't have a problem with our relationship, but it was hard for them to engage with Fatima's family because of my mother's Jewish heritage. I just couldn't understand why the sons of Abraham couldn't make a conscious effort to get along.

One day, when I was at the dinner table with Fatima's family, I couldn't help myself anymore and blurted out my exasperation. "But you are from the same blood!"

Fatima's father, Ibrahim, looked at me with pity in his eyes.

"Issa, you do not understand what you say. I wish it were that easy, but it's not. It's the way of our people."

My life has been shaped by those days. Some were pleasant, and some were not so pleasant. I learned several things that I needed to unlearn from those early years. First, I became very insecure because of my race and ethnicity. I was left always second-guessing myself. To compensate, I outworked and outsmarted everyone. Yet, I still felt like it was not enough. Second, I didn't feel good about myself.

Although my mother constantly reminded me, "Issa, take a good long look in the mirror. You're beautiful and better looking than most girls around you."

*Except for Fatima*, I thought.

Now, Fatima was stunningly beautiful, and she knew it but never flaunted it. She exuded grace and dignity. Fatima and her mother taught me everything I needed to know about caring for myself, from make-up to dress, posture, and how to conduct myself as a graceful and elegant woman.

One of the saddest days of my life was when Fatima announced, "We're moving to England. My dad accepted a position at Oxford University as a professor of Archeology."

That was the second time I cried until my eyes turned red-rimmed and puffed up. Fatima's family's move was both a curse and a blessing. I curled back into my shell, and my insecurities came back to the forefront. I was a loner with very few friends. I trusted no one.

I slowly began to heal as I became more involved in my home church. I became obsessed with learning about the cultures, landscapes, and peoples of the Bible.

One day, my pastor encouraged me in a passing conversation, "Issa, you would make a great archeologist. Combine that with your knowledge of the Bible and your love for Jesus, you could make a great contribution to the Faith one day."

I immediately went home and called Fatima. I spoke with her father for hours about the prospect of me pursuing a degree in archeology.

Ibrahim replied, "Issa, you are one of the smartest girls I know. If you decide to come to England, you will have a place at Oxford. I guarantee it. If you decide to stay in the States, I will write your letters of recommendation."

The rest is history. After graduation, I was headed to John Hopkins University. Ibrahim and I have stayed in contact all these years. Fatima went on to practice medicine as a prestigious neurosurgeon. Fatima's mother sadly passed away from breast cancer. Ibrahim has not remarried and keeps himself busy with his work. We have often shared our work and consulted one another over the years.

I thank God for Fatima and her family. Her father became like a second father to me. They remain Muslim, and I remain a Christian, but we understand one another. Deep down, I believe they understand who Jesus is.

As for me, I gained such a richness and a better understanding of the history of the Bible in its broader context. I would have climbed a mountain for them and they for me. They were my friends. They were my family.

## Chapter 5

## Encounters

*Café LeRuge, Santa Ana, California*
*~ Kasim, My Miriam ~*

I sat sipping coffee, waiting for Miri. I looked around and took in my surroundings. This cafe is quaint, eccentric, and not too far from the university. The people seem friendly enough. I could see why she would like it here. I missed my Miri. *You're the daughter of my heart.* She's mature for her age and capable of running any one of my enterprises. I wasn't sure what Miri would think of this assignment, shadowing Dr. Stevens to see if she's fit for the task ahead. I looked at my watch and noticed Miri was running behind. It's not like her to be late. Then, she appeared out of nowhere.

"Miri, I've missed you. You've spoiled your Papa."

"I've missed you too," said Miriam. "When did you arrive from Jordan? I didn't expect you until next week."

"After speaking with Dean Wright, I moved the timetable up. I want to get to know the renowned Dr. Stevens from afar before we meet."

"Are you going to spy on her?"

"I wouldn't call it that. I want to get to know the real Dr. Stevens without walls or pretenses. This mission is crucial, and we can't afford mistakes. I need to be sure she's the right person for the job."

"I like her, Papa. She is kind, smart, and funny. She loves what she does and is passionate about anything antique. Especially if it's connected to the Bible."

"Good, I expected nothing less."

"You sound like you already know her?"

"Yes. I was going to tell you soon enough."

Miri put her hands on her hips and pouted, reminding me of the expression her mother would make when she was cross with me.

I chuckled, then raised my hands in surrender.

"We met at a summer archeology camp when I traveled to the States in my teens, but I'm sure she doesn't remember me."

"I highly doubt that Papa. You're not a person who is easily forgotten."

"You are correct when you speak of me today. Back then, I was a simple child."

"I know when I'm being fooled. However, I won't press you further, for now at least."

I was glad that Miri dropped this emotionally charged conversation. I wasn't prepared to get into the details about my feelings for Issa. I was still sorting them out myself. I redirected the conversation back to the task at hand.

"So, tell me, have you learned anything from Dr. Stevens's class that would be helpful to our search?"

"Yes. As I mentioned over the phone, she believes the scrolls do exist, but they may be in Egypt. What we have to determine now is whether some political, economic, religious, or catastrophic event would have resulted in our ancestors temporarily relocating to Egypt. And if so, where would they have relocated?"

"Miri, you have grown up so much. You're as beautiful and intelligent as your mother. Now tell me what you've learned about Dr. Stevens's routine, her hobbies, what she likes, and whatever else can be useful for this mission."

"Well, based on our conversations and the few times I spent with her, I know where she lives. I know she jogs in the mornings. She frequents this café and gets her coffee and croissant here before heading to class. She loves to read and possesses a massive book collection at her home. She's also active at her church and has invited me to attend. I told her I would come this Sunday."

"Good. Have you detected anything of concern?"

"No, not at all. She's very dedicated to her work. Quiet, for the most part, unless you're talking about something she's passionate about. Then she comes alive and is very animated. I think her love for all things ancient is related to her Christian beliefs. I'm excited about attending her church, and I'll find out more there."

"I think I'll go too, but we shouldn't sit together. I don't want our identities disclosed yet. Continue your normal activities. I'll be staying at the Ritz. Call me if you discover something new or interesting. Otherwise, keep a low profile and act as if I'm not here."

"Yes, Papa. I sure will be glad when we return home and start the excavations."

"Me too, Miri. Much is at stake. If Dr. Stevens is as gifted as I think she is, we will be one step closer to unearthing the missing pieces of our legacy."

*Next Morning, Café LeRouge*
*~ Kasim, My Reverie ~*

"Double espresso, please, with amaretto."

*Nothing can replace the coffee from home, but this isn't bad for American coffee*, I mused as I sipped from the cup. Then, out of the corner of my eye, I saw her.

Lost in my thoughts, I pondered, *Is that really you, Issa? You're even more beautiful than when we first met twenty-five years ago. I'm sure you don't remember me, the tall, skinny boy from Arabia. I've not forgotten you. Miri's right. You've always been smart, kind, and compassionate. Everything I've always wanted in a woman. If only our lives had turned out differently.*

I was seventeen when my father pulled me out of our summer archeology camp. I found myself back in Arabia in the middle of a crisis. An assassination attempt on my father's life changed me forever—I was his only male heir.

Issa glanced my way, pulling me out of my reverie, but I knew she wouldn't recognize me with my beard and its specks of gray. I'm not the tall, skinny boy with glasses anymore. Nor am I ignorant of my appearance, how my physique draws women's attention.

Now, Issa, she's even more lovely, vibrant, and beautiful than I remember, but her eyes hold a hint of sadness. My investigations revealed that she was married to a university professor named Dave, who passed away suddenly of a heart attack. She also has a daughter, Sky, about Miri's age, who is in her first year at Yale.

This is going to be harder than I thought. I've been trained to keep my emotions in check. Ever since I lost my Abbie—while she was giving birth to Miri—I haven't considered another woman. Due to my precarious circumstances, it's not like I could marry for love.

Father is pressuring me to give him a male heir to carry on the Ma'an bloodline. He would like nothing more than to arrange my marriage to Tirsa, but I could never. She's a distant cousin related to my Uncle Fasim from my mother's side.

Tirsa may hold to our Christian beliefs and understand the secret of our heritage, but I do not love her. Besides, my father is the direct descendant of the Ma'an legacy, not Fasim. I can't let my father compromise his lineage by relinquishing even a hint of power to Fasim.

No doubt, my uncle would delight in usurping my father's position. I can't allow this to happen but at what cost to me? I felt the urgent need to pray.

"Lord, you know I'm committed to supporting my family, but should the rest of my life be governed by the decisions of others? Will I become a shadow of the man I could be? God of my forefathers, can I assist my father, save our family's legacy, and also have a fulfilling life?"

A wave of dizziness swept over me, giving way to a sharp, pulsating sensation in my head—the familiar onset of a migraine. I instinctively began to rub my temples. There's so much at stake, not for myself alone, but for my father and our ancestors. I must find those scrolls and authenticate them. They contain the answers to my heritage and the proof needed to exonerate my forefathers from any wrongdoing. We're devout Christians. Betrayers, never!

I found myself whispering softly, "I need you, Issa, in more ways than one."

I caught myself and sealed my lips but continued to ponder. *Issa, you can help me unlock this mystery and restore peace within my family. But, I'll have to walk a thin line between truth and loyalty for your sake as well as mine.*

I thought about confronting her. Here and now. I thought of the words I would say.

To begin with, "My name is not Kasim Ahkmad. My name is Kasim Fakmad Ma'an, son of Fakmad Ahkmad Ma'an."

Then I thought better of it.

## *Café LeRouge*
### ~ Issa, My Reverie ~

I woke up this morning with a sense of purpose. I jogged my normal three miles without getting winded. After showering, I felt energetic, like my blood flowed through my veins with purpose. I haven't felt this good in years.

I guess I'm still feeling ethereal after last night's prophetic conference. To think, the Lord has an assignment for me in Arabia! I received confirmation last night that the assignment Dean Wright presented was indeed of God. I'm meant to discover something of importance that will change the world.

Since I was early, I decided to eat at *Café LeRouge*. It's a quaint spot I simply love, just a few blocks from the university. I was reflecting on the goodness of the Lord. Then, I looked at my watch and realized I needed to pick up my pace so I would not be late for class. For a moment, I thought

I saw someone I knew. An old friend from the past. No, it couldn't be, could it? No, my friend Kasim Ahkmad moved back to Arabia years ago. In fact, I recall he was abruptly pulled out of our summer archeology camp because of some family crisis. I didn't even get to say goodbye. I had no way of reaching him except by phone, but his number had been disconnected.

Kasim and I were partners in crime. We were inseparable that summer. He was intriguing, mysterious, and romantic at heart. He was tall and skinny but devastatingly handsome. This stranger was handsome, alright, but he was well built with a strong, sleek physique, jet black hair, and a salt and pepper beard. *Impossible,* I thought. *No, not impossible, highly improbable.*

I stared as he sipped his coffee with his pinky raised. It made him look so dignified and refined. From a distance, I could see that his clothes were made of fine material, wool, maybe? His shirt was unbuttoned at the top, and his jacket appeared tailor-made. He looked like a wealthy businessman or a model on the cover of a GQ magazine. His eyes suddenly lifted over the rim of his cup in my direction as if he could read my thoughts. I quickly averted his gaze, but my cheeks were burning red, no doubt.

*Here I go again, not able to control the feelings of loneliness and conjuring up people who I loved from the past.* Loved? Had I loved Kasim? Or was it just girlhood infatuation? If I'm honest with myself, it was one of the best times of my life. I was coming into my own as a woman, and Kasim made me feel alive. I laughed a lot, played hard, felt purpose in my life, and deepened my faith in God. I had no idea that there were Arab Christians, let alone that they love the Lord as much as I do. I was quite naïve back then.

Kasim was the kindest person I had ever met. Every time I looked into his eyes all those years ago, it was as if I were looking into the depths of his soul. And I was pulled in by what I saw. I saw wisdom beyond his years. I saw kindness and love. I saw passion and intrigue. I saw confidence, strength, and dignity. I will never forget one day, when we were talking about our faith in God, the veil behind those eyes revealed a mystery that I could not quite unravel. I knew then that he carried a heavy burden.

As I passed by this stranger, he gave the slightest nod and a hint of a smile. I returned a half smile and chastised myself for conjuring up childhood dreams and for flirting with a stranger. Besides, soon, I would be in Arabia, and maybe, just maybe, I might find Kasim.

## Chapter 6

# Summer Camp

*25 Years Earlier*
*~ Issa, Encountering Kasim ~*

*I'm so excited about this archeology camp. Over these six weeks, I'll learn everything I need to know to have a head start over my peers come this fall,* I thought to myself.

I know, who thinks like that? The fact is, I never made any long-lasting friendships at these camps anyway. But this time, I outdid myself. *To think, I've actually made a few acquaintances in the girl's dormitory. Thank God it's not co-ed!*

I can hear my friends back home, "Issa, you're such a prude."

I didn't care. When I accepted Jesus in my heart, I took a vow of chastity, and I planned to keep it!

"Line up, everyone. We have to review the safety protocols before we commence with the dig," shouted Sam.

"Kasim, come help me with the demonstrations."

"Yes, sir," Kasim saluted.

I turned to Sylvia, grinning, "What a suck-up. But yikes, he's super cute."

"Yes, my type, totally."

Sylvia was outgoing and self-assured, which meant she knew how to garner the attention of any boy. I, on the other hand, never paid much attention to my looks, or boys for that matter. All I cared about were my books and learning. So, I just smiled at Sylvia and resolved within myself to focus on the goal at hand, to learn as much as possible so I could be the head of my class.

Later that evening, Kasim came and sat between Sylvia and me at dinner. Sylvia flirted with him the entire time, but he paid her little attention.

Kasim kept glancing over at me. Right as he got up, he whispered in my ear, "I chose you to be in my group. See you tomorrow."

It was at that moment I became self-aware. For the first time, I cared about how I looked and smelled. I was alarmed at the prospect. I thought I was going to be sick. That night back in the dorm, Sylvia snubbed me. I felt horrible, but I didn't do anything wrong. I certainly didn't intend to hurt her.

I pleaded, "Sylvia, let me explain."

But my pleas fell on deaf ears. So, I went to shower and prepare for bed. While staring in the mirror, I suddenly became conscious about my body and how I looked. I didn't own make-up. I guess it didn't really matter. I wouldn't have known how to apply it anyway.

I didn't feel comfortable talking to the girls my age. I thought about approaching one of the counselors. I talked myself out of it. The most I could do was wash my hair and twist it so it would be wavy in the morning. I wanted to look my best.

The next day, I was placed in Kasim's group, while Sylvia was placed in another.

Kasim commented on my hair—my heart raced, and I looked away.

"Your hair looks different."

"Oh, I just washed it last night."

He lifted my hair off my shoulders and inhaled slowly and deeply.

## Summer Camp

"It sure does smell good."

My face was heated, and I felt warmth course through my body. I was afraid he'd be able to see everything I was feeling. I had never received a compliment from a boy before—that I could remember.

Then he whispered in my ear, "Your cheeks are red. It makes you look even more beautiful."

Before I could gather a response, he took me by the hand, "Let's go digging. This is going to be fun!"

Kasim and I became inseparable. I learned that he had attended this camp last summer. He returned because he wanted to get away from the confines of his life in Arabia.

"Besides," he announced, "I'm enrolling at John Hopkins this Fall."

"Me too! Oh, Kasim, this is so exciting. We will get to see each other every day."

"Well, we are here now, and what I see happens to be very lovely."

"Kasim, you're such a tease. What are we up to today?"

"Issa, didn't you look at the agenda? We're supposed to dig for dinosaur bones."

"Yes, yes, I know that. I mean, what are we going to do in our free time? Do you want to go to the arcade or for a twilight swim?"

"Twilight swim. For now, let's go find some bones."

The sun was scorching, and sweat was trickling down my brow. It seemed like we had been digging for hours. Kasim wiped my face with his hand, leaving dirt streaks across my forehead and brow. We both laughed and decided to take a water break.

Kasim had a grace to him when he was trying to be funny. He was also smart, and it came naturally for him. I imagined his IQ must be off the charts. He had an intellectual humor and could crack a joke innocently while talking about molecules. He had a way of being witty without trying. His sense of humor always made me laugh.

Kasim poured water on a towel and gently removed the dirt from my face. He stared intently into my eyes. I felt butterflies fluttering in my stomach. I wanted to tell him how I felt. He was my best friend. My guardian angel. I wanted him to know that gravity pulled him toward me. My world now revolved around him.

But it made no logical sense, and Kasim was very logical. We had only met four weeks ago. He was like no other person I've met. The gravitational pull was so strong that it was almost frightening.

Then he said, "Issa, you are a ray of sun that shines through the darkness."

Kasim's eyebrows were knit tightly together. Then he smiled. His gray eyes danced with delight as he tapped my nose with his fingertip. I stood speechless. My mouth opened and closed like a fish out of water, but no sound came out. I bowed my head, and my eyes misted over.

Kasim lifted my face and tilted his head, "Habibti, what's wrong?"

He must have spoken in Arabic, for I didn't know what habibti meant.

Without thinking, I blurted out, "I've never felt this way about anyone before."

"And what way is that?"

"Like I've known you all my life."

"I feel the same, Issa."

He took a slow, deliberate breath, reached for my hand, and helped me up. To my surprise, he didn't let go as we walked back to the dig site. We passed Sylvia on the way, and she looked at our hands intertwined. She said hello coolly. We replied hello in return.

We strategized on how to best unearth the bones for the rest of the afternoon. Instead of mindlessly digging, we decided to pretend we were in Arabia at an ancient dig site looking for ancient artifacts. We set up our perimeter and chose our tools wisely. After an hour of digging, we unearthed several dinosaur bones and other planted artifacts.

"We make a good team, Kasim!"

"Yes, we do. In more ways than one!"

I blushed, and then my stomach rumbled, interrupting the awkward moment. We headed back to the dorms to wash before meeting at the cafeteria. While inside my room, I headed straight for my computer to look up the word habibti. I found that it was a term of endearment. It translated, my love.

My thoughts swirled in a chaotic whirlwind as I contemplated whether Kasim's feelings for me were as strong as mine were for him.

I challenged myself. *If he doesn't reveal his feelings, I will broach the subject tonight.*

My only hesitancy was that I'm a Christian, and he is an Arab. I prayed quickly for guidance, showered, and hurried to the cafeteria.

"There you are, Issa. I was beginning to wonder whether I would have to eat dinner alone."

"I'm sorry, Kasim. I got caught up in my prayers, and time got away."

"You seem dedicated to what you believe. Are you a Christian?"

"How did you know?"

"I see you're wearing a cross necklace."

"And you, Kasim?"

"You assume I'm Muslim?"

"I've learned to assume nothing. What I observe is that you're a kind, respectful, thoughtful, intelligent, and fun person to be around. Besides, my best friend and her family are Muslim, and they are like family to me."

"Issa, I, too, am a Christian. There are Christians in Arabia, you know. I live in Jordan in a small town close to the famous city of Petra."

"I didn't know. I thought…well, I guess I did assume. I know that sounds stereotypical. I'm sorry. I guess I just never really thought about it."

"No worries, I usually receive hostile reactions."

"Oh, no. I would never! Besides, our Lord Jesus is of Middle-Eastern descent. He's not a Western man with blue eyes and blonde hair. And, I just wish the sons of Abraham would not fight so vehemently. Didn't Esau forgive Jacob? Didn't Yahweh pronounce a blessing on Hagar's son? I wish it didn't have to be the way it is."

"I agree totally."

"Kasim, you must know that even if you were Muslim, I wouldn't see or think of you differently. Our actions define us most."

Kasim smiled, "Let's eat, my stomach is starting to protest."

After dinner, we walked hand in hand down to the river. We sat on the edge of the dock and talked for well over an hour. We spoke of what we envisioned the future to be like.

Then Kasim turned to me and stared earnestly into my eyes.

"Issa, is there any chance we can have a future together?"

My speech faltered, and all I could do was nod my head.

I closed my eyes and leaned in ever so slightly. Our bodies were in such close proximity that we could hear each other breathing. At that moment, it was as if time ceased to exist. Then, he closed the gap and kissed me with such tenderness. At that moment, I was falling in love.

Kasim held me in his arms, and we lost sense of time. It was only when a breeze came upon us that we realized how late and how cold it was getting. Kasim walked me back to the dorm, and he turned and kissed me again.

As his lips hovered over mine, I thought I heard him say, "I love you."

Then he walked away. That was the last time I saw him. When I woke up the next morning, I went to look for Kasim but couldn't find him. Then, I went looking for Sam. I found him by the makeshift dig site and called out to him.

"Sam, have you seen Kasim?"

He began to fidget and avoided eye contact with me. When I finally got his attention, he had a grave look in his eyes.

Sam hunched his shoulders and reported, "Kasim left for Arabia early this morning."

# Chapter 7

# Church Without Walls

### ~ Issa, My Guest ~

"Miriam, I'm so glad you were able to make it tonight."

Miriam greeted me with a hug, her face bright and eyes sparkling with excitement.

"Thank you for inviting me. This gathering is so huge compared to what I'm used to. Will we be sitting together?"

When I replied no, Miriam's countenance fell. Her eyes roamed over the gathering crowd, and her forehead creased.

"I know this is probably new and a bit intimidating. Come, I've saved you a seat up front. I'm going to help the Pastor with the service tonight, so hold on to your seat."

### ~ Miriam's Experience ~

I wondered what Dr. Stevens could have meant by, *Hold on to your seat?* I looked around and noticed the crowd pouring in. The auditorium was the size of a large warehouse. The stage was centered and set up like a concert hall. There was a band present and there were stage lights highlighting the different activities onstage. The buzz in the air was infectious, and the people were friendly. I caught myself itching for excitement.

"Excuse me, Dr. Stevens. I'm curious about how the services normally are at your church?"

"Do you mean the crowd or the excitement?"

"Both."

"People are excited about what the Lord is doing. They're looking for more than religion or a religious service. They want a personal experience with Jesus."

Dr. Stevens turned to a middle-aged couple behind me and greeted them. She introduced the couple as youth pastors, and they assured her they would assist me if I needed anything. Dr. Stevens went out of her way to make sure I didn't feel awkward or alone.

I made myself comfortable as the music started and the worship team came to the stage. They were singing a song I was familiar with from my youth group back in Arabia. I closed my eyes, lifted my hands, and joined in on the chorus.

"Lord you are so beautiful, so beautiful to me. You are everything I need. You are the joy of my life. You are the inspiration for my soul. Oh, how I love you Jesus."

As the service progressed, I found myself quite enjoying the sincereness of the worship and the people's enthusiasm for the Lord. But what I was about to experience would change my life completely. It reminds me of the ancient stories my Papa would read about on the Day of Pentecost. It reminds me of when the Holy Spirit came upon the believers, and they were empowered and went on to perform many miracles.

I perused the large crowd and wondered, *Where is Papa? Oh, I hope he is here.*

This church was large enough that I couldn't find him, even if I tried. Dr. Stevens caught my attention as she came to the stage. She began to speak about the Apostle Paul's writings to the church at Corinth concerning the gifts of the Spirit.

My father told me that our ancestors were gifted, but it has been over one hundred years since they fully participated in anything like

Pentecost. I think he called it the Azusa Street Revival. The Christian Church in my hometown is Orthodox and very traditional. Although my family partners with the local church to help the small community of believers, we hold our own worship services on our estate in a less traditional manner.

I was drawn back into the worship when I noticed everyone around me erupting in praise. It seemed like the whole church was coming alive, and the gifts of the Spirit began to flow freely, like the days of old.

Then, I heard Dr. Stevens call a woman to the stage. She spoke to her, saying, "God told me you were given a diagnosis of a mass in the liver. This is what is causing your stomach pain. Not only will you be healed of the pain, but when you return to the doctor, their scans will show no mass."

Dr. Stevens then laid her hands on the woman's stomach and prayed for complete healing, saying, "In the name of Jesus Christ our Lord!"

The woman began to weep and jump for joy, shouting, "The pain is gone! I'm healed! I'm healed!"

Unconsciously, I jumped out of my seat and started to clap. The couple behind me put their hands on my shoulder. When I turned, I saw a fire burning in their eyes.

The man said, "Miriam, our God still performs miracles, and he is calling you to do the same."

I nodded but was too stunned to speak. As I turned to look for Dr. Stevens, I saw her lift her eyes upward toward heaven.

At that moment, I could read her lips as she spoke, "Thank you, Jesus, for healing this woman."

Then she closed her eyes and wept. Something stirred deep inside me, and I wept too!

### ~ Kasim's Experience ~

I sat in the middle section of the church, off to the right side, in the back, so that neither Issa nor Miri could see me. I enjoyed the worship and the energy in the room. I haven't felt the Spirit of God move in such a refreshing way in quite some time. Every time I read the stories of my ancestors aloud, they transport me back to the Day of Pentecost and to a time when the gifts of the Spirit flowed freely. But this was different, more like Pentecost here and now.

Then, I saw Issa lay hands on a woman and pray for healing for a mass in her liver.

I uttered to myself, *This is impossible what she's asking.*

The woman began to praise God. Her countenance was so peaceful, almost angelic.

Then, the woman shouted out, "I'm healed! I'm healed!"

She began to jump up and down and yelled, "The pain is gone!"

I sat stupefied. Everything I had ever read and believed without seeing was happening right before my eyes. Even though my rational mind was skeptical of the impossible, I saw a miracle taking place with my own eyes. Words could not describe what I was feeling. It was as if I could feel the healing actually taking place.

For the first time, I can honestly say I understand. I've experienced the excitement of my ancestor Salim. The words on the parchment that I've heard and read so many times are true. God has chosen me to experience them anew.

I tried to process it all. Then I felt ashamed that I hadn't believed like I should all these years. I was supposed to be a partaker in the miracles of God. It's my family that has an unbroken legacy that goes back to the Day of Pentecost.

But our unbelief in this generation has diminished our light and the power for such signs, miracles, and wonders.

In my heart, I rejoiced. *God, you've given me the confirmation I've been waiting for.*

Suddenly, I felt the need to search for Issa. She was still in the same spot. Her gaze was heavenward, and it looked like all the strength had left her. Her focus then shifted to the audience, and it appeared like she was looking for someone. Our eyes connected. It was as if she was looking through me, peering into my soul. There was a godly reverence in her stare like she was communicating a personal message to me from God. Then she looked away and seemed to refocus.

I whispered to myself, *Issa, you are truly a God-send. You are the chosen one, sent to help us unravel centuries worth of mystery. Mysteries that are meant to change Arabia as we know it today.*

Then, I saw tears of joy streaming down her beautiful face. At that moment, something shifted inside me. The pull on my soul for Issa was more than I could bear. I did the only rational thing I knew. I stood to leave, my heart racing like a stallion, my hands trembling like a leaf, my legs pliable as clay.

I don't know how I made it to my car. Slumped over, head resting on the wheel, time stretched endlessly, as I thought about all that had transpired. Then, the one thing I vowed I would never do again, not since I lost my dear Abbie, I wept.

# CHAPTER 8

# SURPRISE, SURPRISE

*~ Issa, Preparing for Jordan ~*

I woke up at the crack of dawn. The day had finally come. Spinning in circles, I laughed with the abandon of a carefree child. My pulse was thumping like a rapid drum beat. I leaped forward, upending pictures on the table and nearly landing face-first on the floor.

Dean Wright told me to expect a limo around nine to take me to the airport. I thought of all the events leading to this trip. The Ma'an family ran the foundation that was funding this expedition. From what I could surmise, they had holdings in several ventures. While doing my research, I found out they are one of the wealthiest families in Jordan, perhaps in all of Arabia, besides the royal families.

The Ma'an family is in the import and export business, mainly dealing with antiques. They procure many artifacts for museums around the world. I couldn't help but wonder if they knew my friend Kasim. After all, he was supposed to start his archeology studies right after our summer camp ended all those years ago.

*It was a long shot*, I decided.

Besides, Arabia is no small place, and I couldn't remember where in Arabia Kasim lived. I shifted my thoughts back to the matter at hand. The Ma'an family were sending an escort, and I would fly to Jordan on their private jet. I was also to be an honored guest at their estate. They preferred that I have lodgings in close quarters because of the delicate nature of the mission. Besides, many of their archeological findings were on the premises.

While packing, I kept looking at my watch. I began pacing up and down the living room, wondering whether this whole excursion was a good idea. Finally, I sat on the couch and heard a car honking. I jumped and ran to the window. I noticed a woman grabbing her son out of the way of a speeding car. I closed my eyes and breathed in and out deeply to rid myself of the jitters. I knew this trip was in God's plan, so I said a quick prayer.

While finishing the last of my packing, the doorbell rang. Inhaling deeply, I answered. To my surprise, there stood Miriam.

"Miriam, what are you doing here?"

"I've been chosen to accompany you to Jordan. Isn't that wonderful? Remember, I'm from Jordan. I will be the perfect escort for you. You will not feel so alone among strangers. Come, the limo is waiting."

I sighed in relief but was puzzled as to why I was just finding out this information. As strange as it seemed, I was grateful Miriam would be coming with me.

"I'm glad you're here. They told me that a woman would accompany me for modesty's sake and to ensure my needs are met. I never imagined it would be you!"

She hugged me, as had become her custom. I didn't mind at all.

"This is going to be the trip of a lifetime, and I know you won't regret it."

Miriam seemed just as excited as me. We began chattering, while I finished packing.

"So, Miriam, what do you know about this project?"

"Do you remember when we first met? I told you that our interests align, and that's why I wanted to take your class."

"Yes. I was quite taken aback. You reminded me so much of myself

## Surprise, Surprise

when I was your age."

"Well, the dig site is not far from where I live. I've been given permission to be your assistant for the excavation. That is, if you'll have me?"

Miriam dropped her head and waited with hesitation for my decision. I couldn't deny her a chance of a lifetime. She was such a bright girl and easy to get along with.

"Yes, of course, you are a God-send. I'm glad you'll be my guide and assistant."

Miriam's face lit up like the sun on a cloudless day. I gave her a reassuring smile as she helped me finish packing. I packed fairly light. I was told all the necessary tools and supplies would be provided for me, including the gear I would need.

Miriam grabbed my suitcase. I carried a backpack with some personal items. Miriam escorted me to the limousine that was waiting. The driver exited the car, carefully loaded my belongings, and opened the door.

To my surprise, staring back at me with a huge smile was my devastatingly handsome café acquaintance. I had to force myself to close my mouth, which presently stood agape in the wake of this surprise.

"Hello, I'm Dr. Ma'an. It's a pleasure to meet you, Dr. Stevens. I know you're anxious to be briefed on this assignment. I will do so as soon as we're aboard my jet. In the meantime, we can spend some time getting to know one another."

Dr. Ma'an's gaze left mine and locked onto Miriam with a warm smile.

"Hello, Papa," said Miriam.

My world tilted at that bit of information. Suddenly, I realized there was more to this story than I had first suspected.

~ *Dr. Ma'an, The Cafe Stranger* ~

Issa froze in place. There were a series of emotions etched on her face when she discovered who I was. I'm guessing she remembered me from our brief café encounter. Her reactions moved from that of surprise to bewilderment to what looked like a scowl. Her left eyebrow was lifted high on her forehead, and the corners of her mouth drooped down in a scowling frown. She recovered quickly, and her face turned to stone—void of any emotion. I needed to gain back control of this situation.

"Dr. Stevens, I must apologize for all the subterfuge. We intended no disrespect. Once I debrief you on the importance of this mission and the need for the utmost discretion, I believe you'll understand."

"I see, please continue," Issa replied with a smirk on her face. It was as if she enjoyed seeing me squirm under her control.

I alighted from the car, towering over her. It was my only way of regaining some semblance of control.

"Please make yourself comfortable, and I will explain everything."

As I proceeded to help Issa into the car, she bit her lower lip and looked at me with hesitation. She promptly regained her composure, lifted her head, and pasted a brave look on her face. She then took the seat opposite where I was sitting. I couldn't help but smile. It reminded me of my Issa, the one I remembered from summer camp all those years ago.

Miri took a seat next to Issa, and I was left facing the two most beautiful women I knew. Issa's eyes were boring into mine, so I commenced with my defense.

"Yes, Miriam is my daughter, and she was sent here for two reasons. First, to learn from the best. Second, to ensure our partnership would be beneficial to all involved. Miri speaks highly of you, Dr. Stevens, and admires you greatly. Her judgment is sound, and based on our research, you are the best person for this assignment. I know you must have a lot of questions. Perhaps I can answer one or two before the flight to put your mind at ease."

~ *Issa, My Retort* ~

I asked Dr. Ma'an the first two questions that came to my mind,

## Surprise, Surprise

"You look familiar, like we've met before. What did you say your first name is? And why do you and Miriam have different last names?"

Dr. Ma'an's eyes met Miriam, "You see, Miri, our dear Dr. Stevens is a sharp woman, and nothing gets past her."

He then addressed me, "That's two questions, and I will answer them both for you. Miri's full name is Miriam Fakmad Ma'an. Second, my name is Kasim."

My world shifted again. It couldn't be the same Kasim. Maybe Kasim was a common Arabic name, like John or David is a common American name? Besides, my Kasim's last name is Ahkmad, not Ma'an. Something told me to probe this man some more.

"So, is that your full name?"

Dr. Ma'an laughed softly, a deep, rich laugh, with a smile that sported pearly white teeth and caused his eyes to crinkle on the sides. He was captivatingly handsome.

He said, "That's three questions, and you were granted two. We'll revisit your questions later. For now, I'd like to know what your thoughts are on the lost scrolls of the Apostle Paul that were allegedly written to the Arab Christians?"

"Well, many believe Paul wrote to the Arab Christian community to encourage them when he returned to Damascus."

"Yes, Miri told me you had some interesting theories. What facts or assumptions are you basing your theories on? I've done some extensive research myself but continue to run into dead ends."

"It's well known that the Apostle Paul frequently wrote to the churches he established or assisted. The Holy Scripture tells us that Paul took a journey to Arabia. After his conversion, he did not go straightway to Jerusalem to those who were called apostles. Instead, he went to Arabia and later returned to Damascus. Second, there was a discovery during the Crusades, artifacts in the general area where the Arab Christians were purported to live. The artifacts had the symbol of the fish, which, as you know, was a widely used symbol among Christians to identify their faith in times of persecution."

I hesitated a moment before continuing. Dr. Ma'an's face showed rapt attention. After I mentioned the Crusades, there was a shift in his countenance. I couldn't put my finger on it.

Instead of trying to figure him out, I continued, "I'll be more than happy to share my research with you."

"Dr. Stevens…" Dr. Ma'an's face showed a mixture of awe and trepidation.

"You may call me Issa, Dr. Ma'an."

"Alright then, and you may call me Kasim. I'm sure you're aware very few scholars have published on this subject due to the sensitive nature of the findings. The potential harm it could bring to Arab Christians in today's political and religious climate is not to be taken lightly. This is especially true if there indeed exists a continued line of succession from the Ancient Arab Christians and the findings are deemed not conclusive enough to protect them."

"Kasim, I'm sure you've done your research and know that I am a devout Christian. I've sought the Lord on this matter for quite some time. However, I had not received any guidance as to how to proceed. When I received this invitation, I took it as a sign from the Lord that the time had come. I take it that you are a Christian too? I know Miriam has professed her faith in Christ, and of course, you are partnering with a Christian university."

"Yes, I've done my research. And yes, we are Christians. However, this is not common knowledge in our country. There are many who would use such information to strip my family of its wealth and prestige."

All I could do was nod and turn away from the grave look in Kasim's eyes. The more information he divulged, the more uneasy I felt. I had heard the stories of excavations gone wrong. The kind you encounter in the movies. They indeed do exist. But what Kasim was talking about was of epic proportion. It could change political and religious landscapes, even to the brink of war and bloodshed. I did the only thing I knew to do. I closed my eyes and prayed.

*~ Kasim, My Concern ~*

## Surprise, Surprise

Maybe I said too much, too soon. Issa ceased her questions, turned her head, and closed her eyes. I knew she was praying, and I was glad. We were all going to need it. Maybe I should never have dragged her into my world. But what was done was done. The only thing I could do at this point was close my eyes and pray too.

*~ Issa, Plane Ride to Jordan ~*

After boarding the luxurious private jet, Kasim continued to brief me on the state of affairs in Arabia. He explained the plight of the Arab Christians. He told me about his import and export businesses. He also revealed that his foundation is the holder of many of the artifacts that his family businesses have acquired over the centuries.

"So, have you been involved in the recent excavations for the lost scrolls?" I asked. It was more of a statement than a question, but it didn't seem to faze Kasim.

"Yes, but to the outside world, we are merely interested in the excavations for what they can add to our wealth, nothing more. Issa, you must know how important it is that our identity not be revealed. Not yet, at any rate. I can't lie to you; this mission is fraught with danger. I'll do everything in my power, with our Lord's help, to keep you safe."

"I will not back down, and I will not lie to you either, Kasim. This scares me half to death! Nevertheless, I'm here on assignment, personally and professionally. More importantly, I'm on assignment for the Lord."

"I'm glad to hear that, for raiders, grave diggers, and the like still exist in the twenty-first century. They come in many faces, and frankly, no one can be trusted in this line of business. I have briefed you thus far because I want to give you an opportunity to decline my offer. If you choose to decline later, you can stay at my estate for as long as you like. Call it a vacation, courtesy of the Ma'an family. But if you choose to continue, I want you to go in with your eyes wide open."

*Eyes wide open*, I thought to myself.

There is much more to this story than meets the eye. For all intents and purposes, my eyes were wide open, and I was blind as a bat. As much as I wanted to run away, with equal intensity, I wanted to stay.

The Spirit of the Lord gently whispered to my spirit, *I have called you to this task, and I am with you.*

I steeled my resolve, looked Kasim in the eyes, and told him with as much courage as I could muster up, "I'm committed to you and your mission and will help you in whatever way I can. But remember this, I can only be as good a help to you as you are to me. If you withhold information, I can't take responsibility for a failed mission."

There, I said it. With as much honesty and humility as possible, I revealed what was niggling at my core. I didn't want to offend Kasim, and although he was a Christian, he was an Arab man, most likely steeped in his culture, which said that a woman must remember her place.

Kasim looked deep in thought as he looked away. He stayed that way for a long time. Then he looked me in the eyes with such intensity that shivers coursed through my body.

Finally, he announced, "Issa, it's me, Kasim Ahkmad. Or rather, Ahkmad is my father's middle name. My birth name is Kasim Fakmad Ma'an. I've missed you so much."

My eyes must have enlarged, rivaling the size of the moon. Joy coursed through my body, and my eyes crinkled on the sides. My lips softened, and I began to smile deeply. Then, my face must have flushed crimson. I felt anger well up in me at the thought of Kasim abruptly leaving me on that dreaded day in summer camp. I had not heard from him again, until now.

### ~ Kasim, My Regret ~

I saw several emotions cross Issa's face, but the last one was definitely the look of hurt and betrayal. My emotions were equally all over the place.

I softly replied, "I'm so sorry, Issa. I understand if you want nothing to do with me or this mission."

Her face seemed to soften, so I continued.

## Surprise, Surprise

"I was swiftly taken from the States back to Arabia after an assassination attempt on my father's life. I'm his only male heir. His only child, for that matter. My father feared that the people who were after him would find and use me as leverage to get to him."

"Oh Kasim, was anyone hurt?"

"No, no, Issa. To this day, we haven't found who ordered the assassination attempt. There have been several over the years. Our advisors would have us believe it's a rival faction who sees our family as a threat because of our growing wealth."

"And your abundant resources have led you to a dead end?"

For a moment, I looked away and was deep in thought.

I replied, "My father believes otherwise. His guess is that it's the opposing religious factions who want to suppress Christianity in Arabia at all costs. Although, not many know our heritage, which makes me wonder if the threats are from within."

I turned my attention back to Issa. Her face was still flushed, but I could see she was making an effort to tamp down her ire. It pained me to see her this way. It dredged up memories of the pain I felt when I abruptly left her. I gathered enough courage to continue.

"After a while, my family convinced me that I could never forge any significant relationships with those outside of our immediate circle. Primarily because of the threat it would bring to our family and to our legacy. I've never forgotten you, Issa."

*I just couldn't allow myself to love you,* I mumbled under my breath.

Truth be told, it was too late. I fell in love with Issa that summer. But I was just a boy and there was nothing I could do about it. My family needed me, and I wrestled with that for a long time.

My father knew it, too. By the next year, I was married off to the daughter of a close family friend, who was also a believer. I wasn't in love with my Abbie at first, but we grew to love one another. And I had her to thank for my precious Miri.

Abbie's family were Bedouins who converted to the way of Christ under my father's tutelage. They were also able to trace their lineage to the Arab Christians, as far back as the Crusades. That was enough for my father to give his blessing. He would have done anything to keep me away from the thought of Issa and returning to the States.

### ~ Issa, My Resolve ~

It took me a moment to recover from the shock of being told that this wealthy, influential, handsome man was indeed my Kasim. We proceeded to fill each other in on the details of our lives for the past twenty-five years.

I had felt betrayed and alone when Kasim left. It wasn't until I met Dave three years later that my life regained some semblance of normalcy. Kasim was the first boy I had ever kissed. My young brain somehow thought that meant we would be married one day.

I don't know if Kasim felt the same way because he never declared it, and he disappeared from my life shortly after. I sure hope he doesn't remember any of it. I was feeling pretty awkward. He, on the other hand, acted as if nothing was amiss.

Kasim proceeded to brief me on the political climate in his country and what was expected of me as a woman. He told me that I would be respected because of my status as a renowned scholar and his personal guest but that I should uphold the customs of his people to the best of my ability.

*How dare he belittle me as a woman,* I mused.

My temper got the best of me, and I challenged him.

"I'm just as qualified and educated as any man associated with this excavation, and you want me to act like a silly girl with no sense."

"Issa, you misunderstand. I'm telling you this for your safety and the safety of my family and to prevent drawing any unnecessary attention to this project."

I blinked rapidly, and my face turned beet red. I felt so imprudent.

## Surprise, Surprise

I humbled myself and apologized, something I didn't like doing. I hated being proved wrong about anything.

"Kasim, please accept my apology. I meant no offense."

"None taken. This must all be overwhelming for you, and rightfully so. Let me tell you a little more about myself."

Kasim told me that his mother had died five years ago and that his wife died while giving birth to Miriam. He confided in me about the assassination attempt on his father's life. He told me I would get to meet his father, his uncle, and his cousins while staying at the estate.

About three hours into the flight, we finally had our meal. We decided to watch videos of some recent excavations, all headed up by Kasim.

"I see you've put the skills you learned from our archeology camp to good use," I teased.

Kasim's face lit up, and he replied, "I'm looking forward to working with you again, Issa. It's been a long time, but I remember everything like it was yesterday."

I gasped, a barely perceptible intake of air. But nothing seemed to get past Kasim. I had hoped he had not remembered any of it, especially the dreaded kiss. It was definitely time to change the subject. Seeing as this flight was going to be a long one, I suggested we watch a movie.

"Indiana Jones," offered Kasim.

I put my hands on my hips and chided, "You would choose that movie."

Kasim gave me a boyish grin, "What's wrong with this movie?"

"You know very well what's wrong with this movie, SNAKES!"

"Oh, yes, snakes. You'd better be glad I was there to save you. I told you not to turn over stones with your bare hands. You were so stubborn and feisty back then."

Kasim's eyes were dancing with pleasure, and he chuckled as he walked away to retrieve the movie.

Talking over his shoulder, Kasim added, "And I can see little has changed."

I was furious, but Miriam couldn't contain herself and burst out laughing. I found myself laughing too. When Kasim saw that I was laughing, the laughter became contagious to the point where we were all holding our sides.

The remainder of the flight was carefree. Between Miriam and Kasim, they kept me busy playing board games and laughing. As nighttime drew near, Miriam slept on a couch nearby. Kasim was reading over some documents. I listened to worship music with my earphones and closed my eyes.

Suddenly, I felt a large, warm hand cover my own and Kasim's voice saying, "Wake up, Issa, we're here."

# CHAPTER 9

# Saul's Journey to Arabia

*~ Saul, The Escape, A.D. 35 ~*

After my encounter with Jesus on the road to Damascus, I had a burning desire to tell my countrymen about Jesus. For far too long, I had a zeal for the wrong thing. I stood by and watched innocent people get murdered for confessing faith in Christ.

I remember when the Synagogue of the Freedmen brought accusations against Stephen. They accused him of blasphemy, saying Jesus would destroy the temple and change the customs of Moses. He was taken out of the city to be stoned. He spoke with such conviction and authority. Like the others, I, too, was deceived. I, too, wanted him dead. However, his last words have remained with me to this day, "Lord, do not charge them with this sin."

I, Saul, even had women and children imprisoned. It became a thorn in my side. Falling to my knees, I tore my clothes, poured dirt over my head, and moaned in agony, for the pain of my past sins was far too great.

I prayed, "Lord, I feel so unworthy to be considered your servant. I had your very elect killed. I've sinned against you and others. My heart is heavy with shame and guilt."

I wept without restraint. How long I stayed there, I could not say. I finally managed to resume my prayers.

"Please help me receive the forgiveness you offer on the cross. You are the spotless Lamb of God, who takes away the sin of the world. From this point on, I vow that my latter zeal will be greater than the former. But this time, it will be for you, Jesus."

The believers of the Way were reluctant to receive me at first. Once they saw my sincerity, they embraced me. On the other hand, my fellow Pharisees, those who were in bondage to the Law, those who missed the signs of the coming Messiah, plotted to kill me.

Certain leaders of the synagogue had already dispatched a missive to Jerusalem informing the High Priest that I had gone mad. And the Temple guards had made it back too.

They reported, "Saul is preaching in the name of Jesus in the synagogue."

This caused such an uproar that I had to be taken from the Damascus synagogue and hidden among the followers of the Way.

"Saul," implored Ananias, "it's no longer safe for you to preach in the synagogue. You must leave as soon as possible. I bid you, do not go to Jerusalem or Tarsus until this all settles."

"I must go to Jerusalem to meet with Peter, John, and the others and tell them about my encounter with Jesus."

"They will not receive you, and if the High Priest gets wind that you're in Jerusalem, he will not hesitate to kill you."

"I'm not afraid of death. For me to live is Christ and to die is gain."

"Listen, I'll get word to the disciples in Jerusalem. Give them time to consider all that has happened and prepare to receive you. In the meantime, we must help you leave Damascus."

"I must go to Tarsus to tell my family about Jesus and get them to safety. Besides, all my belongings are there. I will need my tent-making equipment to earn wages."

"I'll send some believers to Tarsus and make sure your family is safe. We'll relocate them and your belongings if necessary. We'll explain to them your encounter with Jesus and teach them about the Way."

The believers had been so concerned for my safety that they concocted an idea of how to help me escape Damascus. They found a basket that was sizable enough to fit me in. Then, at night, they lowered me down the city wall. I barely escaped with my life.

My first thought was to go to Jerusalem and meet the disciples of Jesus. Ananias had warned me that they would not be ready to receive me. Instead, I followed what Jesus told me, to bring the Gospel to the Gentiles. So, I fled to Arabia.

Before they lowered me down the wall, I confessed, "I'm afraid of heights."

Ananias said, "God is sending you to the Gentiles, my friend, so no harm will befall you."

Ezra replied, "There will be fellow Jews in Arabia because it is a thriving trade center with trade routes between Arabia, Egypt, and the Mediterranean Sea."

"I don't recall the High Priest ever speaking of a synagogue in Arabia. If there is, I will bide my time. I'll mingle with the Gentiles and seek out fellow believers," I said.

I had enough provisions for a ten-day journey, and I still had the coins I carried from Jerusalem. We calculated the trip to be about a ten to twelve-day journey by foot, depending on the weather and the terrain. I would eat what I could find from the land if needed.

"Saul, if you cross paths with a caravan, negotiate with the caravan master. It will be much easier for you," suggested Ezra.

"Yes, I will do as you say. In the meantime, I'll use the time alone to pray and seek the Lord's direction for Arabia."

"We've collected enough coins to help you settle there. Take it and add it to your purse. We will not take no for an answer," urged Ananias.

I started to protest but thought better of it.

Instead, I embraced my brothers in the Lord and pronounced, "The peace of our risen Lord be with you."

"And also with you, brother Saul."

As they lowered me down the wall, all I could do was pray. My stomach felt like it was mimicking the frantic movements of fish caught in a fisherman's net. The basket jerked a few times, then stopped. My breath hitched, and I could feel my heart thumping against my chest. I thought I heard a commotion at the top of the wall. Fear gripped my heart like the talons of a bird holding onto its prey.

The basket hit the ground with a thud that rattled my bones. There was no time to investigate what was going on behind the walls. I grabbed my provisions and ran for a thicket of trees in the distance. Once I found safety, I would gather my bearings and pray some more.

I traveled until the moon was high in the sky. Then, I stopped to set up shelter and pray. I lost track of time, and the clouds were now obscuring my only source of light. It was dark. I couldn't discern if I was praying to the East as was customary or in some other direction. The moment the sun kissed the horizon, I knew what direction I needed to go. The sun rises in the East and sets in the West. I knew Damascus was north of Arabia. I needed to head South, so I set off in that direction.

*~ Saul, Pray, and Prey ~*

The first day, my journey was uneventful, but the second day proved to be challenging. A sandstorm hit, causing me to take shelter near a hillside, which shielded me from the worst of the storm.

I prayed in earnest. "Lord, you gave me this assignment to take the gospel to the Gentiles. I know it's not your will for me to perish in this wilderness. I'm entrusting you with my life."

When the storm settled, I sighed in relief. I bowed my head to the ground, "Thank you, Lord, it could have been worse."

Unfortunately, the residue of the sand caused me to crave more water than I'd anticipated. This left me with a dwindling supply of this precious resource. Whenever I came across a tree, I inspected its leaves for signs of moisture and siphoned off as much as I could.

I knew there should be an underground stream that nourished these trees. I had neither the time nor the tools to locate it. Instead, I pressed on with a determination that brokered no argument or opposition.

The terrain proved to be arduous the closer I got to Arabia. When possible, I traveled close to the mountain range to avoid being detected by two-legged or four-legged predators. The rock-strewn paths and uneven ground slowed my progress. I found a thick tree branch that had long lost its vitality. I fashioned it like a walking stick, which proved invaluable over the unstable desert floor.

The hot desert sun beat mercilessly on me as if I were its only target. My tallit soaked up the sweat and deflected some of the sun's rays, but it was also suffocating. I was running out of water. My mouth was parched, and my tongue tasted like grit from the dust. I couldn't even smell properly because the sand was embedded in my nostrils.

There was not a soul in sight, human or animal. I did see a flock of vultures circling about three thousand meters back, which made me wary and alert for any four-legged predators. Then, as if I conjured up the danger in my mind, I fell upon a pack of wild dogs. These dogs were ravenous. Their rib cages were sunken in, which proved the lack of prey in these desert parts. They bared their teeth and growled menacingly.

I began to wave my stick and make loud noises in an attempt to scare them off. The pack did not seem phased by my antics as they began to encircle me. One dog started to bark viciously as it closed in on me. I sent up a swift prayer and called on the name of Jesus for protection.

"Lord, you are the Creator of Heaven and Earth and everything in it, please settle your creation."

I thought of the story of Daniel in the Lion's Den and how Yahweh shut up the mouths of the lions. Then, I remembered the story of the angel who would not allow Balaam's donkey to cross the road.

Then, I prayed again, "Lord, shut up the mouths of these dogs, and send an angel to block their path."

Immediately, the dogs began to yelp, and they turned and ran. It was then that I knew without a doubt God was with me, and I would make it to Arabia alive.

The evenings were surprisingly cold. I had to wrap myself in my cloak and the pallet I used for sleeping. From time to time, I noticed a group of trees with sparse vegetation. At least it was enough to take shelter and siphon for water. The stark change in temperature from day to night was taking a toll on my body. By day six, I became feverish and was nearly out of water. I knew I needed to press on.

I noticed the rock face changing colors from gray-white to reddish-brown the closer I came to the rugged mountainous terrain. I knew this to be the ancient territory of Esau, the brother of Jacob, who was the father of the Edomites. This was also ancient Moab and the mountain where Moses died, according to the Torah.

"Lord, allow me to speak to this rock so the waters may gush forth as it did for your servant Moses when he struck it."

I dared to speak to the rock, but nothing happened. I was tempted to strike it but thought better of it. I was about to give up when, out of the corner of my eye, I saw a clump of trees with green foliage jutting out of the mountainside far off in the distance.

By noonday, I reached the mountain floor. As I made my way to the trees, I could feel the moisture in the air. I placed my hand on the mountain and could feel wet moss on the rocks. The scent of fresh water reached me, and I allowed it to guide me to its source, which was between the rock crevices around the bend in the mountain.

I located a brook, where I guessed the mountain goats drank liberally. It was as if the Lord gave me the sense of smell, like that of the mountain goat, for I found the water quickly. I drank deeply and went through ritual cleansing. I spent time in prayer and reading from a scroll the words of the prophets concerning the coming Messiah. I must have fallen asleep, for when I opened my eyes, the sun was soon to set. I could feel the difference in temperature. I began to shiver. It was only then I realized my skin was ablaze with fever.

A quick plea slipped from my lips, "Lord, do not allow your servant to die in this wilderness."

I was feeling weak but needed to get some distance from the brook. No doubt, the creatures of the night would come to satiate their thirst.

I found a cleft in the mountainside, which provided sufficient defense against the biting winds and frosty night air and shelter from creatures that roamed in the desert night. I dared not start a fire, as it would only attract night predators.

By morning, I was delirious with fever. I thought I was seeing things as two men approached me. They looked like Bedouins, but maybe they were angels sent by Yahweh? When they addressed me, I noticed they were speaking in an Aramaic dialect that was familiar to me. Although they were close in proximity, their voices sounded distant. Then, everything went dark.

When I awoke, my nostrils were assaulted by the smell of camel dung, spices, and sweat from the drivers. I found myself surrounded by camels laden with wares and men milling about. I noticed my fever was gone.

A lanky man with a white beard approached me and spoke in Aramaic.

"We nearly lost you, sir. We found you over there on that remote mountain. Where are you from, and where are you headed?"

My voice was hoarse, but I managed to say, "I'm Saul of Tarsus, and I'm headed to Arabia."

The man replied, "You'll have your wish indeed. We should arrive within the hour."

## Chapter 10

# The Ma'an Estate

*- Issa, Settling In -*

We landed on a private airstrip somewhere in Jordan. There was a limousine waiting to take us to the Ma'an estate. Kasim and Miriam exited the plane, both smiling broadly, happy to be home, I presumed.

I looked at Kasim and inquired, "How far are we from your estate?"

"It's about a thirty-minute drive."

I peered out the window of the limousine, and history began to unfold before my eyes as I took in the ancient landscape. Some of the views were breathtaking. The sun was rising in the East. I knew Jerusalem was nestled in that direction. The first tendrils of dawn began to weave through the tapestry of the night.

"Look, Kasim, it's beautiful!"

Slowly, the colors in the sky began to shift—a gradient of deep purples and blues giving way to the soft blush of dawn. The world seemed to hold its breath, anticipating the grand unveiling of a new day. With each passing moment, the sun ascended, painting the sky with hues of pink, orange, and gold. In that ethereal moment, as the sun completed its ascent, I felt a surge of hope for our mission. It was as if the sunrise held promises untold, whispers of new beginnings and uncharted journeys that awaited ahead.

Miriam interrupted my thoughts.

"Welcome to Ma'an, Jordan, Dr. Stevens."

I noticed we were approaching the estate. It was breathtaking and monumental in its size. The intricate carvings on the face of the structure made it look ancient, like a castle.

"This is such a beautiful place," I said. "Are the excavations to be here in Ma'an or in Petra?"

Kasim replied, "Petra is approximately thirty-six kilometers from Ma'an, about a forty-minute drive. Much of our property isn't developed and extends outward and borders Petra. There are other properties within Petra. The excavations will primarily take place there."

We passed by a guard house and entered the primary grounds of the estate through an iron gate that creaked as it opened. The gate had an intricate design of grapes in full bloom on vines, surrounded by lotus. The grounds were immaculate with a profusion of flowers. The inside was equally astounding, with expensive rugs strewn across marble floors and relics gracing table tops. The paintings looked like they were from before the sixteenth century.

Kasim excused himself to attend to some urgent matters. Miriam and I were escorted to the residential section of the estate by a servant.

"Here we are, Dr. Stevens. Your room is down the hall. Papa's room is at the end of this corridor next to mine," said Miriam.

"Please, when we're alone, call me Issa. I think of you as a friend and my trusted guide."

"I'd like that very much, Issa. You can call me Miri, like my Papa does."

"Thank you for helping me settle in, Miri. I don't know what I would've done without you. It's all a bit overwhelming. I'm probably just jet lagged."

"I'm here to help, however I can. How about I take you to the

## The Ma'an Estate

bathhouse? It's set up in the Roman style with a caldarium, steam room, jacuzzi, and a masseuse."

"That sounds amazing."

"I will get you up to speed on the dinner arrangements for tonight and who will be attending. I think that advantage will help put you at ease. My family can be intimidating sometimes."

"Any information you can give me will be great. I don't want to be behind the curve on this one."

"I agree. Now, off to the baths we go. And, after the baths, it'll be siesta time for both of us. Then, my handmaiden will apply her craft and help us prepare for dinner."

The baths were everything Miri described and more.

"Oh Miri, I could indulge in this hot tub for hours."

"Wait until you meet Rajah, my handmaiden. The massage alone will keep you here forever. It will put you to sleep for sure. But that's okay because we'll need to be well-rested for tonight's dinner."

"So, tell me about this guest list for tonight."

"Well, my grandfather, Fakmad Ahkmad Ma'an, will be there. I think it would be appropriate to address him as Mr. Ma'an. My Uncle Fasim will be there as well. Be careful around him, Issa. I don't trust him. If he had his way, he would be paterfamilias, the head of the family as the Romans called it."

"Oh, thank you for warning me."

"My grandfather has been pressuring my Papa to remarry so that he can have a male heir and keep the succession of our line to our paternal side. A pure line, they call it. In other words, so my uncle doesn't usurp it."

"Miri, why did your father never remarry?"

"My Papa wants to marry for love. His marriage to my mother was an arranged marriage. But over time, he grew to love her. He will not admit it, but I know he feels guilty that their love didn't have an opportunity to blossom. They married so young, and it was only a short time before my birth and her passing."

"Miri, I'm so sorry. We don't have to talk about this if it's too painful."

"I didn't know my mother except through the eyes of others. Papa speaks highly of her and tends to put himself down without even knowing it. It makes me feel sad for him. I want nothing more than to see him happy. After my mother passed, he vowed never to marry again unless it was for love. I want that for him too."

"And, this puts your family legacy in jeopardy?"

"Yes, in the sense that the right to succession will fall to my Uncle Fasim's family if my father should die without a male heir. The problem is that Fasim is my mother's brother and, therefore, not a direct descendant of the Ma'an family. The only living male of the Ma'an line, other than my grandfather, is my father."

"I see the dilemma."

"Also, Fasim is not a Christian like we are. His primary religion is money. He wouldn't betray his family, though, not so much because of his loyalty but because of our wealth and what he stands to lose if our faith in Jesus were to become common knowledge."

"Who else should I be concerned about?"

"You have no need to worry. Papa will be there."

"I'm not worried, more curious than anything."

"Fasar, my father's maternal cousin, will be there as well. He is a flirt, so watch out for him. Although, he would not dare insult you in my father's house. You are under his and grandfather's protection. Akhab often joins us for the evening meal. He helps with the excavations and runs the family's import and export business. He lives alone. His wife died a few years ago, and he has no children. Grandfather treats him like a son."

"So, you and I will be the only women?"

"Yes, to my knowledge. But don't let it intimidate you. You'll be seated with me and Papa. We will help you with all the social and cultural niceties."

After a long nap, I stretched my arms out wide and yawned even wider. Miri greeted me with a sweet smile, and Rajah followed behind her. Rajah was assigned to apply her craft to my face and hair. She expertly applied my makeup, which brought out the color of my green eyes. She then curled my hair and set it with pearls at the nape of my neck.

Miri walked in with a lovely and expensive-looking gown that could easily be worn at a formal event. The dress was long and flowing, with sequins at the neckline and sprinkled throughout the dress, which made it sparkle. The dress had a trim of lace embroidered with a design that looked like lilies at the hem and on the seams of the dress. It was a deep, rich, forest green that set my eyes ablaze.

"It's beautiful, Miri, but I'd prefer not to give the impression that I'm trying to impress someone. After all, in a few days, I'll be in trousers knee-high in dirt."

"On the contrary, first impressions are everlasting, and we must show the men that you are as formidable off the job as you are on the job." A giggle escaped Miri's lips. "Besides, I don't get to dress up often, so indulge me a little."

When Rajah finished applying my makeup, I couldn't believe what I was seeing in the mirror. Who's this lovely lady?

"Miri, I feel like an imposter. This is not who I am."

I used my hands to gesture from the top of my head to the soles of my feet to stress my point.

Looking in the mirror, I repeated, "This is not who I am. I prefer to be a simple woman with an average appearance who happens to know a lot of stuff."

"Issa, why do you say such things? You're beautiful inside and out. Why can't you see that?"

"Humph, you mean after Rajah finishes working her magic on my face?"

"No, you're beautiful and smart without all this." Miri gestured at my ensemble for emphasis.

"You just don't know it. My Papa thinks so too."

Stuttering in disbelief, I countered, "I think you misunderstand, Miri. Your father and I actually met a long time ago at a summer camp. We were young. It was right before going off to college. That's why we are so familiar with one another."

"Yes, I know. Papa told me all about it. That's why I know he cares for you deeply."

I was sure a deep crimson red filled my cheeks at that revelation. I hadn't expected Kasim to share our childhood encounter with his daughter. I wonder just how much information he told Miri.

He couldn't be aware of the depth of my emotions for him—for during that period, I don't believe I fully comprehended my own feelings. And I doubt he felt the same for me, or else he would've tried to contact me at some point after he left. It would be useless for me to believe otherwise.

So, I gave Miri the safest reply I could think of, "Oh, I see."

"You're very modest, Issa, and that's what my Papa likes best about you. You're a formidable woman, wise and knowledgeable, wrapped in grace and humility. You have a strength that brokers no argument for triviality. You're the kind of woman I want to become."

"Thank you. I will take that as a compliment. Although, I don't really know who this woman is that you're describing. And even if it were true, I don't know how far that compliment will get me in Arabia. I'm not ignorant of the cultural differences here, and I'm bound to get myself in trouble in one way or another."

"That's exactly why I'm here to help."

"But Miri, I don't know if dressing up like the Queen of Sheba is going to help any of us here."

"You will grace us with your presence and enchant us with your beauty. Besides, our men need to know women can have beauty, brains, and brawn."

I wasn't as convinced as Miri, but for her sake, I smiled. However, I felt like an imposter inside. I felt like a wrecking ball about to hit its target.

~ *Kasim, The Dinner Fiasco* ~

I was deep in conversation with my father discussing the upcoming excavation when, at the periphery of my vision, I saw the most beautiful, exquisite, regal woman I've ever seen on this side of Heaven. As I turned to greet Issa, my breath hitched, and my heart kicked into overdrive. I tried to slow down my breathing so that I could speak without faltering.

Father nudged me, "Kasim, will you introduce me to our lovely guest?"

Issa, indeed, was beautiful. Miri looked just as lovely. I bet she put Issa up to this. I'll have to thank her later. Issa looked like royalty with her deep, rich, forest green dress, which accentuated her emerald green eyes. She smelled like roses with a hint of jasmine. Her hair was decorated with pearls. Her lush lips were ruby red, reminding me of the too few kisses we shared before I was abruptly removed from her life. I would prefer nothing more than to take her in my arms and tell her how much I've missed her, how I've never stopped thinking about her.

I knew exactly what Miri was up to. She wanted her grandfather to be so impressed with Issa that he would give up his nonsensical idea of trying to arrange a marriage for her Papa. *Could Miri be trying to do her own match-making*? I wondered. My life was too complicated and full of danger. I had no intention of dragging Issa into its drama. Or putting her in harm's way more than I already have.

Besides, Issa was my age, and to bear a child at forty-two would be dangerous for her. But just the sound of it…Issa and I married with a child of our own. Lord knows I would give up my wealth to be with her. But my legacy, that was too weighty a matter to think about. God would have to make a way.

I was brought out of my reverie when I heard Miri introducing Issa to everyone. I quickly recovered and escorted Issa to her seat.

I leaned in and whispered in her ear. "You're as beautiful as the day I first met you."

She took in a sharp breath and smiled.

To my surprise, she whispered back, "You're still as devastatingly handsome as the first day I met you."

"Touché," I replied with a smile as I proceeded back to my seat.

Uncle Fasim turned to Issa and began his interrogation. Thankfully, Father interrupted him.

"Fasim, we will have time for business later. Let's eat and enjoy our new friend and our family."

Fasim frowned, but Father acted as if he didn't notice.

Fasim turned to Miri and, with contempt, he squawked, "Miri, where is your hijab? You forget your place. You've become too Americanized."

Miri looked at Issa and spoke in earnest, "I'm so sorry, Dr. Stevens. I will return."

Then she ran out with a look of distress on her face.

How dare he speak to my Miri that way? I glanced at Issa, and her face was stricken. Her brows were knit together, and she looked as angry as I felt.

I intervened and voiced to my uncle, "She meant no disrespect. She will return with the appropriate headcovering."

*~ Issa, The Gift of Healing~*

I could see Kasim's eyes smoldering with anger as he addressed his uncle. There's definitely more to this family than meets the eye, and I'm determined to find out what it is. I had a suspicion there was as much danger within as there was outside the walls of this estate.

As dinner came to a close, Fasim turned to me and asked, "Why are you really in Arabia, Dr. Stevens? Halfway around the world? An American woman all alone in an Arab country? What do you stand to gain from the Ma'an fortune?"

"I beg your pardon, sir. Until a few weeks ago, I had no knowledge or intention of being here. I was sought out by your nephew to assist in an archeological project. I accepted the invitation because it aligns closely with my area of expertise and my academic interests."

Fasim frowned, and I thought I heard a low growl that accompanied his look of disgust.

His next words almost unhinged me. "You're not welcome here."

"Uncle, enough! I will not stand by and have you insult my guest."

"Can't you see, Kasim? She's trying to spin you in her web to gain your fortune. You know our plans must move forward as your father has declared. It must not; it cannot be any other way."

Suddenly, Kasim's father yelled out in pain as he gripped his chest and fell from his chair.

"Father!"

"Grandfather!"

"Fakmad!"

They all exclaimed at once!

I felt the Holy Spirit nudging me to lay my hands on Fakmad's heart. Even though I knew that would break every rule of etiquette in Arab culture. Fakmad began to sweat profusely. His face was pale, and his skin felt cold and clammy. I began to pray for the Lord's healing power in the name of Jesus.

As I laid my hand over his heart, my prayer was inaudible at first. Then, as my lips began to move, I found my voice. The strength of it even sounded strange to me. I prayed as one with authority and the power to arrest the spirit of death that tried to grip Fakmad. I knew it was the Spirit of God through me praying life into him.

It was those final words I spoke, "Death, you have no power here, and you must leave in the name of Jesus Christ the risen Savior."

At that moment, the grip of death released its ugly talons. Fakmad, with his eyes still closed, smiled weakly and whispered, "I'm healed, the Lord has healed me."

Everyone stood motionless. I was drained of all my strength and fell backward on my heels. Silently, I began thanking God with my eyes closed. Kasim rushed to my side and placed his arms gently on my shoulders.

"Issa, are you alright? Do you need water?"

"Yes, please, I would like that very much."

Fakmad looked at Fasim with a faraway look in his eyes and said, "This is what we call a miracle. The miracles that our ancestors told us about. Miracles that are still possible today. I believe our plans are about to change."

# Chapter 11

# Old Feelings Die Hard

*~ Issa, Danger Lurks ~*

Old feelings die hard. I found myself staring into Kasim's all-consuming gray eyes. Those eyes bored into mine with an intensity that made my insides burn. As he leaned in, I succumbed to the temptation and welcomed his kiss. I felt like twenty-five years of pent-up desire was unleashed in that one passionate kiss. He held me in his arms, keeping me warm and sheltered from the night's chill. He whispered in my ear, "Issa, I love you."

Suddenly, I jerked up in my bed, gasping for air and drenched in sweat. Was it all a dream? It seemed so real. Disappointed, I yawned and stretched my arms, slowly coming back to reality. I reminded myself of something Kasim told me earlier. His father was trying to arrange a marriage to a distant cousin for him to save his legacy.

What did that mean? Then, it dawned on me. Kasim mentioned that his unbroken legacy is tied to the mission of the excavations. I must help him find the connection. This is the key to unlocking the mystery. And maybe it will explain why his family is so opposed to us being together.

After my dream, it was proving impossible to go back to sleep. The darkness outside was gradually receding, and dawn was on the verge of breaking. I decided to find my way to the kitchen to brew a cup of coffee. The servants were not awake yet, so I fumbled my way through the dark corridors of the eerie estate in search of the kitchen.

As I turned a corner, I saw a shadowy figure cross my path. My heart lurched in my chest. I ducked behind a wall so as not to be seen.

*What if it's Fasim?* I thought in horror.

I'm sure he'd find the means to do away with me and call it an accident. My heart was racing like an express train. I was sure whoever was on the other side of the wall could hear it. I molded myself into a crevice. The shadowy figure passed and looked my way. I saw a pair of sinister yellow eyes that looked like a cat's eyes peering in my direction.

I held my breath. Then, a quick prayer for protection slipped from my lips. The eyes seemed to look right through me. A shiver ran down my spine, and I could sense an evil presence, demonic in nature. Suddenly, an unexplainable peace descended upon me. At that moment, I was sure I was taking refuge under the wings of the Almighty, and he was covering me.

I couldn't help but wonder what sort of evil lurked in the halls of this estate and whether Kasim was even aware of its existence. When I no longer sensed the malevolent presence, I sighed in relief. I stood still as a statue for about ten minutes before I felt it was safe to return to my room.

Then, I heard his voice, "Issa, is that you?"

"Kasim, you nearly scared the life out of me. How long have you been standing there?"

"I just rounded the corner. You're up early."

"I couldn't sleep. I thought I'd get some coffee."

"I'm headed that way too."

"I've been standing here for ten minutes waiting for a safe time to return to my room."

"What do you mean a safe time?"

"Well, it felt like someone was following me. Then, I saw a pair of yellow eyes staring in my direction. It felt like an evil presence."

"Issa, this estate is well guarded. However, to be on the safe side, I

## Old Feelings Die Hard

will move your room next to Miri and me, though the accommodations are smaller."

"I don't mind at all."

"I also want you to call me if you need to leave your room unescorted at night."

"Yes, I would appreciate that very much. I hope all of this doesn't sound foolish, but I know what I saw. I know what I sensed."

"I take what you say seriously. I will alert my security team of your encounter."

Kasim held out his arm like a gentleman, and I grasped hold immediately. I felt his warmth and his muscular frame next to mine. His entire presence cocooned me, and I leaned into his side. I felt safe in this man's company.

Before we reached the kitchen, Kasim stopped. He turned to face me, his piercing gray eyes meeting mine with intensity. We stood there, the passing seconds stretching out into what felt like an eternity.

"Issa, your faith and quick action helped save my father's life. I'm indebted to you. You must know that," said Kasim.

"I only obeyed what the Spirit of the Lord told me to do. God is with your family, and he has sent me here to help you in whatever way I can."

Kasim took a deep breath, the release of tension visible. Then he leaned in and kissed me on the forehead and pulled me into his embrace. He smelled of sandalwood and spice. His touch, his warmth, his embrace left me dizzy.

"I'm here for you. After all, remember you're my partner in crime," I said.

Kasim chuckled, with that deep, husky voice, and replied, "Now for that cup of coffee. I'll make it for you. After all, you are my guest."

Kasim winked at me.

"Thank you, kind sir." I jested, exaggerating a low curtsey.

The smell of coffee brewing was delectable. Arabic coffee was not for the faint of heart.

We sat and made small talk for a short time. I laughed at a joke he told. It felt like we were back in summer camp and had not been separated all those years.

Kasim abruptly changed the topic.

"On a serious note, I will take you on a tour of the grounds this week. I will show you some interesting artifacts we've acquired. I think this mission will make more sense once you see them."

I peered over the rim of my cup and smiled.

"I would like that very much. I'm here to help."

"You may not be so eager after today."

"And what is that supposed to mean?"

"There are things about me that you aren't aware of. I know now—I must tell you. But herein lies the dilemma—to tell you is to put your life in peril. And I wouldn't be able to live with myself if anything happened to you, Issa. You mean too much to me."

Kasim reached for my hands and grasped both of them. A tingling sensation shot up my arms. I began to have what could only be described as a hot flash. I'm sure he noticed the tinge of pink on my cheeks.

Trying to compose myself, I said, "Kasim, I'm not here by accident. It's the Lord's doing. It's his will, and he will protect us all."

"Your faith is admirable. My ancestors had your faith. Their faith was strong enough to survive nearly two millennia. Now, that faith is in danger on my watch. After last night, my father is convinced you are sent by the God of his fathers to help restore our legacy. But enough about that. It will become clearer to you over the next few weeks."

"I will pray and ask for the Lord's guidance," I said.

"You are a light in darkness, Issa. You must know I care for you deeply."

All I could do was nod my head. I was at a loss for words. After all

## Old Feelings Die Hard

these years, he still cared. A stubborn tear escaped my eye, and Kasim gently wiped it away with his fingertip. He then placed the palms of his hands on both sides of my face. He leaned in and kissed me on the lips.

His kiss started out soft, then built up in its intensity. In that kiss was the innocence of our youth. There was affection, warmth, and caring. Then, there was something more: need, desire, and craving.

As his lips hovered over mine, he said in a hushed tone, "This is to finish where we left off all those years ago."

Kasim settled back in his chair and looked away as if remembering something in the distant past.

"I'm sorry I had to leave you like that. I know I've told you this already. If it weren't for the assassination attempts…"

I nodded my head, but I knew better than to push for more information. When he was ready, he would tell all.

"Well, both you and your father are alive and well. And here we are, right where we left off," I said.

"Yes, indeed. And, the last thing I remember is that endearing kiss we shared."

"I've not forgotten. I was angry at first, when you abruptly left. Then, the anger faded, and I felt sad, then all alone. I was looking forward to starting college together. I was hoping for so much more."

I hesitated a moment. "Kasim, I thought you didn't care. You just disappeared from my life. You never once contacted me. I had no way of reaching you."

I lowered my head and whispered, "Where do we go from here?"

"Let's go for a walk, Issa."

Kasim held out his hand to help me stand. To my surprise, he didn't let go. We walked through a garden located on the estate grounds. That garden, what a beautiful place. I almost forgot I was in the desert because they had the most beautiful rose bushes of varying colors. The smell was intoxicating.

There was a water fountain made of marble in the center of the garden and a statue of a little girl in the midst of the fountain. The child was holding her hand extended outward. There was a sparrow perched in her palm. The sparrow appeared ready to take flight. It looked so real. I sat down to observe the detailed work of the artisan who sculpted this exquisite piece of art.

The girl carved into the statue reminded me of a younger version of myself. She looked so self-assured. As a young girl, I knew what I wanted, and I was focused. I was determined to do what was necessary to complete the tasks to accomplish my goals. Yet, I was also attentive to the needs of others. I cared for people, just like the girl in the statue cared for the bird.

The bird reminded me of this older, unsure version of myself. A widow, all alone, trying to live life again. But, not quite sure how, or even if I'm up for the task. The bird looked ready to take flight, but there was also a hesitance to it. I, too, want to take flight but find myself too frightened to spread my wings and fly.

Kasim also seemed to be lost in his thoughts. So, I sat on the bench reflecting on my life. I was encouraged as the words of Jesus came to me, "You are more valuable than many sparrows."

My countenance lifted, and I smiled. For I knew, no matter what happened, the Lord would take care of me. Out of nowhere, I heard the sound of birds awakening as they began to softly chirp. I marveled at how the Lord takes care of his creation.

I finally said, "It's so peaceful and beautiful here."

"Not as beautiful as you."

Kasim took a rose, entwined it in my hair, and placed it behind my ear.

He leaned in and whispered, "My beautiful, sweet Issa. I've never forgotten you."

I responded with yearning, "I never forgot you either."

"My wife knew of you. For the first few years, I'm ashamed to say, her life was miserable. She felt like she was competing for my affection, even though you were thousands of miles away, and we never spoke."

"Kasim, I'm so sorry, I didn't know."

"I was so young when we married. I didn't know how to be a good husband. I take responsibility for my actions. My mother prayed for me often and spoke gently with me about the ways of women. As I matured into manhood, I grew to love my Abbie."

Kasim's eyes were glazed over. He stared into the distance as if he were back in time, reliving the events. He had my complete attention. I wanted to tell him he didn't owe me this explanation. He didn't have to talk about his pain—it seemed too deep. Before I could say anything, he continued on.

"It took a while for her to conceive. When she did, something shifted in me. Maybe it was the responsibility of fatherhood. It meant a lot to my family as well, because I needed a male heir. When we found out we were having a girl, Abbie felt like she let me down. I kept telling her over and over again I was happy no matter what. Still, I saw the sadness in her eyes. When Miri was born, there were complications, and I lost my Abbie."

Regret etched on my face, and I lowered my gaze and whispered, "Kasim, I'm sorry for your loss."

Kasim pressed on, and I wondered if he even heard me.

"She was able to hold our baby before she died. She named her Miriam after the patriarch Moses's sister. I was thrust into fatherhood alone and left to manage emotions that ranged from guilt to failure to loneliness. I threw myself into my work and learned to run my father's businesses. It was not until my mother chastised me for not spending enough time with Miri that I came to my senses. From the age of eight onward, Miri went everywhere I went. I made sure she had the best tutors and learned alongside me."

"I can see you love her dearly," I replied.

"She became my life, my confidant, and closest friend. I couldn't fool Miri. She knew I was lonely, but she's against the idea of another arranged marriage for me. She would see me marry for love."

Kasim took me by the hand and led me along a tranquil trail surrounded by a profusion of colorful flowers and trees. There were anemones, black iris, and plenty of wildflowers leaving a heavenly fragrance in the air. Jacaranda trees formed a lively procession, painting a vibrant path of purple hues.

I finally broke the silence and began to tell him about Dave and Sky. We sat on a bench near the end of the garden.

"Kasim, I waited and waited. You never even called. My mother and father were supportive at first, but then they became angry, saying I was wasting my life."

"Issa, I'm really sorry. Everything was out of my control."

"I'm not telling you this to lay blame or make you feel indebted to me. I just want to share the trajectory of my life. All my experiences, good and bad, have made me who I am today."

"It was all my fault, Issa."

Kasim buried his head in his hands. I instinctively began to rub his shoulders. Then he pushed his hair out of his face with the palms of his hands. He left them on top of his head and leaned against the wall, eyes misting and forehead creased.

He inhaled deeply, letting air fill his lungs, "Please continue, Issa."

"My parents weren't convinced that you were truly a Christian. I was upset with my mother because she has a Jewish heritage. I had to remind her how hard it was for Christians to accept her at first. Her family wanted to disown her for becoming a Christian and for marrying a man of Afro-Caribbean descent. I pointed out the hypocrisy and inconsistencies of their arguments, and they finally let me be."

"Issa, I didn't know you had a Jewish heritage. I guess we didn't have enough time to get to know one another on that level."

"Yes, that would have been the next obvious step," I conceded.

"Please continue, I didn't mean to interrupt."

"Well, I slowly began to engage with old friends and made new ones at college. I met Dave during a summer excavation class where I enrolled at Yale. He was always so cheerful, optimistic, and funny. He was a brilliant man with a photogenic memory. He was handsome and nerdy with a funny sense of humor. We eventually fell in love."

Kasim cleared his throat and said, "It seems like you found happiness."

I leaned against the wall and continued, "When we graduated, Dave became a professor at Harvard. We married soon after, and I became pregnant with Sky. Sky is so much like her father. She has a brilliant mind. She's funny, spontaneous, and loves adventure. When Dave passed away, Sky and I mourned in different ways, which made us drift apart in some ways. I regret she went off to college before we could navigate our grief together."

We talked until both our stomachs protested, reminding us we had missed breakfast and it was now time for lunch. As we walked in the dining area hand-in-hand, Kasim greeted his father and uncle in his Arabic dialect.

"As-Salaam-Alaikum Father, Uncle Fasim."

"Wa-Alaikum-Salaam, Kasim."

Fasim's gaze lowered to our laced hands, and he glowered at us. Lifting his head with daggers in his eyes, he snarled, "I see you two have reacquainted yourselves." Kasim made no move to untwine our hands.

Conversely, Kasim's father beamed and bid us to join them. "Perfect timing, we were just speaking about you two. Our timetable for the excavations has moved up. We commence tomorrow."

"But father, I haven't properly briefed Issa."

"Then I suggest you spend the rest of the day doing so."

I blushed, confused by Mr. Ma'an's statement and annoyed by Fasim's comment and unseemly behavior.

Mr. Ma'an, sensing my distress, reassured me, "Don't worry, Dr. Stevens, my son will explain everything to you. Soon, it will become clear why you are here. You will understand the gravity of the situation from our perspective and why time is of the essence."

## CHAPTER 12

# NOTHING BUT THE TRUTH

*~ Issa, The Truth Unfolds ~*

The events of the past weeks left me exhausted, resulting in my unexpected absence at breakfast. Between the flight to Jordan, Fasim's perpetual foul mood, the miraculous healing of Kasim's father, and my roller coaster of emotions—I was bone-weary. However, lunch proved to be delightful. Fasim was not present, which contributed to a cheerful atmosphere. Mr. Ma'an was in good spirits, no doubt, because of the Lord's healing power.

I bit into a sumptuous pastry topped with fresh peaches and various sorts of berries. I purred as I tasted the sweetness of the fruit bursting on my tongue. Instinctively, I licked my lips. The sweet smell of the fruit mingled with the fragrance of roses from the large vase at the center of the table was enchanting.

Kasim interrupted my indulgence.

"Issa, I would like to show you something of importance that will help during the excavation. I must ask you to take a solemn oath to secrecy until the time is right to reveal what I'm about to show you."

"Yes, of course."

"Good. I just needed to hear you affirm it. We will rest before we go."

After lunch, Kasim escorted me to the bowels of his estate, which were only accessible through a secret door leading to an underground passageway. As we descended the stairs, I held onto the wall and noticed how it transformed from smooth rock to what felt like limestone, damp and full of moss. The further down we descended, the air grew cool and stale-smelling.

As the light grew dim, Kasim grabbed what looked like a torch from the side of the wall. He dipped the end in pitch and lit it with a pocket lighter. I felt the intensity of the heat immediately, but what came next, I didn't expect. As my eyes grew accustomed to the source of light, I noticed we were in some sort of cave.

Suddenly, there was a flapping noise and screeches everywhere. I screamed and waved my hands over my head. Kasim covered me with his body while waving the torch overhead. At first, I thought there was a flock of birds taking flight. As I cautiously peeked out from under his arm, my breath caught in my throat at the unsettling sight before me.

"Kasim, why are there bats under your home?"

"You'll see. I promise it will all make sense."

Finally, the bats flew through a crevice in the rock, and Kasim released me from his hold.

"Are you ok?"

"Yes, just a bit shocked is all. Anything else you want to warn me about?"

"Well, nothing as dramatic as this. You'll see soon enough."

Kasim and I walked down a spiraling staircase for what seemed like forever. Then, we exited in what looked like catacombs. Kasim handed me a handkerchief as the air was now assaulting. There was a staleness mixed with the odor of spices. I knew that odor from a previous excavation I assisted in Egypt. *Frankincense and myrrh*, I surmised.

To my surprise, I saw the sign of the fish engraved into the stone walls at what appeared to be equal distances. Kasim interrupted my thoughts and explained that these were the tombs of his ancestors.

"My ancestors built this estate."

"Your estate seems more like a fortress."

"Yes, I can see your point. This added protection is necessary. As I was saying, my family built this estate on top of an ancient grave site."

I choked, but it all made sense now.

"How has it been maintained so well after all those years?"

"It's nothing less than a miracle. This site is known to have been in existence for close to two millennia. It has been passed down from generation to generation. However, it's only been in my father's father's lifetime that the grounds have been expanded."

"This is monumental and expensive to maintain, I would imagine."

"Our wealth has grown exponentially through our various businesses and investments, allowing us to expand and purchase key real estate extending to the Ma'an-Petra border."

"This is all so fascinating, Kasim."

"Our modest living, other than this estate, has kept us out of the sight of those who would seek to destroy us for what we possess. As you know, my family has a Christian heritage that dates back to the first century."

"Tell me more."

"It all began with my ancient Saba Kasim, whose namesake I possess. Prior to becoming a Christian, he had become a circumcised Jewish proselyte with the help of a rabbi he met on one of his merchant trips to Jerusalem. It was on the road to Emmaus where Saba Kasim encountered Jesus after his resurrection. That's when my ancestors became Christians. He took the message that Jesus is the Messiah back to Arabia. He also sent his grandson Salim to Jerusalem for Shavuot to celebrate the Feast of Weeks. This is the place and time Jesus told his disciples to wait for the promise of the Holy Spirit. Salim was filled with God's Spirit that day."

"Kasim, such information is prodigious. It's groundbreaking."

"Yes, but there is not enough evidence to take to the Department of Antiquities to prove there is a link to our legacy. We'll need to find something of substance that connects the people in this gravesite to the first-century Arab Christians."

"Kasim, we can authenticate an approximate dating of the skeletal remains. The connection of your ancestors to first-century Christianity would be a huge achievement and would validate our Christian faith in so many ways."

"Yes, and herein lies the heart of our mission. However, we do not want to tip our hand too soon. My countrymen will not take kindly to any findings that will substantiate Christianity, which makes this mission dangerous. We believe we're close to finding the location of the scrolls that contain letters the Apostle Paul wrote to the Arab Christian community in Petra. This would be a compelling historical find."

"There are others who are in the preparation phase to find the scrolls you speak of."

"Yes, I'm aware, but they do not have the advantage that we do. There are two working theories we have considered. Some believe our ancestors hid the scrolls somewhere near the caves in Petra during a time of persecution under King Aretas IV. Others believe the scrolls were hidden in an unknown location by our ancestors during the tenth-century Crusades. They believe the scrolls were hidden from both the Christians and Arabs of that day."

"Interesting theories," I replied.

"Arab Christians were forced to fight alongside their countrymen against the Crusaders who marched through Syria to get to Jerusalem. The Crusaders called themselves Christians and proclaimed to fight for the same God we serve. It was the worst of times, but we felt justified in helping save our land and our people. After the attacks against the Arabs, our countrymen could no longer tolerate any Christians among their people. They united against us, even though we fought alongside them."

As Kasim was speaking, my mind was imagining what it was like in those days.

## Nothing But the Truth

*I could hear the clanging of swords and fierce battle cries. The cacophony of sounds was deafening. The air itself seemed to vibrate with the discordant symphony of war. There was smoke everywhere, and burning embers were raining down. The cries of the wounded and dying rose like a haunted melody. I could smell the metallic odor of blood, and there was death everywhere.*

"Issa, did you hear me? You looked as if your thoughts were far off."

"Yes, yes, Kasim, that's awful. I didn't know. They didn't teach us any of this in school. Your ancestors' voices are suppressed, and the world needs to hear their stories."

"My ancestors escaped with nothing more than the clothes on their back. They escaped to Egypt and slowly came back to Arabia, settling in Ma'an and the bordering areas of Petra. There is evidence that there may have been two Exoduses to Egypt. One under King Aretas IV and a second during the Crusades. Our beliefs were suppressed to ensure our survival. We worshiped in private and relied heavily on oral tradition until after the Crusades."

"Does this explain why the number of Arab Christians are so few?"

"Yes and no. We were too few in number to fight and win a war. Instead, we established ourselves in public as a strong merchant family. It was the skills we acquired in Egypt that made us stronger and more knowledgeable in the trade of rare spices, and wool, and the discovery and sale of ancient artifacts. Unfortunately, as our family's wealth has grown, some of our people's faith in the Christian God has waned. Uncle Fasim is an example of this."

My face paled at the mention of that name. I whispered, "I'm afraid of him."

"You need not fear him. Fasim and I may have our differences, but he's not foolish enough to harm you or give up our family secret. In doing so, it would strip us of all our wealth and our strength, including himself."

"I'm not so sure about that, Kasim."

"Issa, the real danger is if we are unable to locate and authenticate the letters that the Apostle Paul penned to our ancestors. We believe he would have penned these letters on parchment and secured them as scrolls when he returned to Damascus. A find of this magnitude would tie our family to the ancient families of Arabia."

"Kasim, maybe I watch too many detective movies, but I believe your threat may originate from within. At least in part."

Kasim's body tensed, and he instinctively shielded me, pulling me behind the wall of his rigid frame. His posture transformed into a firm and upright stance, magnifying the full measure of his height.

"What's wrong?" I whispered.

"I heard a sound. No one comes down here, not even my father."

Kasim began slowly backing away.

"Maybe it's more bats?"

"Or rats," mumbled Kasim.

"Literally or figuratively?"

"Both."

We managed to find our way to the stairs in backward motion and made it to the surface in haste. Kasim called for his security team to explore the catacombs and report back to him. He faced me and spoke as if we had never been interrupted.

"You are correct, Issa. I've given this much thought, and my eyes are open to all possibilities. Even if my father doesn't agree with me, I would prefer that everyone believes I'm looking for an enemy from the outside. It will give me a much-needed advantage. No one knows that I'm watching them."

"I'll be watching too, and praying," I added.

"Finding the scrolls remains the priority. This discovery will not only vindicate my family, it will put us in a position to reveal our heritage as Christians. It will also ensure our continued legacy and our freedom to worship in public."

We ambled through the gardens and made our way back to the

residential area of the estate. Kasim's guards reported that they found nothing in the catacombs. Kasim's shoulders visibly relaxed. He massaged his neck, and a subtle sigh escaped his lips. A sense of ease settled over him, and I continued our discussion.

"How exactly will the scrolls protect your family from retribution?"

"The Arabs have a deep reverence for their ancient history. They will not harm my family if we should be exposed for our Christian heritage in connection with our ancient history. And the fact that we fought with our countrymen against the Crusaders shows our loyalty to our country and our people."

"I pray you are right, for all our sakes. I do know one thing. I have a contingent of people praying for the success of this mission. While they don't know details, they do know my work often entails some degree of danger. Especially when it takes me out of the country."

"Issa, I'm grateful for the prayers. They'll give us an added layer of protection and the wisdom we need to succeed. We have gathered much research and have strong evidence that the scrolls might be buried near one of the excavation sites. When my family relocated back to Arabia, we slowly began to buy land in strategic locations where we believed our ancestors lived. We began excavations and have unearthed many ancient artifacts that have informed us more about our heritage."

"This is helpful information," I said. "If you allow me access to the artifacts, I can analyze what time periods we are dealing with. I can also decipher if there was a synagogue or some place of worship where the scrolls might have resided at some point."

"You'll have complete access. We ran into some difficulties during our last excavation. That's when I convinced my father to enlist your help against my Uncle Fasim's advice. I've followed your work throughout the years and have longed to reach out to you."

"Why didn't you?"

"My family knew I had developed a strong bond with you. You were all I talked about. They expected me to marry within my clan to maintain our family secret and our legacy. They required me to cut all ties with you, and they arranged my marriage soon after I returned to Jordan."

"So, I wasn't good enough for you? For your family? What makes you think I'm good enough now?"

"You were always good enough for me. I argued with my father relentlessly to no avail. Soon after I arrived in Jordan, there was another attempt on his life. I felt the weight of responsibility fall on my shoulders. My father almost died. I didn't want to disrespect or dishonor him. I didn't want to be the one responsible for breaking a legacy that has existed for nearly two millennia."

Kasim was right. I was being selfish. My tears betrayed me. I didn't know if they were from anger or some other emotion I couldn't identify. He gently dried my eyes with his kerchief and continued.

"When my wife died in childbirth and left me without a son, my father insisted I remarry so I could produce a male heir. If I cannot accomplish this, then the right of succession falls to my Uncle Fasim. As you know, that's a dangerous prospect. As a compromise, my father and Fasim would have me remarry a distant cousin, and I have put them off for far too long."

"I see," is all I could manage to say.

"Issa, now that you're back in my life, I cannot imagine being with anyone else. I know what I want, but there is danger everywhere. First, the assassination attempts. Second, our business rivals and the wealthy families with long histories in Arabia. Third, a likely threat exists from our government because of our wealth and influence. As well as the current political and religious climate in our neighboring countries. Our adversaries only know in part what our wealth consists of."

*Just how wealthy is this man?* I asked myself.

Kasim continued, "And as I mentioned before, very few people know about our heritage. The fact that you do poses a risk to my family and a threat to you. My family knows who you are and why I sought you out. Although, I was conflicted for so many reasons."

"You didn't want me to come?"

"To the contrary. I wanted to see you at any cost, and that was selfish on my part, because of the danger I have placed you in. I wouldn't be able to live with myself if any harm came to you. And, I, well I just, I mean…I was conflicted because I knew what was expected of me."

*- Kasim, Truth Be Told Once -*

I fought the instinct to tell Issa everything. How I loved her. How I regretted having left her. How a piece of me died that day our friendship was cut off. That day, our future ended. I knew in my heart that she still cared for me. Maybe even as deeply as I care for her. But I couldn't allow this to go any further without telling her the whole truth.

Her eyes never left mine. In the depths of those brilliant green eyes, I saw concern, weariness, and some other emotion that looked like longing. Inhaling deeply, I steadied my breathing. With steely resolve, I poured out my heart to this woman whom I fell in love with in my youth.

"Truth be told, Issa, I love you. When I made the decision to bring you here, I needed to resolve within myself that I couldn't bear to lose you again. And, I prayed that somehow you would feel the same way about me."

In quiet rebellion, a lone tear escaped from her eye. With all the tenderness I possessed, I lifted her chin, leaned over, and pressed my lips to hers. To my surprise, her kiss deepened, and she clung to me with what seemed like the same desperation and desire I was experiencing. I returned the favor.

How long we stood there eludes me. But one thing was certain in my mind: *I must marry this woman whom I've loved, lost, and found again. The only woman I could see spending the rest of my life with. The only woman I want to carry my child.* But I knew that now was not the time. I had to let her explore her feelings and think through all the possibilities before entangling her life with mine.

*- Issa, Truth Be Told Twice -*

When Kasim let go, I felt bereft. Truth be told, I could spend the rest of my life with this man if God so willed it. I knew he felt the connection too. After all, he declared his love for me. But he faced so many obstacles. I couldn't allow him to put himself, his family, or his legacy in jeopardy. I couldn't impose my desire or divulge my feelings to him. Not while he was in such a fragile state, in conflict with family, duty, loyalty, and love.

I would have to be content with keeping our relationship on a professional level. I knew it would tear me apart when the time came to leave.

*Oh Lord, I don't know if my fragile heart can bear it. But I know that I can do all things as you strengthen me. And if it be your will, please grant me the desire of my heart. Please give me Kasim.*

# Chapter 13

# The Legacy

### A.D. 33, Petra, The City of Raqmu
### ~ Salim, The Legacy ~

I ran to Saba Kasim and hugged him tight.

"Salim, Abdi, I thought you would never return! Come, sit and sup with me."

"Yes, Saba, it's good to see you too!"

"You, over there, bring us some water and take care of those camels for me," I said.

Abdi interrupted. "I will take my leave and let you two recount the stories of our journey."

"Abdi, I will tell your father what a help you have been to Salim and how you have brought honor to my household this day," replied Saba.

"Thank you, sir," Abdi said and scurried off.

I sat next to Saba, drawing circles in the sand and contemplating the events that transpired on this life-altering journey.

"Now, start from the beginning, Grandson."

"Well, as you know, Benjamin gave us lodgings at his Inn. Then, Abdi and I went looking for John, the disciple of Jesus. We were looking for the meeting place Jesus spoke of to celebrate the Feast of Weeks. John directed us to the Upper Room, where the disciples meet. In the courtyard below, there were Jews, proselytes, and God-fearers from Jerusalem and from other nations. They were all gathered for Shavuot."

"Is this the same place Jesus told the disciples to wait for the promise?" asked Saba.

"Yes. It was like nothing I've ever experienced! I heard a sound like a windstorm. The sound was even more fierce than a haboob. It originated from the heavens and swooped in like a sandstorm with a force so great that I stumbled and nearly fell. I began to speak in an unknown tongue. I had no idea what language I spoke until the person next to me inquired, 'How do you know the language of Rome?' Then, I turned and heard someone from Rome speaking the language of our countrymen. They were praising and speaking about the wonderful works of God."

"Slow down, Salim. So this was the sign of the promise of the Holy Spirit?"

"Yes. It was nothing less than a miracle to hear Romans speaking in our dialect. We were all in awe and began to inquire what this meant. Peter gathered us and explained that this is what the prophet Joel spoke of. 'In the last days, says God, That I will pour out My Spirit on all flesh.'"

"Ahh, the prophet Joel, yes, yes! He also declared, 'And your daughters shall prophesy, your old men shall dream dreams, your young men shall see visions.'"

"Saba, that's exactly what the disciple Peter announced. He began to preach, boldly proclaiming that God raised Jesus from the dead. He told us that Jesus has returned to Heaven. He is now sitting at the right hand of God and is pouring out the promise of the Holy Spirit to all who believe."

"Amazing! Salim, continue."

"Peter preached the message of repentance and baptism. He said, 'Repent, and let every one of you be baptized in the name of Jesus Christ for the remission of sins; and you shall receive the gift of the Holy Spirit.'"

"You received the gift," Saba said with reverence, tears flowing down his cheeks, each one finding refuge in his white beard.

"Yes! The gift is for everyone. We are to spread the good news. This is a promise to our children, and our children's children, and to as many as the Lord God will call. It's a legacy that is given to everyone who believes."

"Grandson, this legacy is to be the legacy of the Ma'an family! Through the power of the Holy Spirit, we will proclaim Jesus and his gift of salvation. We will proclaim the promise of the Holy Spirit to each generation as a perpetual legacy until Jesus returns."

### *Twenty-First Century - Ma'an-Petra, Jordan*
### *~ Kasim, A Perpetual Legacy ~*

Today, we decided to make productive use of our time in the library. My family's book collection was extensive. Issa had pleaded with me, hoping to dedicate some time to peruse its vast offerings.

She climbed the ladder attached to the large circular bookshelf and reached the top. The ladder loosened from its track, and I ran to steady it.

"Issa, grab hold of the top shelf!" I yelled.

She dangled from the narrow ledge and held on for dear life. "I'm okay!" she yelled back.

I secured the ladder in its track, and Issa grasped it.

Holding the ladder steady, I snapped, "Next time, let me help you."

"I'm sorry, Kasim."

"Stubborn girl," I mumbled under my breath.

Issa climbed down slowly. Her foot slipped on a rung near the bottom, and I caught her by her waist. Her nearness unsettled me, causing me to let go abruptly as if my hands were scorched by molten iron.

Issa managed to stumble across some annals containing our ancestry from that top shelf. What she found was no coincidence. From those annals, I began to recite the oral traditions from my ancient Saba Kasim, which was customary in our community during Pentecost.

"Issa, this is our oral tradition. Without proof of Paul's letters, the ones he wrote to my ancestors, we will be considered heretics, infidels in our own country. To claim that Arabs were Christian centuries before they were Muslim, and rightful heirs to this land, will only increase tension in our nation."

"But Kasim, it's common knowledge that the Muslim faith did not exist until the beginning of the seventh century in the common era. And the Koran gives honor to Jesus, albeit only as a great prophet."

"True, Issa. However, this is not common knowledge. This information is primarily known to those who have higher education, not among the common people. Besides, the older generations prefer to hold on to tradition and see any new information as heretical, created by Western Europeans, or infidels as they are called."

"I do see how that could be a problem. Kasim, please help me understand more about the Christian community here in Ma'an and Petra."

"The Christian communities are small in number but significant compared to our neighboring Arab nations. Arab Christians are well-integrated into Jordanian society and enjoy a high level of freedom. Nevertheless, there are still those who oppose us. Our neighboring Arab countries and splinter factions within Jordan resist such freedom."

"This explains the need to be discreet. But why all the subterfuge?"

"For the sake of peace and to be left alone. Many Arab Christians would rather practice their Christian faith in silence and melt into society. They keep to themselves and congregate in small groups. Many are not verbal about their beliefs outside of their communities for fear of retribution. Bedouin Christians consist of those nomadic tribes who mostly live life outside of the mainstream culture and protect themselves by seclusion. In this regard, we are silenced and have silenced ourselves from freely proclaiming the good news of Jesus Christ."

"Isn't there any protection for your people?"

"Our government can only do so much to protect us. They are obligated to protect and hold fast to what is most important to them.

## The Legacy

That is, the very thing that holds the fabric of their being together: Islam. Our goal is not to upend centuries worth of tradition that this country has come to know as a way of life. Our goal is to present the facts as we know and have experienced them and to offer hope in our God and a peaceful coexistence."

"Kasim, do you think this is even possible?"

"Our people have a right to know their history and decide for themselves. And we have a right to inherit the land of our forefathers and live in the place that we cherish so dearly."

"This must be hard for you and your family. Wouldn't it be easier to just leave?"

"My family could easily pack up and leave. We have the resources and connections. However, there are many who are unable to do so. And there are others who would not leave even if given the chance. We cannot leave them to an unknown fate."

"I'm beginning to understand your dilemma."

"Issa, we have preached the truth of Jesus to many in our community who have come to depend on us for spiritual guidance. We also provide resources for a small community of believers, much like the apostles did in the first century. For these reasons, we cannot leave."

"Kasim, that's awe-inspiring! You carry so much on your shoulders. Your family has a strong sense of what the Lord has called you to do. And you have been faithful to that calling for close to two millennia. But, it's a dangerous undertaking."

"No less dangerous than what the first-century church faced. Many of our people do not know that Jordan contains some of the oldest Christian communities in the world, dating as far back as the first century. A number of Arab tribes and kingdoms accepted Christianity, including some of the Nabateans who built Petra. Petra is one of the seven wonders of the world as we know it today. Our ancestors told the stories of pre-existing Christian communities adopting the Arabic language. And of pre-existing Arabic-speaking communities adopting Christianity. The Nabateans are an example of the latter."

"Yes, I read about this when I was researching Paul's journey to Arabia. Kasim, please continue. I think this information can be useful to our excavations."

"Well, you may already know that a small percentage of Jordanian Christians are also ethnically Bedouin. According to the Orthodox Church, Jordanian Christians number around two-hundred fifty thousand, all of whom are Arabic-speaking. This doesn't include the minority Christian groups and the thousands of Western, Iraqi, and Syrian Christians residing in Jordan."

"And your family belongs to the minority group?"

"Yes, because we believe the miracles of the Bible and the gifts of the Spirit are still alive in the church. However, we have not exercised our God-given authority to operate in these gifts for over a century. As a result, practically speaking, we have aligned ourselves more closely to the Orthodox way of doing things."

"I see. But, what do you hear the Lord saying now?"

"Issa, when you exercised your faith and laid your hands on my father, as he lay dying before my eyes, and you declared healing in the name of Jesus, the trajectory of our mission changed. Not only must we find and authenticate those scrolls, but we most boldly proclaim Jesus Christ to our people and connect them to hope in God. Over time, we have adhered to the Orthodox ways. But I believe the Lord would have us look to Pentecost, to rely on the Spirit of God to help find the answers we need."

"Kasim, this is a huge undertaking, a dangerous one. I know God has sent me here to help, but politics, religion, civil war, nations warring against nations, that sounds like an end-time prophecy of epic proportions!"

I grabbed Issa and held her tight. She trembled in my arms and clung desperately, as if her very existence depended on it. The unspoken plea in her touch resonated, a silent call for reassurance in the face of an unseen storm.

"I won't let anything happen to you, Habibti. The Ma'an family has survived these threats for over twenty centuries. This is why we must find the scrolls. God will vindicate us as he has in times past. I have faith, you have even greater faith. Together, we can do this."

## CHAPTER 14

# THE WADI MUSA

*~ Issa, Excavation Progress ~*

We drove about forty minutes from the estate. Kasim gestured to his driver to pull to the side of the road. We were several miles away from the center of town. To my surprise, I saw a myriad of houses and business establishments, but I didn't notice an excavation site anywhere. I saw elaborate homes carved into the sandstone cliffs. These homes were intricately detailed structures that looked to be chiseled by hand out of the rocks. They were covered with what looked like stucco and painted to enhance the rose-red colors of the rock. The homes at the base of the mountain were just as elegant and painted with bright colors. They were also further apart in distance. The smaller homes on the valley floor were of varying sizes.

Kasim had mentioned his family owned several of these homes, which were scattered about. The houses were simpler the further they were away from the mountain. Some were made of mud-brick, unpainted, with no elaborate designs. I stepped out of the car, breathed deeply, and took in the beauty of the landscape.

"Kasim, where are we?"

He chuckled, "We are a few meters away from the headquarters for the excavation site."

Then I remembered something Kasim told me. *We have several dig* sites. *They're in confined locations on our properties and we dig down.*

"Which properties do you own?"

"My family owns five properties in this area." Pointing, he continued, "One in the section of that rock face, two at the base of the mountain, and the others in the center of the city."

"This is so amazing! I'm guessing your properties are fronts for the excavation sites?"

"That sounds more like a statement than a question, Issa."

Kasim's eyes danced with amusement. His grin and throaty laugh revealed a hint of teasing and sarcasm.

Kasim briefed me on the previous excavations and their intricate connections to our current project. He shared with me the rich history and geography of the land. Much of this information was not found in any of the research books or journals I had read. Kasim further enlightened me about the city of Ma'an, which proudly carried the name of his ancestors for centuries.

"Despite the government's claim of sovereignty over the land, they graciously allowed the city to retain its name to avoid conflict with the Bedouin tribes," said Kasim.

"That was a magnanimous gesture on your government's part. A diplomatic response to avert civil war, no doubt."

"You are correct in what you say. The people were ready to take up arms and fight."

"So, tell me more about the conflicts. Are they real or perceived? Let's look at this from multiple angles. Who has the most to lose, and who has the most to gain from our discovery?" I asked.

"Ok Issa, let's look at this strategically. If we find and authenticate the scrolls, we risk enraging the religious community in our country and abroad. We also risk land disputes with neighboring tribes and our government. This all translates to a shift of power and wealth. For this alone, there are many who are willing to kill and be killed."

## The Wadi Musa

"Who has the most to gain from our discovery other than your family?"

"The marginalized Christian communities in Jordan would gain greater religious freedom. Perhaps also in neighboring countries. A find of this magnitude would also inform history and add to the cultural knowledge and awareness of our Arab heritage."

"Good, Kasim, now let's narrow it down a bit more. Do you know of any one specific person or group who would want to come against your family?"

"No one has overtly declared war against our family. I don't want to chase shadows. The assassination attempts on my father's life were all clandestine. When the time comes, we will know. God will reveal it."

"Ok, fair enough. Tell me more about the excavation sites."

"The primary excavation site is in Petra, roughly thirty-seven kilometers from the primary grounds of the estate in Ma'an. I pointed it out earlier: the one built into the rock face. As I mentioned previously, we also own a smaller-sized, modest property at the base of the mountain and in the center of town. This area is called the Wadi Musa."

"What does your government think of all the properties you own?"

"Many of our properties are in the name of our various companies or family members."

I was beginning to understand the breadth and depth of this man's wealth, and it intimidated me. *I don't belong here. I could never fit into Kasim's world.*

Kasim continued, "The smaller properties were used in conjunction with past excavations, and they'll be used as outposts during our digs. The rock-faced property will be set up as one of our headquarters stations."

"Kasim, I don't know if I'm the right person for this job."

*- Kasim, My Gaffe -*

I could kick myself for divulging too much information too soon.

If the deep ridges now forming on Issa's forehead were any indication of how she felt, I wouldn't be surprised if she caught the first plane back to the States. Issa wasn't accustomed to living in my world. I had to act quickly.

I did the first thing that came to my mind. I pulled her into my arms and whispered in her ear, "You are exactly the right person for this job. Aside from your academic prowess, you are the only person I trust to be here with me right now. Besides, I believe you told me the Lord sent you here on this assignment?"

*~ Issa, Prep Work ~*

After hearing Kasim's endearing words, I buried my head into his shoulder. I held onto him tight, and I didn't want to let go. Time stretched as we lingered there. Then Kasim interrupted my momentary bliss.

"We must journey to the headquarters before the sun pierces the horizon."

When we arrived at headquarters, Kasim escorted me to a vaulted area and showed me a captivating display of artifacts unearthed over the past three years. These phenomenal treasures had been discovered in various locations throughout Ma'an and Petra. They dated back anywhere between the early first century to the fourth century. Since these artifacts were found on the land owned by Kasim's family, they had not yet reported them to the Department of Antiquities. What caught my attention were the tent making tools among the artifacts.

"Kasim, do you realize the significance of these tools? You know what this means, don't you?" I asked.

Kasim replied with a touch of reverence in his voice.

"These tools could have been used by my ancestor Youssef and the Apostle Paul."

"Have you conducted radiocarbon dating on the artifacts yet?" I inquired.

"Yes, we've confirmed that the artifacts date back to the first century, strengthening our belief that they belong to my ancestor Youssef."

"That's incredible!"

"One of the properties, close to the base of this mountain, was strategically built near an ancient Nabatean home known today as the Ez-Zantur House, whose findings date back to around A.D. 20. Our excavation efforts began directly beneath our own property, uncovering fascinating artifacts dating back to the fourth century."

"Now, I understand the magnitude of what you mean about possible land disputes," I interrupted.

"We strongly believe the Ez-Zantur House had once been the dwelling place of my ancestors. One of the inscriptions we found bore the symbol of a fish."

"How far down do you think we need to dig to find artifacts from earlier centuries?" I asked, my curiosity piqued.

"Several homes were constructed on top of our site over the centuries. We've been able to determine this through the dating of the jewelry, pottery items, the transition from sandstone to limestone in the building structure, and the coins we found. The coins unearthed in the most recent dig were dated around A.D. 363. This was around the time of the great earthquake that destroyed much of Petra. We also found human bones and glass artifacts. Remarkably, we even recovered several intact ceramic vessels, oil lamps, and perfume bottles."

"Does the government know of your findings?"

"The Department of Antiquities only knows about the one site we excavated that had findings from the thirteenth century forward."

"That was a bold move, Kasim. No doubt it drew attention to you and your family?"

"Yes, but ethically, we felt it was important to do so. The artifacts are late enough in history not to cause disruption to our cause. Besides, these were findings on the outskirts of the land, not beneath the structure."

"A find of the thirteenth century is just as significant, but I see your point."

"Our work was disguised as basic upgrades performed to modernize the land surrounding our home. Some entities offered us money to buy the land outright, but we exercised our legal right to cease all engagements. The government set up dig sites close to our home but didn't find anything of significance, so they discontinued the project. I believe they simply didn't dig deep enough, and their staff was not as thorough or knowledgeable as ours."

"Scattering bread crumbs that lead to a trail in the opposite direction is a stroke of genius," I said.

"We didn't report the artifacts found near the Ez-Zantur House," replied Kasim. "The items found adjacent to that property were specifically dated to the time Paul visited Arabia. Once we can conclusively prove our family lineage and their connection to the first-century Arab Christian community, we will be more amenable to sharing our findings with the authorities."

"So, help me understand. Are we talking about three excavations that have taken place already, with significant evidence?"

"Yes. I'm speaking of three separate digs."

"Why isn't this enough to prove your lineage?"

"The evidence is not sufficient because there are no written records to corroborate the findings. We need the letters Paul wrote to our community as further proof. The danger we face is that any evidence found on or near government property runs the risk of being confiscated, or it may fall into the wrong hands or disappear altogether."

"I understand. So, we won't let that happen. We must ensure the preservation and integrity of our findings at all costs."

"Yes, Issa! The good news is that the primary estate on the border of Ma'an and Petra, where the underground tombs are located, have been in our possession for centuries, and we have the papers to prove it. This is why the tombs remain intact. Unfortunately, many tombs have been carved into the mountain face. Those tombs have been raided over the centuries."

## The Wadi Musa

"Have there been any sanctioned digs in those areas?"

"Little has been done by way of excavation, which means we have much work to do. This also creates a more complex problem."

"How so?"

"If any of our sites are deemed historical locations due to our archeological finds, some sort of agreement will need to be made between my family, the government, and other international entities."

Akhab interrupted our discussion, nodding his head at Kasim and greeting me with a smile. Kasim excused himself.

While at the main headquarters, I learned that Kasim's crew worked the outside perimeters—undercover as maintenance—from the early hours of five in the morning until ten in the morning. They carefully planned their schedule to avoid the scorching heat of the afternoon sun. The remaining hours were dedicated to excavating within the structure. The most recent artifacts discovered were stored in nearby caves where their Bedouin families dwelled and where the team also found shelter for rest.

The findings were astonishing, artifacts from the era of the Edomites, who had inhabited the area more than a millennium ago before the Nabateans, around the thirteenth century B.C. These artifacts were discovered closest to the Bedouin caves on the outskirts of the city.

The fact that they had found the catacombs at their primary estate was nothing less than a miracle. It provided a valuable clue in narrowing down the geographic location of Kasim's tribe's ancestral roots to at least the second century based on the artifacts discovered. The decision to construct their estate in such close proximity to the various archeological sites proved to be a stroke of genius. This allowed them to keep the excavations a secret, shielding them from prying eyes and inquiring minds. And it was an act of brilliance to disperse the artifacts in varying locations in case of a siege of any one property. However, there was still a measure of risk. There were a select few non-family members that Kasim had hired to assist in the mission.

Kasim reassured me, "These are trustworthy people who have worked with me on previous sensitive projects."

When Kasim returned, he escorted me down an elevator shaft to the dig site. We were approximately three stories below the foundation of the property. The terrain beneath my feet was uneven and rocky. Kasim had purchased all the necessary equipment I needed, including my attire. How he knew my pants, shirt, and shoe size down to the exact measurement was a mystery to me.

My face flamed with embarrassment the day he showed up at my bedroom with the apparel. I thought him pretentious at first. However, today, I was grateful. I was instructed to wear normal attire, including my hijab, en route to the site. I was to change into my work gear on site so as not to draw attention.

"Issa, over here," I heard Miri call my name.

Kasim and I walked over to where Miri was working.

"Miri, you're here early."

Miri winked. "I wanted to have everything perfect for you when you arrived."

"That was thoughtful."

Kasim interrupted, "Akhab is working over there. He runs the Ma'an family's import and export business, and you met him during dinner. He's also a Christian and works closely with us at the excavation sites to determine what artifacts can be curated and what remains in the vaults as a part of our personal collection."

"Hello, Dr. Issa. It's a pleasure seeing you again."

"Thank you, Akhab, the pleasure is all mine. Will we be working closely together during this expedition?"

"Yes. Miri and I will bring you up-to-date on our progress and findings."

"Thank you."

"Issa, I will take my leave now," said Kasim.

## The Wadi Musa

"I can manage just fine. You have things well organized here. It's quite impressive," I replied.

Kasim left the site to take care of business. He told me it was imperative that life proceed as usual so as not to arouse any suspicion. We worked underground most of the day. Our day proceeded as any normal day would in the world of archeology. Each site was marked carefully with a full description of the various artifacts that were found.

The painstaking work of removing dirt to uncover new layers was laborious and time-consuming. However, their progress had been remarkable. I familiarized myself with the layout of the site and the location of where each artifact was found. There was one particular section that caught my eye.

"Miri, I need your help. Please hand me that trowel and a hand broom."

"Have you found something new?"

"Yes, these pottery shards look like they could be stone water jars used for ceremonial washings. There aren't enough shards to piece together, so I'm looking for any inscriptions, letters, or markings of any kind."

I turned on my headlight, and Miri grabbed the Laser-Stimulated Fluorescence light. Miri moved like a pro. Each step she took was deliberate, a testament to her experience. Her motions were smooth, efficient, and spoke of a practiced ease that only comes from years of doing something over and over again. Her genuine excitement was contagious. I found myself caught up in the moment, mirroring her enthusiasm. Kasim taught her well. I couldn't help but smile.

I began the tedious work of dusting off the broken pieces and trying to put them together like a puzzle. My gasp drew the attention of others. Miri looked at me, eyes sparkling with wonder.

"What is it, Issa?"

"Miri, pass me that trowel over there and go find Akhab."

Akhab was at my side in no time. I pointed to the corner of the larger pottery piece, and using the fluorescent light, I explained, "Look at this marking here. We need to continue digging. There must be more."

"Dr. Issa, we've already excavated the breadth of this area within our borders."

"Then, we dig deeper."

Akhab nodded and left to carry out my instructions. I proceeded to run my own test and analysis on a few of the pottery and jewelry findings. I spent the remainder of the day corroborating my research with the data obtained from the other artifacts.

Akhab approached me and announced, "We've found something."

As the area came into view, two things immediately drew my attention: a nearly intact vase and what looked like the starting point of a boxed dirt structure that was shaped like a rectangle, *a mikvah*, I thought.

"Do you think there is a temple nearby?" asked Miri.

"Not a temple as one might typically envision, but rather a place where they likely engaged in worship," I replied.

"Miri, Akhab, I'll need to work the perimeter outside the building."

"Dr. Issa, we don't have the appropriate papers and permits to excavate the grounds beyond this property," cautioned Akhab.

"I only want to get a visual of the exterior of the property."

"Miri, you and Dr. Issa will have to change clothes. Do you have your hijab?"

"Yes, I do. Issa, let's change quickly before we lose sunlight."

When Kasim finally returned, he found Akhab, Miri, and myself outside the building, admiring the wonder of God's majesty. The sun was setting on the horizon, casting a warm glow over the ancient land. We couldn't help but feel the weight of history resting upon our shoulders. Our mission was far from complete, but the journey we embarked upon promised to unveil a captivating narrative. A story intertwined with faith, heritage, and the unyielding pursuit of truth.

## Chapter 15

# Saul's Arrival in Arabia

### A.D. 35
### ~ The City of Raqmu, Called Petra ~

When I arrived in Arabia, in the city of Petra, I was taken aback by the flurry of activity. The aromas of lamb, onions, and various sweets wafted through the air. The smells were tantalizing; my mouth was watering, and my stomach began to growl. I had to remind myself that most of what they offered, I could not eat, for the food was ritually unclean.

Our entrance into Petra was grand and reminded me of a procession into the courts of a king. The mountain range was devastatingly beautiful. There was a structure that looked like a temple built directly into the rock face. The beauty of this place could only be compared to a well-adorned bride on her wedding day. The red rock with its smooth ridges screamed out, *Caress me.*

The opulence of this city was quite evident. There were several caravans laden with wealth entering into the city. They carried exquisite, colorful jewels such as lapis lazuli and red granite. There were also aromatic and expensive incense, spices, and perfumes from the East. I indulged my senses for a moment and imagined myself in the banquet halls of King David. I was sitting with the nobility, eating like a prince. I was smelling the perfumes and gazing at the adornments of the nobility.

I quickly snapped out of my reverie when the caravan master

informed me, "The marketplace is where we part ways, Saul."

"Shufa, what is this place called?"

"Raqmu, as you can see, the city is surrounded by red rock, but the Greeks and Romans call it Petra."

I was lost in my thoughts for a moment, reminiscing on the patriarchs of old.

Then I replied, "This geography is not unknown to me, for it is ancient and has been mentioned in the writings of Israel's prophets thousands of years ago. It was called Moab back then, and our great prophet Moses died on that mountain where you found me. In days old, it was called Mount Nebo."

"This is the first I've heard of this, Saul."

Before departing, I broached the subject to Shufa about payment for my passage with the caravan. He had not mentioned a word to me about it.

"Please accept three denarii for the travel protection and the care you provided me."

"Saul of Tarsus, I can see that you are a Pharisee by your clothing and the constant prayers you pray to your god. Give me two denarii and pray to your god that he prospers me and my family."

"You are most gracious, and I will entreat the One true God of Israel on your behalf. He has sent His Son Jesus, the Messiah, to take away the sin of the world. The greatest blessing I could bestow on you is that you come to believe in Jesus and inherit the Kingdom of God, which has riches untold."

"Saul, you must tell me more of this Jesus. My gods only offer wealth and prosperity in this life. They do not speak of an eternal kingdom with eternal riches. Besides, they often exact a great cost on their servants. What price does your Jesus require?"

"My friend, Jesus paid the price in full by dying on a Roman cross, and the salvation he offers is free."

## Saul's Arrival in Arabia

"We must talk again before I depart."

"That we will, my friend. In the meantime, can I trouble you for a moment?"

"What do you need?"

"Where can I find adequate lodging and a good meal among my fellow Jews?"

"There's an inn less than two thousand cubits east of the marketplace, I believe you will find what you are looking for there."

"Shalom Shufa, until next time, and may you and your family prosper."

I noticed the sun high in the sky and gauged the time of day. I began walking through the marketplace, noting the exchanges among the people, the clothing they wore, and the languages they spoke. I was grieved by the number of idols. I would have to be tolerant of this blasphemy. At least, until I could preach Jesus and set them free from the oppressive bondage to carved images. Wood and stone that cannot speak or hear, much less ensure a harvest or send the rains.

When I arrived at the inn, I was greeted by a friendly voice that spoke in Aramaic.

"How can I help you, sir?"

"I mean no offense, but is there a Jewish quarter in this city?"

"We are everywhere," was her reply.

"Then, you are Jewish?"

"Yes, my name is Anna, and my husband and I own this Inn. By the looks of it, you are a religious leader, no?"

"Yes, I'm Saul of Tarsus and a Pharisee."

"Then what are you doing in these parts? We have no synagogue here. King Aretas is tolerant of our people as long as we don't interfere with the city's commerce or the worship of its gods."

"Do not worry, I'm not here to start a synagogue. However, I will need regular lodgings. I will be here for some time. Can you accommodate me?"

"Yes, sir. I will have my husband make the arrangements."

"Simeon!" she yelled. "Please come help our guest to a room. He will be with us for a while."

"Shalom Simeon, do you have a room with a wash basin and a window that faces East?"

"Yes, sir. Anna says your name is Saul of Tarsus, a Pharisee?"

"Yes, indeed, and a servant to the Messiah, Jesus."

"I've not heard that our Messiah has come. We're so isolated in these parts without a synagogue. I'm sure that I can gather our people to meet here at the inn to learn more of this Messiah. However, we must be careful."

"Yes, your wife has told me about your King. Is he not tolerant of other religions?"

"Yes and no. He does not force his gods on us. But he expects us not to force our God on him or do anything that would decrease offerings at the temple."

"Simeon, if it's acceptable, I will teach our people here and see how things work out."

Simeon stroked his gray-streaked beard and nodded, "Follow me."

My room was accommodating, with a raised bed, clean linen, a wash basin, and a window that faced toward Jerusalem. The latrines were located down the hall. It would suffice. Besides, I was used to living the bachelor life.

At that moment, I thought of Rebecca, the woman to whom I had been betrothed, and the life we could've had together. She was the daughter of one of the elite families of a fellow Pharisee in Jerusalem. She was beautiful, with flawless skin like alabaster and long honey-brown hair that reached to her waist.

## Saul's Arrival in Arabia

I thought back to the challenges I faced when brought before the council. I was an excellent student of Torah and excelled beyond those I studied with. I even sat at the feet of Gamaliel. But the one thing I lacked was a wife.

I would've been comfortable without one for a while, but deep inside, I knew I needed one. Shortly after the betrothal was announced, I was made a Pharisee. And not long after that, Rebecca died. Sitting here alone in this room, away from all I know and cherish, makes me long for Rebecca. It makes me long for a wife. I shook myself out of my ruminations and began my prayers, "Hear, O Israel, The Lord is our God, the Lord is One."

The next day, during the noonday meal, I took some refreshments and spoke with Simeon.

"I'm a tentmaker by trade. Are there any opportunities for work in this city?" I asked.

"Yes, old man Youssef Ahkmad Ma'an. He's a tentmaker. The best in these parts. Kasim Ahkmad Ma'an is his brother, and he's a trader. He sells his brother's tents as well as spices and expensive linen and wool. He makes several trips to Jerusalem each year. They are Arabs, but proselyte Jews and have even submitted to our ritual of circumcision. After you eat, I will take you there."

"Your wife Anna, she's a good cook."

"Yes, when we opened the Inn, we decided to serve our native food, hoping the change of pace would be acceptable to the palate of the people here. Truthfully, there are so many people that travel these parts that our food was hailed as delectable. Anna's secret is in the spices she uses. We purchase them from the caravans that travel through the city, particularly from the Far East."

While chewing, I managed to say, "Yes, Simeon, this mutton and chickpeas are the best I've ever tasted!"

"Wait till you eat the sweetcakes. You'll become addicted instantly, my friend."

"Have you thought about returning to Jerusalem and opening an Inn?"

"No, there are no good memories for us there. The Romans killed our only boy. They stormed the marketplace one day, looking for one of the zealots. One of their horses reared in fright, and my boy panicked and ran. The horse's hooves came down and trampled him."

I could see Simeon's eyes well up with tears as he shook his head. His face was chiseled with anger, then anguish, and finally defeat. Whenever the Romans came out in force, innocent people were always caught in the middle of their rampage.

Simeon spoke again, "Our only consolation was the Roman centurion—who was responsible for the accident—was truly remorseful. His fellow officers chided him for having sympathy, saying if it wasn't for the zealots, this would never have happened. The centurion paid them no attention. He quietly pulled me aside and promised to render compensation for the burial of my four-year-old son. He sent his servant over the next day with coins sufficient enough for the burial and to purchase this Inn. We never turned back. When I asked his servant why he would do such a thing, he simply said, 'My master is a Godfearer.'"

Anna walked in with a plate and handed it to Simeon. "Please give this to old man Youssef with my greetings. He's lost so much weight since his dear wife passed, and he doesn't look out for himself as he should."

After the noonday meal, Simeon escorted me to see old man Youssef. He was in his shop preparing the leather hide for a tent.

"Hello Simeon, what brings you to my humble business? Are you in need of an awning for the shop?"

"Hello Youssef, I don't need an awning just yet, but Anna sends you food with her greetings."

"She's so kind, please send my regards. Is it that obvious, Simeon?"

"You've lost too much weight, my friend. Have you thought of remarrying?"

"I have given it much prayer. We shall see what the Lord says. So,

## Saul's Arrival in Arabia

who is our friend here?"

"This is Saul of Tarsus. Saul, this is Youssef Ahkmad Ma'an."

"Shalom Youssef, Simeon tells me you're a proselyte."

"Yes, my brother Kasim sat under Rabbi Joseph of the Capernaum synagogue. His son Benjamin has an Inn in Jerusalem."

"I know the Capernaum synagogue well. There are some leaders there who are sympathetic to the believers of the Way."

"What do you make of this, Saul?" responded Youssef.

"My brother, I thought you would never ask!"

"I was on my way to Damascus to round up the believers of the Way when Jesus appeared to me in the midst of an intense light. He asked me why I was persecuting him. I was blinded by the light, and the Lord Jesus instructed me that a man named Ananias, a believer of the Way, would come and restore my sight. All of this was fulfilled. Afterward, I went straight to the synagogue to preach Jesus and barely escaped the city with my life. I was told to go to Arabia, and here I am."

"Blessed be our risen Lord! We, too, are believers of the Way. My brother Kasim encountered the risen Lord on the road to Emmaus. My nephew Salim was present during Shavuot and received the promise of the Holy Spirit. Jesus had told his disciples to go to Jerusalem and wait for the promise. He said they would be endowed with power from on high."

"Saul has agreed to teach about Jesus to the Jewish believers at the Inn," interjected Simeon.

"Now I know why the Lord instructed me to come to Arabia! I'm supposed to preach to both Jews and Gentiles and tell them about our crucified and risen Savior," I replied.

"I must take you to meet the others. But first things first, what brings you to my shop since you didn't know I was a believer?" asked Youssef.

"I'm a tentmaker by trade, and I'm looking for work in order to pay for my lodging and meals at Simeon's Inn."

"I can surely use the help. Do you work with leather as well as linen?"

"Yes, I can also make strips of cloth from goat and camel hair."

"Magnificent! Consider yourself hired. Can you start the day after the Sabbath?"

"Yes, of course."

"Good, that will give me time to introduce you to my clan. We've all been circumcised as proselytes, and we are now all believers of the Way. We are anxious to learn of the Messiah and how Jesus fulfilled the prophecies of old. It would be an honor to hear this from a notable Pharisee as yourself."

"I would be honored. After a time, I'll need help devising a strategy on how to get the Good News of Jesus to the Gentiles in this region."

"That, my friend, is going to be a difficult task."

"Yes, Simeon has informed me of King Aretas's policies on this matter. I do not fear him because our Lord has called me to teach Gentiles about the Way. Nevertheless, I will pray for wisdom and rely on the advice of the believers here in the city."

~ *Saul, Meeting Kasim* ~

Kasim lived in a mud brick home of substantial size. He was a traveling merchant dealing in rare spices, linen, and wool. His home did not represent the wealth he owned, I imagined. Youssef told me his family worked alongside him in business, and they all shared in the profits. His clan are Bedouins from Arabia and shepherds who sell fine wool. I learned that they had been living in Arabia before the Nabateans laid claim to the region before King Aretas IV assumed kingship.

I must have been steep in thought, for I did not hear Kasim approach.

"The infamous Saul of Tarsus. I've heard many stories. I'm Kasim," he said.

"Brother Kasim, it's a pleasure to meet you. I'm afraid the stories you've heard are probably true, and for this, I'm deeply sorry."

## Saul's Arrival in Arabia

"I meant no disrespect. I'm pained that you must live with those memories as a thorn in your flesh. I'm equally in awe of what our God can do in transforming your life so thoroughly."

"Thank you, your words touch me deeply. I know I must live with the memory of my actions, but our Lord has nailed my sins to his cross. He did what the law could not do, imputed my sins, and has given me his righteousness."

"You must teach us, Saul. There are many in my clan. We have a large number of brethren who still live as Bedouins outside of the city. They live the simple way and enjoy much more freedom in their worship."

"You're a wise man, Kasim. Perhaps we can fellowship and break bread outside of the city. You can tell me all you know of Jesus. I'll start with the Torah, and we can learn together of our Messiah and how he has fulfilled the Scripture."

On the Sabbath, we gathered in the low-lying mountains in a secluded area. To my surprise, Kasim's clan were well versed in the Torah, and they worshiped Adonai. The songs of David were soothing to my soul. Simeon and Anna had joined us, along with ten other families from the city. Besides Simeon and Anna, there were three Jewish families, and the remainder were Arab believers who lived in the city.

Kasim led the prayers and spoke on the teachings of the disciples. That is the eleven who had been with Jesus. He recounted the story of Shavuot, which they referred to as the Day of Pentecost, when the promise of Jesus was fulfilled. They were all filled with the Holy Spirit.

Then Kasim shared, "It was my grandson Salim who experienced this wonderful promise. When he returned, we were all baptized in the name of Jesus. We also prayed for the promise of the Holy Spirit and the Lord was faithful to fill us with his Spirit. We, too, began to speak in other tongues, not of our own language. Saul, can you please share with us the Torah and show us the fulfillment of our Messiah."

"First, I must say that I, too, was baptized and filled with the Holy Spirit."

I recounted the story of my experience with the Lord Jesus on the road to Damascus. I explained how Jesus sent Ananias to lay hands on me and how I received my sight, was baptized, and was filled with the Holy Spirit.

Then I stood and prayed, and the word of the Lord came over me from the prophet Joel. "'And it shall come to pass afterward, that I will pour out My Spirit on all flesh.' I believe this is what your grandson Salim experienced on the Day of Pentecost, the promise of Jesus."

A collective gasp rose from the crowd. Kasim proceeded to speak about partaking of the Lord's Supper and of fellowship and the breaking of bread.

I asked Kasim, "Please explain the Lord's Supper to me. The Sanhedrin received reports that the followers of the Way were eating flesh and drinking blood, which is forbidden by Torah."

Kasim eagerly responded, "We take and eat of the bread and drink of the vine as a representation of fellowship with our Lord. Jesus told his disciples on the Passover before he was crucified to 'Take, eat; this is My body.' Then He took the cup, and gave thanks, and gave it to them, saying, 'Drink from it, all of you. For this is My blood of the new covenant, which is shed for many for the remission of sins.'"

"Yes," I replied. "We are to remember his body on the cross and the blood he shed. He became the once and for all sacrifice. We no longer need the blood of bulls, lambs, and goats."

~ *Saul, You Don't Work, You Don't Eat* ~

"Youssef, I learned so much last night!"

"Yes, my friend, we have much to teach each other. We have the experience. You, Saul, have the experience and the knowledge of Torah."

"I will pray and seek God on this matter so the Lord will give me the words to say. That I may have the opportunity and the boldness to speak it to the Gentiles, whom he has called me to."

"Enough of this—we have tents to make," said Youssef.

I replied in good humor, "You don't work, you don't eat."

Youssef and I sat for hours cutting leather and cilicium to make tents. The women of Youssef's family stitched them together so they could hold up to heavy use and repel moisture. This was a skill I was familiar with, but I was more accustomed to working with goat's hair. It's more affordable for the common people. It also breathes in the hot weather, and the hairs swell in the rainy season to keep out the moisture.

My face must have shown my contemplation, for I heard Youssef say, "Saul, what are you thinking?"

"Leather seems to be popular in this region."

"Yes and no. The traders that come and go prefer the sturdier tents made of leather. The locals and Bedouins mainly use tents made of goat's hair."

"I have skill in both techniques. I can even stitch. Although, I mostly leave that to the women."

"I'm thankful for it all. I know the Lord sent you here to help a fellow brother with his work and fellow believers with their faith."

"Yes, and there's much to do. I'll be here for a while, if you'll have me."

"Saul, you're a welcome addition to my family."

"Thank you, my brother, thank you."

# Chapter 16

# Guess Who's Coming to Dinner

*Issa, The Unwanted Dinner Guest*

I was growing accustomed to dinner being a family affair. I didn't mind so much, as I enjoyed speaking with Kasim's father. He was a wealth of knowledge concerning ancient Arabia.

"Issa," he shared, "Our ancestors were nomads who settled in Petra before the Nabateans came to power."

Loud noises interrupted our conversation, and everyone's attention shifted to the entryway. Kasim's Uncle Fasim and his Cousin Fasar were joining us for dinner this evening along with Akhab.

As usual Fasar was a bit raucous and flirtatious, but he was easygoing and kept us all laughing. On the other hand, Fasim always managed to ruin the evening in one way or another.

Fakmad continued to recount the stories of old, "My ancestors dwelled in Arabia for centuries until the Nabateans came to power. We were mountain-dwellers-turned-traders. I must concede the Nabateans were geniuses when it came to architecture and trade. This is how they became a formidable nation. They also brought their many gods, which eventually cursed the land. But the Lord God of Israel was gracious enough to reveal his Son Jesus to us, and here we remain almost two millennia later."

Fakmad spoke boldly and with authority to everyone seated at the table. He flailed his arms in every direction, proclaiming God's protection from his enemies and the coming vindication of his seed. He proclaimed Jesus to be the Son of God, the Messiah, the One who is to come and gather his people as the last days draw near.

"Listen everyone," he declared. "I should have died three times over, yet here I am. We serve the true and living God, maker of Heaven and Earth. The Lord will see to it that his will is accomplished. We'll find the scrolls that contain the Apostle Paul's letters to our ancestors. We'll proclaim Jesus in the land of our forefathers!"

Looking directly at Fasar and Fasim, Fakmad snapped, "And you two would do well to revere the Lord in word and in deed!"

Fasim had a look of chagrin on his face. Fasar bent his head in remorse. Fasim quickly changed the subject.

"Dr. Stevens, how much closer are we to finding the scrolls? Isn't that supposed to be your expertise?"

Akhab, looking directly at Fasim, chuckled, "I'm beginning to believe the sour look on your face is a permanent feature."

Akhab evidently had a long history with the Ma'an family and was not afraid to speak his mind. I secretly applauded him. I didn't want to give Fasim the pleasure of an answer. Instead, I shifted my attention to Kasim and began to summarize the events of the day. Fakmad and Akhab joined in the conversation, and we all accounted for the progress of the mission. Kasim was the first to elaborate in detail.

"I spent most of my day brokering a deal with the Louvre Museum in France. They're interested in the artifacts from the fourteenth century that we unearthed at the sanctioned dig site in Petra."

Akhab continued, "Dr. Issa and I scouted the perimeter of the building today. I must admit at first, I was not sure what we could accomplish. Then, she made some excellent observations. Dr. Issa, tell them what you told me."

"I was examining the different building structures in the nearby vicinity when a thought came to mind. We need to do cross-analyses

## Guess Who's Coming to Dinner

of the artifacts that have been discovered thus far. Compare what you have found at each of the sites in Petra and at the Ma'an-Petra border. Categorize them by date and catalog them by the depth of the find. If we find patterns, and I believe we will, it will help us to further our search in strategic geographic areas."

"Issa, that's brilliant!" exclaimed Kasim.

"Why didn't we think of this earlier?" asked Fakmad.

"I think we'd better wait and see what the data reveals before we get too excited," I advised.

Just then, the smell of succulent roasted lamb caught my attention. Dinner was always an elaborate affair at the Ma'an residence. It consisted of a four-course meal. I could smell an array of spices that were used to season the lamb and vegetables. Hummus and pita bread were served. The hummus was well-seasoned and tasted delicious. My stomach rumbled, and my salivary glands were overreacting to the variety of tantalizing smells.

In the periphery of my vision, I saw a woman enter the dining hall. There were the occasional guests who dined with us. Usually, close family friends and associates were invited. But I was not ready for tonight's guest. One of the most beautiful women I've ever seen walked into the dining room. She was tall and slender with dark raven hair that peeked through her hijab. She had flawless olive skin and handsome facial features with a beauty mark on her left cheek. She had the most amazing hazel eyes.

Kasim had just returned from speaking with the chef when this tall beauty threw herself into his arms. She gave him the customary greeting of a kiss on both cheeks that was far too close to his lips for decorum and lingered more than was customary.

Kasim stood rigid. Finally, after dislodging her hands from his arms he said, "It's good to see you, Cousin."

Kasim's gaze sought mine, "Issa, forgive my rudeness. This is my cousin, Tirsa. Tirsa, this is Dr. Stevens. She's a close friend and is here to help with the excavations."

Fasim's facial features transformed from his usual perpetual scowl to the most benevolent smile. I felt so uncomfortable and out of place that I found myself fidgeting in my chair. Kasim and Miri turned to me simultaneously, "Issa, is everything okay?" asked Kasim.

I blushed with embarrassment, my feelings a mixture of outrage and anger. And something more—jealousy. After all, Kasim was a handsome man and a sought-after bachelor. From what I understood, he was practically betrothed to that beauty of a cousin. That is, if Fasim had any say in the matter.

I paled in comparison to Tirsa's beauty and elegance.

As if Fasim could read my mind, he said, "So nephew, have you given any more thought to the merit of marrying your dear cousin."

~ *Kasim, My Ire* ~

My uncle was irritating my last nerve. I took an exaggerated breath and exhaled. I was about to give Fasim a retort that would've been out of character even for me.

My father interrupted, "Fasim, leave Kasim be. This is neither the time nor the place."

Tirsa replied, "It seems as if Kasim's interests lie elsewhere. I am, of course, the most logical choice. You're safe with me, Cousin."

"She is correct! We have discussed this over and over again and have all agreed it's the most reasonable course of action," emphasized Fasim.

"Thank you, Uncle," said Tirsa.

Tirsa smiled at Fasim. Then her countenance changed to a scowl—her tone laced with disdain—as she addressed Issa. "I mean no disrespect, Ms. Stevens."

"Her name is Dr. Stevens," Miri corrected.

"Yes, yes. Dr. Stevens. I understand you teach at a small Christian college. Are you really up for a work of this magnitude?"

"Tirsa, I'm the one who decides who is qualified to represent the Ma'an family. Your criticism of my choice is a direct criticism of me. Are you sure that is what you mean?" I replied.

"No, Kasim. I'm merely concerned—as we all are—regarding the importance of this mission. I meant no disrespect."

*~ Issa, My Defense ~*

The fact that these people were talking about me as if I were not sitting at the table was beyond irritating. *Maybe this is how the wealthy and privileged behave*, I thought.

*Well, I'm not going to stand for it.*

I mustered up the courage to reply to the taunts.

"Ms. Tirsa, let me assure you I know exactly what I'm doing. My calling to this mission goes beyond being hired to do so. The Lord has commissioned me to this task and to help this family."

"Oh, that's very noble, Dr. Stevens." Tirsa retorted. "What do you stand to gain from this commissioned assignment?"

"I get to see history in the making. I get to experience the very hand of God directing the future of his beloved Church. I get to be a partaker of God's divine will for your family. This, my dear Tirsa, is priceless!"

Fasim interrupted my speech, "So you think you win the affections of my nephew as your reward? It's common knowledge that he is wealthy."

Fasar came to my rescue, "Uncle, if you took the time to get to know Dr. Stevens, you would not say these things."

"Fasim," implored Akhab. "You have misjudged Dr. Issa. Her expertise has been invaluable to our progress. Her research alone helped us get this far before she even stepped foot in Arabia."

"Her expertise is not in question, it's her ulterior motives. I'm only trying to protect my nephew, to protect this family!" shouted Fasim.

"And what are your ulterior motives, Uncle?" asked Kasim.

With a coy smile, Tirsa interjected, "Uncle Fasim is just trying to protect us all. Besides, he knows how much I care for you and our family.

We only want you to be happy and for our family to remain safe."

"Again, you belittle me. You forget your place. I can take care of myself without you or Uncle Fasim's help. I'm capable of deciding who can make me happy and how to keep my family safe."

"Kasim! Apologize to Tirsa. I've never known you to be so rude. That is, until Dr. Stevens entered this household," Fasim replied.

Fakmad answered with a stern voice, "Enough! I'm seeking the Lord's will on this matter, and I'll reveal my decision when the time is right. Now, let's eat."

~ *Kasim, My Remorse* ~

The remainder of the evening was quiet. I saw the horrified look on Issa's face. I was not proud of myself. She must think we're a bunch of spoiled, privileged brats. Certainly, my family's behavior tonight was not a reflection of Christ. Neither was mine. More like a drama on prime-time television, full of intrigue and deception. I wanted nothing more than to whisk Issa away from this place and cradle her in my arms. I want her to know she is loved and safe in my embrace. But I feel like I'm losing control of my own destiny. Am I being selfish and unreasonable?

~ *Issa, My Misery* ~

The remainder of the evening was unbearable for me. I couldn't help but notice how Tirsa looked at Kasim with longing. Oh, she was in love with him alright. And could I really blame her? What was there not to love about him? He was a gentleman, kind, attractive, smart, and attentive. Kasim had a charisma that unwittingly drew you to him. What in the world was I thinking? This beautiful woman was who his family wanted. It's the most logical choice, and that's who he would choose if I were not here distracting him from his mission—from his legacy. I tried hard not to show the myriad of emotions that I was experiencing.

I guess I failed miserably because Miri placed her hand on mine and squeezed tight. Fasar gave me a sympathetic smile and winked at me. Akhab gave me a look that said, "I'm sorry." Fasim and Tirsa had smug smiles on their faces. Fakmad was enjoying his meal as if nothing was amiss.

Kasim's face was devoid of any emotion. Maybe he's come to his senses. Maybe now he realizes that what we experienced all those years ago was simply infatuation.

I abruptly stood and excused myself from the table.

Apologizing to Fakmad and Kasim, I said, "Please excuse me. I'm not feeling well. I think the heat was too much for me today."

Kasim called after me, "Issa, I'll check on you shortly and make sure you are well."

I nodded because I feared if I spoke, the distress I felt inside would seep through my voice.

"Miri," Kasim said, "Please accompany Issa to her room and make sure she is well."

### ~ Kasim, Confronting Father ~

After the meal, I pulled my father to the side and demanded an audience with him in his office. I was livid. I was appalled. I was done with it all! I'm no longer going to allow this family to ruin my life or the people I love. Nothing about their actions tonight resembled Christ-like behavior. I wasn't willing to pretend to defend a legacy that claims to cling to Christian values and faith but lives opposite of them.

I've done everything that's been required of me since I was a child. Now, I'm a man. I'm capable of thinking for myself. I'm not here to fight for position, power, or wealth. Jesus came against the Pharisees and Sadducees of his day for seeking such things and for oppressing God's people. What has my family legacy come to?

I rehearsed this diatribe in my mind over and over again while I waited for my father in his study.

"Kasim," my father interrupted me mid-thought.

"Father." I nodded my head curtly.

"What is on your mind, son?"

"Since you raised the question, I will respond honestly. Let me first ask you a question. What are we all really doing here? What is our true mission? I can't continue to be a part of something that doesn't bring glory to God. And this family's attack on Issa brings no glory to him. It was shameful and doesn't display Christ at all!"

"Son, calm down, please."

"I will not marry Tirsa!"

"Kasim, going against my wishes brings dishonor."

"I would rather give up my wealth, prestige, and power before dishonoring you."

"My son, to give up your inheritance, and thus your legacy, would bring the worst kind of dishonor. What is troubling you?"

"Father, were you not sitting at the same table this evening? Fasim has been plotting and manipulating us to gain wealth, power, and position. He seems to have bewitched poor Tirsa into doing his bidding. Mother would be appalled at his actions."

"Son, you think I'm so old that I'm dull of mind? I believe Tirsa is the best choice for you, and I think your mother would approve."

"Father, that's not fair."

"If only my dear wife were here, she would be able to temper her brother. We must somehow get Tirsa out from under his spell."

"You just don't get it. I don't want to marry Tirsa! I don't love her. I was the obedient son when I married Abbie. I will not have my life ruined again by the choices of others."

"How dear you speak ill of your dead wife. She gave us one of our greatest gifts, and don't forget that!"

"That's not what I meant. Miri means the world to me, and I grew to love Abbie. I grieved her and had to try to raise a daughter at such a young age. The difference is I'm no longer seventeen. I'm forty-two. I'm a grown man and capable of making my own decisions concerning what's best for me."

"Oh, Kasim, where did I go wrong raising you? All I ever wanted was the best for you. To leave a continuous legacy for you and your descendants."

I sighed in exasperation.

"Father, I know you only want the best for me. But you must hear me. Issa is what's best for me. Have you prayed and asked the Lord about Tirsa?"

Father dropped his head. I didn't want to bring sorrow to him in his old age, but I had to continue.

"Well, I've prayed and sought the Lord on this matter. Not only do I love Issa, I feel a sense of renewed purpose with her by my side. I feel at peace, and I'm happy. She loves the Lord and is committed to helping us, because she's obeying what God told her to do."

"Son, I'm forever in her debt for obeying the Lord for my healing. And I've given it much thought. I performed a background check on her."

"Father!"

"Sorry son, but it was necessary, and you know it! I have concerns because, culturally, there will be a great disconnect for her. And what we require of her may be too much to ask. Second, her ethnicity and biracial status may raise issues among our people. Her mother is of Jewish descent."

"That's a bit hypocritical. Our ancestors were Jewish proselytes."

Father raised his hand to stop me, "Let me finish. We also know nothing of her biological father. She was raised by her stepfather from around the age of three. We believe her biological father is Afro-Caribbean, although he was born in the States."

"And what difference does any of this make?"

"We must keep our lineage as pure as possible."

"Says who, Father? Is that what Jesus preached? Is that what the disciples taught? No! They advised us not to be unequally yoked with those who don't believe as we do. What you speak of are traditions of men. When you speak this way, you make us sound like an Aryan race, trying to keep a pure line. We are citizens of Heaven, and our family extends to any who believe in the Lord Jesus Christ."

Father turned his back on me and looked out his window. I saw him peering at the mountains, lost in thought. He stood there for a long time with his arms firmly across his chest. I prayed silently, hoping, pleading with the Lord to speak to his heart. Father inhaled deeply, then exhaled. His brows were knit together, and his facial expression was grave. I felt my heart drop to my stomach, and my pulse raced. I didn't want to go against my father's wishes. But this time, I would, no matter the consequences. I'd rather obey God than man, even if that man was my father.

I felt a moment's regret as there was a voice speaking in my head saying, *Isn't it written you must obey your father?*

Then another voice countered, saying, *Satan also spoke to Jesus saying, 'It is written.'*

The voice continued, *Take heed to what I have told you to do, Kasim.*

At that moment, I knew it was the Lord speaking to me. I now know what I must do, even if it breaks my father's heart. I must marry Issa.

Abruptly, my father spoke, "Son, I will give you my blessing."

I must have been holding my breath, for when he spoke, I finally exhaled.

## Chapter 17

## All is Not as it Seems

*~ Issa, Later That Evening ~*

Miri walked me to my room and apologized for the third time. I felt beyond humiliated.

"Issa, are you going to be okay?"

"Yes, Miri, I'm just tired."

Just before closing the door, she said, "I will come back to check on you."

What was I thinking? I don't belong here. These people are elitists with a history that is tied directly to an ancient society. And who am I? An average-looking American woman in a foreign land. A biracial misfit. A bygone professor at a small Christian college who hasn't even earned tenure yet. My daughter barely speaks to me, and my husband has left me here all alone!

I lowered my head in my hands and began to wail. I was trembling. The tears spilled forth uncontrollably, and I cried frantically, swept away by the intensity of my emotions. At first, I felt sorry for myself. Then, I became angry. I continued my diatribe, and with bitterness, I aimed it at God.

*Why me? I'm never good enough! Always second best. Did you bring me to this foreign land for me to be mocked? Laughed at? Berated and told I'm not good enough? How could you allow this to happen? I thought you loved me. Everyone who says they love me, leaves me. I've done everything you've asked of me. I pray, I read my Bible, I'm active in my church. I love you, Lord, with all my heart, soul, mind, and strength. I dropped everything to come here. I thought this was what you wanted. Now, I don't even know if I hear your voice.*

Maybe it was just me hanging on to a childhood fantasy. I deserved what happened at dinner. I should never have come here. But how could I have known I would be working with Kasim?

I yelled, "Just get me out of here, Lord! I want to go home." Then a sob escaped my lips. "I don't want my heart to be broken again."

I finally fell asleep. Then, a noise woke me. I thought I was dreaming when I first heard Kasim's voice. My bed dipped from the weight of his muscular frame, and he softly called my name.

"Issa, it's me, Kasim."

My eyes fluttered open. His face was contorted as if in pain. His eyebrows knitted together with a look of concern. No doubt he was shocked at what he saw. My face was probably blotchy and swollen. I was sure my eyes were red and puffy like I had been assaulted.

He quietly said, "I knocked. When you didn't answer, I became concerned and let myself in."

He bent down and softly kissed me on my forehead.

"Issa, I'm sorry that you had to experience the selfishness and scheming ways of my uncle."

I sat up and looked him in the eyes. It seemed like time was suspended. Neither of us flinched.

With all sincerity, I responded, "But it's the most logical choice. You must do what is in the best interest of your family—to preserve your legacy."

"You mean what is in the best interest of my uncle. I will decide what is in my best interest. Of course, with my father's blessing."

Kasim unceremoniously slid off the bed, reached into his pocket, and pulled out a silk cloth.

As he opened the cloth, he asked, "Issa, will you marry me?"

To my surprise, there was a diamond ring, the size of which I had never seen. It was a pear-shaped brilliant diamond set upon a prong with an array of smaller stones. They looked like Alexandrite stones as the colors changed when the ring was turned in either direction. The ring was set upon a band of yellow gold. Tears of joy welled in my eyes as I absorbed the moment.

"The ring, it's beautiful," I said.

"It was my mother's."

Then, my countenance fell, and my voice trembled, "Kasim, I can't see how this will work for either of us. I don't want to come between you and your family."

"Tell me you do not love me, and I will not pursue this any further."

I lowered my head and squeezed my eyes shut. A throbbing pain formed at my temples, and I instinctively began to rub them.

"Issa, please tell me what your feelings are for me?"

After some time, I whispered, "I love you, too."

"Remember, Habibti, love never fails. It is the greatest of all."

I closed the distance, wrapped my arms around Kasim, and squeezed him with every ounce of my strength.

I whispered in his ear, "I love you so much."

In my excitement, I shrieked, "I want to make you the happiest man in the world. I want us to grow old together, and…"

My excitement quickly ebbed.

I wanted to say, *And have your children.*

But could I have children at my age? Could I provide Kasim with the male heir he needed? I suddenly stiffened in his arms.

Kasim pushed slightly away, keeping me within arm's reach, and asked, "What's wrong, Habibti?"

A stubborn tear escaped, "What if I can't give you what you need most? A son."

Kasim sat on the edge of the bed, lifted my chin, and answered in a gentle voice, "My sweet Issa, I'm marrying you because I love you with every fiber of my being. I have no desire to be with any other woman. My father has given us his blessing. We both agree that this is the will of the Lord, and we are expecting signs, miracles, and wonders to take place—just as they once did with our ancestors. We believe and are trusting God on this matter."

Suddenly, there was a soft knock on the door.

"Who is it?"

The voice beyond replied, "It's me, Miri."

"Come in, Miri."

She opened the door and ran and enveloped both Kasim and myself. How the petite girl managed to encircle both of us in her embrace, I'll never know. We all laughed. Miri looked at me in earnest and asked the question.

"So, what's the verdict?"

Kasim smiled, "She's ours forever."

Miri screamed with delight.

"Papa, Issa, I'm so happy for both of you. And Papa, I'm glad you will not be alone anymore."

"Well Miri, I guess we have a wedding to plan. Kasim, you need to go do whatever bridegrooms do."

Kasim chuckled, "We have a few weeks to get ready. The household has already begun preparations. In the meantime, you and I must continue with the excavation."

"What about Fasim and Tirsa?" I asked.

## All is Not as it Seems

"My father has spoken to them both. They're not happy, of course, but they'll not cross my father in this matter."

"I'm afraid of Fasim. I fear he'll try and harm me to get his way."

"You are my betrothed now. And although we will forego all the traditional waiting periods and the pre-ceremony celebrations, you're considered my wife once we sign the wedding contract."

"Oh, like Ketubah?" I asked.

"Yes, exactly!"

"When do we sign the contract?"

"Within the next few days."

"How will you keep me safe until then?"

Miri replied, a wide grin spread across her face, "You can sleep in my quarters with me. It's certainly large enough to give you your space, and my room is adjacent to my Papa."

I smiled and hugged Miri. She was always a thoughtful girl. Her face beamed as she took her leave. Miri was always so perceptive. I knew she left to give Kasim and me time to process our emotions. Kasim looked at me with longing, and my insides felt like a tangled ball of yarn. Why did I feel as though this was the first time I'd ever been courted by a man? I felt like a high school girl being asked out on a prom date.

Kasim cleared his throat, interrupting my thoughts.

"There's much to do. However, I don't want to take away from your special day. I feel terrible that we must still work on the excavation and plan a wedding at the same time."

I interrupted him, "You don't have to bother with an elaborate wedding. You can forget all the formalities. I'd be content with an informal ceremony in the beautiful gardens."

"I know you would prefer to avoid all the fanfare. But I will give you what you deserve and so much more."

"I can't help but feel like an imposter. I know you are marrying below your station. I don't know how to navigate in your world of power and wealth."

"A life dedicated to the Lord, prayer, and the knowledge that all we have comes from him. That's how we navigate together, Issa."

I whispered softly, "I love you, Kasim."

"I love you too, Habibti."

Kasim leaned in and softly kissed me on my nose.

"Now, I must let you sleep. We have to be at the excavation site in the morning. We have a lot to accomplish in a short period of time. But don't worry, we also have lots of people to help us."

Kasim kissed me again, this time on my brow, and I nodded. For the first time since arriving in Arabia, I knew I would sleep well.

~ *Issa, The Sky is Falling* ~

An Arabic Christian wedding is no small affair.

*How am I supposed to manage an excavation and plan a wedding in such a short time?*

I called Sky first thing the next morning, not knowing really what to expect. My spirit told me to brace myself.

So before calling, I kneeled at my bed and prayed, "Jesus, thank you for knowing me better than I know myself. Thank you for knowing what I need most and providing it. You love your children and are a good Father. I praise you because you are the maker of Heaven and Earth. You created humankind and called your work good. Help me always to remember this and to learn to see the good in people, even in Fasim and Tirsa. Now, I ask that you take care of Sky. Heal her heart and help her not to be too disappointed in me. Give me the words to say, so she can feel how much I love her. In Jesus's name. Amen."

"Hi Sky, it's mom. How are you doing?"

"Hey Mom, I'm fine. How about you?"

"I'm doing well. Tell me about school."

"I'm enjoying it. I'm quite the controversial figure. You know, always challenging my professors' worldviews."

"Sky," I exclaimed in horror. "You must watch what you say."

"Don't worry. They respect that I always back up what I say with more facts than just the Bible. If they only knew some of the things they teach are right out of God's Word. They just bend the interpretation to make it mean what they want it to mean. The kicker is they don't even back it up with facts, just philosophical rhetoric."

"Be careful, Sky. You're as smart as your dad. But I don't want to see you get treated unfairly because you are a fearless woman who expresses what she believes. After all, the Bible says to be wise as a serpent and as harmless as a dove."

"I know, Mom, you don't have to worry about me. So, is everything okay? You usually don't call for small talk."

"I need to know if you can get permission from your professors to take maybe seven to ten days off?"

"Why? Is there something wrong?"

"Well, no. It's just that I'm getting married, and I really want you to be here."

"Married! To whom? I didn't even know you were dating anyone!"

"Sky, it's a long story. The man I'm marrying, his name is Kasim. We have known each other since our teenage years."

"Oh. You never mentioned him. Did Dad know about him?"

"No. Kasim had to abruptly leave the country when we were seventeen, and I've not seen him since. Until recently."

"He lives overseas?"

"Well, yes and no. His primary residence is in Ma'an, Jordan, near Petra. He has an international business, so he also has residences in the States."

"Oh, okay. I'm sure there is more to the story. I don't think there should be a problem. I'll have to complete a few minor projects, but the work here is not hard for me."

"Sky, I think you may have surpassed both your dad and I in your level of intelligence. Well, at least mine. I struggled at every turn to maintain my honors status. Nothing comes easy to me."

"Mom, really. You're too hard on yourself, and you know it. You have one of the most brilliant minds I know."

"Well, enough about me. Kasim is sending his family's jet to pick you up. Will that be okay with you?"

"A private jet! Just who are you marrying, the prince of Arabia?"

"No, not quite. I'll tell you everything when you get here."

"Mom, you surprise me."

"Well, I'm hoping that is a compliment?"

"Well, we'll have to wait and see, won't we?"

"Sky, please don't be upset with me. You are and will always be my first priority."

"I know, I guess. I'll see you soon. Will Grandma and Grandpa be coming?"

"No, Grandpa has not been feeling well. His eyesight is getting worse, and the arthritis leaves his knees stiff and painful, making it hard to move around. We will be recording the ceremony, and I will send them a copy."

"I'll have to give them a call and check on them. I need to look in on them more often. They're just so independent. I forget how old they really are."

"Yes, me too. I'll let you get back to your studies. I'll send all the details for your trip later today. I love you, Sky."

"Love you too, Mom, bye."

The following week, Kasim and Miri decided to fly to Connecticut to pick up Sky. Kasim thought it would give them time to get acquainted. I prayed it would be a game-changer for her. Kasim left me with a contingent of guards, and I spent the week with Rajah, enjoying beauty treatments and planning for the wedding. I wanted everything to be perfect for Kasim. I would've been happy to exchange vows in a small, intimate setting and begin my new life with my husband. But the Arabic Christian wedding was more than a wedding. It was an ingrafting into the legacy of the Ma'an family.

I studied all I could about Kasim's family, culture, and traditions in the short time I had. I paid attention to every detail and how each tied together. I focused on the significance of each intricate part of the elaborate ceremony. I didn't want to bring shame to Kasim or his family. I must get this right! If not, they'll wish they had married him off to Tirsa.

It was while studying Kasim's family history that it dawned on me. The family's traditions are what knit them cohesively as one unit. These traditions held the family together and preserved them for close to two millennia. If they had managed to escape to Egypt with the scrolls, they would have learned how to preserve them from the Egyptians.

I gave voice to the words as they formed in my mind, "Perhaps the scrolls were taken to Egypt, preserved there, and then brought back to Petra. Perhaps there are some clues they left for us, and we are missing what's right before our eyes."

"Dr. Stevens?"

I was drawn from my monologue when a servant informed me that Kasim, Miri, and Sky had arrived. I made a mental note to talk to Kasim about my theory, and I hurried to meet them. I ran into Sky's arms and embraced her.

"Oh, how I've missed you, Sky!"

I turned and thanked Miri and kissed Kasim lightly on the lips.

I whispered in his ear, "Thank you, this means so much to me."

Kasim and Miri excused themselves to give Sky and me some time alone. We started walking toward my room.

As soon as we were out of earshot, Sky spoke, "Your friends, they are lovely people."

Her voice sounded dry, and I felt a knot form in the pit of my stomach.

"Sky, I know this all seems sudden to you, but Kasim and I knew each other before I met your father."

"Yes, he told me. I can tell he loves you."

"Listen Sky, no one will ever be able to replace your father."

Silence greeted me, so I continued.

"I miss him too, but he would not want us to grieve for him forever. Your father believed that we must live our lives to the fullest with the time God has given us on this earth. He believed, as we both do, that we live to live again. He is with the Lord. He lived, loved, laughed, played, and prayed hard while his time was served here. One day, we will see him again. Your father would want to see us laugh and love again."

"I know, mom. It's just that I don't know how I'm going to fit into your new life."

"That, my dear, is entirely up to you. You can continue school and then start your career. You also have the option of living with us until you get on your feet. Kasim spends half of his time in Arabia and the other half in the States."

Sky interrupted, "Miri seems fond of you. She'll make a good daughter."

A pool of tears blurred my vision, "What are you saying? You're my daughter, my flesh and blood."

"Mom, don't cry. It's just that I don't know you anymore. Miri seems to know more about you than I do."

"Sweetheart, you've been away, and I've changed some as well."

"Yes, I see."

Sky looked around at the opulence of the room.

"Sky, it's not about the money. Kasim and I were best friends before he was taken from the States back to Arabia. His family was in crisis, and we lost contact. When we reacquainted, I found that we had so much in common. It was as if we were never separated all those years. We share the same passion for our work, and we both love the Lord."

"I don't blame you, mom. I just have to adjust to the changes."

"Would you like to help me finish planning for the wedding?"

Sky gave me a half smile and answered, "Of course."

"Well, it's off to the baths with you, then we can plan to our heart's desire."

When we emerged from the baths, Sky admitted, "I could get used to this."

"Wait until you receive your massage. You'll truly not want to leave this place."

Sky smiled again, and this time, it seemed to reach her eyes. Over the next week, Sky and Miri became quite close. At first, Sky seemed reserved, angry even. After a few days, she seemed more relaxed and accepting of the marriage. The truth is, she spent more time with Kasim, Miri, and Fasar than she did with me. It didn't bother me in the least. I was happy to see her smile. I sensed, deep in my soul, all would be well.

# Chapter 18

# Excavation Plans Interrupted

*- Issa, The Unexpected -*

I heard knocking on a door in the recesses of my mind. Then I heard my name. I reluctantly lifted my head off the bed and inquired of the culprit behind the door.

"Who is it?"

"It's me, Miri. We're going to be late for the excavation. Papa asked that I let you sleep a little longer today. He's already left for the site."

I immediately jumped out of bed to open the door.

"Miri, I wish your father would have woken me. I'm so embarrassed. This is business, and I'm a professional. I don't slack on my duties."

Miri walked in with the biggest grin on her face. She was so easygoing. She exuded joy and could keep you laughing all day.

"Laughter does good like a medicine," she would say.

"Papa didn't think it was necessary for you to be present for the actual digging. Whatever is found will be secured at the location it was discovered and the necessary testing performed. This is where your expertise will be most helpful."

"I will dress quickly. Where is Sky?"

"She left with Papa and Fasar. They're giving her a tour of Ma'an and Petra. Then they'll meet us at the dig site. Sky will accompany us until lunch, then she and I will return to the estate to assist with the wedding preparations."

"Sounds like a busy but fun day."

Kasim's security guard escorted Miri and me toward the dig site at the Ma'an-Petra border. We were in a Mercedes sports utility vehicle that set out for a rugged ride. We took an alternate route so we could get a wider view of the perimeter of the dig site.

Suddenly, my head jerked back, and I realized we had been hit. The car spun around. It seemed like the spinning would never come to an end. Then, the car rolled over and came to a dead stop. My ears were ringing. Miri and the driver looked unconscious, but I could tell they were still breathing.

Suddenly, my car door was yanked open.

*Thank God!* I thought.

Someone pulled my arm and unceremoniously dragged me out of the car. My eyes widened, and a knot formed in my stomach. I realized this was not a friendly rescue. Two men happened upon me. Each grabbed one of my arms and dragged me like a rag doll. I began to kick and scream. From behind, I could hear a man's voice speaking in an Arabic dialect I didn't know. I was able to make out one word, kidnap! Next thing I knew, someone grabbed my hair from behind and yanked my head back. They slapped a rag over my nose and mouth. My vision began to fade toward nothingness.

### ~ Miri, My Ordeal ~

The sun was peeking over the horizon when I finally regained consciousness. I turned and stretched my neck to check on the driver. There was blood trickling down his head. From my angle, I couldn't tell if he was breathing. I frantically turned to look for Issa but couldn't find her. My pulse quickened. I was stuck and couldn't get my door open. Yelling seemed futile. Then I remembered my phone had a tracking device.

In retrospect, I'm glad Papa was so cautious. He would always say, *Miri, I must know where you are at all times. Your life is my most valuable possession.* If I could only alert him, he would know where to find me.

I tried to reach my back pocket, but the seat belt was locked in position. I tried to free my hand, but I was twisted in the most awkward position. It was almost impossible to move in any direction. My breathing became erratic, and my lungs felt like they were on fire. I couldn't get any air into them. My throat felt like it was closing off, and the heat was unbearable. I began to sob. I thought for sure, *I will die this day.*

Then I heard a small, still, voice whispering, *Pray, Miri, pray.*

My voice was barely above a whisper. "Lord Jesus, help me to calm my breathing."

*Be anxious for nothing, my daughter.*

"Help me to think clearly, to find a way to escape."

*No harm will come to you.*

"Please Lord, give me the wisdom to break free from this death trap. Give me a witty idea."

*Move your right shoulder forward seven degrees, then upward seven degrees, then lean to the right seven degrees.*

I did as the voice instructed me.

*Now, slowly wiggle your arm upward until it is freed.*

I began to slowly wiggle my right arm. Inch by inch, it seemed to move. My heart leapt.

*One last wiggle*, I thought.

"Yes, yes! Thank you, Lord! My arm is free. He who the Son sets free is free indeed, literally!"

I reached into my right back pocket and pulled out my phone. My left hand was still stuck, but thanks be to God, I'm right-handed. I immediately dialed Papa's number but couldn't get a signal. My heart picked up its pace again, and I became dizzy.

I began to give the Lord thanks for the miracle of freeing my arm, and it calmed me. I waited for the guidance of the Holy Spirit. I didn't hear the voice I first heard. I closed my eyes and physically leaned forward. Then, I leaned in, into the Spirit and waited. I heard the voice, barely a whisper.

*Closer to the window.*

Immediately, I typed my Papa a text and sent it. It didn't go through, but I knew once I got a signal, the text would send off. I switched to the location app and put my hand on the send button. I placed my phone as close to the window, as far up as my arm could reach, and waited for a signal.

I waited and prayed. Discouragement set in. My arm was getting tired. I couldn't hold the phone up any longer. I put my hand down and groaned inwardly. It was stiflingly hot, and I was sweating profusely.

I told myself, *Just one more time.*

I raised my phone to the window one last time.

One bar. My phone had one bar! I pushed the send button and prayed that one bar was enough to send the signal. Papa would know something was wrong and come search for us. We had agreed the only time I would use the tracking app was in an emergency. As the time passed, I felt like I was suffocating. My head was pounding. My chest felt like an elephant was sitting on it. My advanced training in first aid kicked in, and I concentrated on slowing my breathing. I began to sing in silence, "Great is Thy Faithfulness." Then, I started to fade.

*~ Kasim, Rescuing Miri ~*

"Akhab, help me get her out!"

"It's going to require the jaws of life, Kasim."

"No, we don't have time. My driver is already dead, and I don't know how long Miri has been like this."

"I have an idea. Let's tie this chain to the front of the car and pull it apart slowly," said Akhab.

## Excavation Plans Interrupted

I yelled to my men, "Do as he says! Has anyone found Issa?"

"No, we've searched everywhere. If she was ejected from the car, we would have found her by now," someone replied.

I was rattled to the core. I had to keep my cool. I couldn't lose it now, that would only endanger Miri. And I needed to remain calm and level-headed to find Issa.

"Slowly, slowly. We don't want to tear the car apart. Just enough to get to Miri."

Akhab called to me, "Kasim, I almost have her. I just need a knife to release her seat belt."

I ran toward him, yelling, "Is she breathing?"

"Yes, I see her chest moving up and down."

I cut Miri free from the seat belt and carried her gently to the air-conditioned Escalade. I brought emergency supplies, including a portable oxygen tank. I immediately put the nasal prongs into Miri's nostrils and started the oxygen. Her pulse was rapid and bounding.

"Akhab!" I yelled. "Get me cold, wet, cloths. She has a heat stroke."

I began to cool her body temperature by placing cold cloths on her head and neck, under her arms, at her groin, and at the bottoms of her feet. After ten minutes, Miri began to groan. She lifted her right arm to her forehead, and then it flopped back down.

"Miri, Miri, are you okay?"

"Yes, Papa," Miri croaked.

"Miri, where is Issa?"

"I don't know. When I regained consciousness the first time, she was gone."

"Kasim, over here, I see marks in the dirt. It looks like Issa may have been dragged. And here, it looks like there was a struggle based on the pattern in the dirt," said Akhab.

Someone yelled, "Over here, it looks like another set of tire tracks! A van, maybe?"

I bowed my head in my hands and began to wail, "No, no! Oh God, help me!"

"Kasim, someone has taken her," said Akhab.

"Then why is there no note? Why has no one contacted us with a demand?"

I felt a pair of petite arms encircle me. I knew it was Miri.

"Papa, we will find her. The Holy Spirit spoke to me in the car when I was trapped. He gave me the instructions I needed to get loose and send the emergency call. I'm sure the Lord will do the same for Issa."

"Should I contact the authorities?" whispered Akhab.

"No, not yet."

The last thing I wanted to do was involve the authorities. They must not know Issa is here for any archeological exploits. This would raise too much suspicion. I must work fast. I knew if I could not locate her safely in the next twenty-four hours, I would have to go to the authorities.

"Cousin!"

"Kasim!"

I was squatting in the sand, looking for clues, when I heard Fasar and Sky call out to me.

"What are you two doing here?"

Fasar answered first, "We heard about the car accident and came to see if everyone is ok."

"Miri suffered a mild concussion and heat stroke, otherwise she is going to be well. My driver, unfortunately, did not survive the accident."

"And my mom?"

"Sky, we don't know where your mom is at the moment. We are looking for some clues that might alert us to her whereabouts."

## Excavation Plans Interrupted

"My mom is the most intelligent woman I know. Although she doesn't believe it about herself, I know her. Wherever she is, she will leave us clues. I will help you."

Sky surprised me. I thought she would unravel. I should've known better. She's certainly her mother's daughter.

Sky immediately went to work with Miri and Fasar to unearth clues that might lead us to Issa. This gave me the time I needed to make calls to my contacts to widen our search.

I noticed Fasar's dirt bike in his pick-up truck. Smart boy. Before I could say anything, Fasar and Sky mounted the bike, engine revving.

"Sky and I are going to see where the second set of tire tracks lead, and then we'll circle back around."

"Papa, I will look around for any clues Issa might have left."

"Miri, only if you feel up to it."

Slicing her hand in the air, she replied, "I'm fine Papa, but Issa may not be. She needs us."

Miri was the first to notice something. She had a keen eye, and her archeological skills were more advanced than most.

"Papa, look here. These are fibers from a dirty piece of cloth. It's barely perceptible, but I think I smell chloroform. You know what this means, right?"

I felt a knot in the pit of my stomach. Chloroform, if inhaled in very small doses, can keep a person unconscious anywhere from twenty minutes to two hours. Or even more, depending on how concentrated it is.

*Why would anyone want to kidnap Issa?* I wondered.

"I know what you are thinking, Papa. Someone either knows what we are looking for and knows Issa is the key to finding it, or someone knows how much she means to you and is using her as a pawn."

"Miri, I have already commissioned our team to send out the drones to search for her. We will find Issa, but we must move quickly."

Miri went back to scouring the perimeter. If Issa was unconscious, she wouldn't have been able to leave clues until she regained consciousness.

Fasar and Sky zoomed by on the bike and skidded to a stop.

Nearly panting, Fasar said, "They're heading toward Petra."

We all jumped in our vehicles and headed toward the city. We switched to walkie-talkies to keep each other updated.

I radioed everyone, "If this truly is a kidnapping, we need to search any and all abandoned buildings. Fasar, you go east. Akhab, you go south. I will have my men go west. I will search each of the dig sites. I have asked our Bedouin family to search the caves to the north."

"Have there been any ransom demands yet?" asked Akhab.

"No, we haven't heard a word."

It had been two hours since we all went our separate ways. There were no clues to be found. No one heard or saw anything. Issa wouldn't be difficult to miss in a crowd of any size, even if she wore a hijab. Those emerald green eyes wouldn't go unnoticed.

# Chapter 19

# Issa's Trials

*~ The Perpetrator, The Ride to Siq ~*

"We must hurry to our destination."

"Where are we taking her?"

"The hidden caves near the Siq. First, we need to change her into Bedouin clothes."

"Why is that necessary if she's going to the caves?"

"Kasim has family and friends among the cave-dwelling Bedouins, and he will have alerted them by now."

"You men drive! I will handle this."

I began to fumble through the pile of clothes the men had managed to acquire.

"Who gave you these clothes? I told you Bedouin, women's clothes. You give me a hijab that looks like it's made of royal Phoenician purple dye!"

"Sorry. We grabbed what we could."

"We must hurry before Kasim sends out the drones in search of her. He's very resourceful."

## ~ Issa, My Ordeal ~

"What happened?" I said, rubbing my temple. "I feel so dizzy. Where am I? Where are you taking me?"

"Stuff the cloth back in her mouth," said my perpetrator. "You are in Petra, dear Dr. Stevens, far away from Kasim, where you'll not cause him any more trouble."

"Why are you doing this?" I gagged. "Please take this cloth out of my mouth."

"Calm down. I don't intend to harm you, unless you give me reason to do so."

"Is Fasim behind this kidnapping? You know it will not work. Kasim will find me!"

"Ha, ha, ha. No, my dear, you'll be out of Jordan by the time he finds out what happened."

The van stopped at the base of a mountainous structure that was so splendid it took my breath away. The mountain was swirling with various shades of red rock. "Oh Lord, your majesty is beyond measure," I whispered.

We were on what seemed like the backside of the mountain, on a well-worn path that led upward.

"Keep climbing. We don't have time for this delay. We need to get to the cave swiftly. Then, we fly out at first light."

"I can't move any faster," I mumbled through the cloth.

There were so many rocks. The sun was beating mercilessly down on the hard-packed mountain dirt. Blisters were forming on my feet. The sun was reflecting off the ground and onto my face, intensifying the heat. I could barely breathe, much less talk.

"Hey, I'm thirsty," I mumbled again. "Can we stop just for a few minutes?"

My perpetrator mocked me. "Oh, our dear Dr. Stevens is having a hard time with our way of life. And you think you can marry Kasim and live among us? You are a fool to think you could come to Arabia and marry one of the richest men in our country. You usurper!"

"You have it all wrong," I pleaded.

"Someone, give her a few drops of water. She doesn't deserve any more than that. But we need her alive."

*They're not going to kill me.* I sighed in relief.

"She cannot be damaged goods, or we will not be able to sell her to the highest bidder."

*Sell me?* My frantic thoughts betrayed me. I bit my lip, and tears silently fell down my cheeks. *Kasim, I need you, where are you? Hurry, come quick!*

I thanked God when we finally reached our destination. It seemed like we would never make it up this mountain. They escorted me to the back of a cave, and surprisingly, it was cool inside. After a while, I must have dozed off because someone poked me with a walking stick made from a thick tree branch.

"Time to eat," said one of the miscreants.

"Why are you doing this? I'm nobody to you. Let me go."

"To the contrary, you are somebody. You are the person who is in the way of all my plans, and I intend to get rid of you for good!" said my perpetrator.

"You will not get away with this. Kasim will never stop looking until he finds me."

"Confident, aren't we? You think more highly of yourself than you should. Yes, he'll look for a while. When he doesn't find you, he will abide by his family's wishes and move on."

"You're so cruel! Just send me back home. I will stay out of your way. You'll never hear from me again."

"Oh, I believe you, Dr. Stevens. Kasim, on the other hand, will find you in no time, if I allow you to return home."

I buried my face in my hands and began to weep. The voice became slightly gentler.

"Eat, you will need your energy."

They were right about that. I would eat so I could have enough energy to escape this awful place. I kept hoping all of this was just one big nightmare.

The voice repeated. "Here, eat, Dr. Stevens."

I was thankful for my meager meal. It tasted good—all things considered. I had pita bread with goat cheese, olives, and something similar to hummus. I could also smell lamb roasting, and it made my mouth water and my stomach stir. I wasn't provided any. After I finished eating, my hands were tied behind my back once again.

"Please, I have to use the restroom first."

"Take her to the cleft in the mountain outside and give her privacy. But guard the passage."

As we walked to the area outside the cave, I stumbled a few times.

"I can't use the bathroom with my hands tied," I said.

The guard loosened the ropes, "No funny business or else!"

I quickly relieved myself. Then, I used the remaining time to set clues about the bushes. I wrote in the dirt, "Help Issa." I tore off a piece of my hijab and then tore that piece in two. I left one piece on a bush and tucked another in my back pant pocket. I would leave this clue inside the cave.

"Let's go, you've had enough time."

I walked toward the guard submissively. Then, a thought formulated in my head. I would run and hope the drones they spoke of would pass by me. If I was caught, they would not kill me. It appeared they just wanted me to disappear and be out of Kasim's life.

*It must be Fasim trying to move me out of the way so Kasim will be forced to marry the beautiful Tirsa*, I thought.

As soon as we rounded a bend in the mountain, I ran.

The guard yelled, "Stop, or I will be forced to hurt you!"

I began to pray, "Lord, send the drone, send a miracle!"

Mid-thought, I stumbled on some rocks, twisting my ankle. I fell to the ground and hit the side of my head hard on a rock. I put my hands to my head to assess the damage, and sticky liquid met them. I began to heave and wretch at the metallic smell. I looked at my hands and saw what I feared—blood. I could hear laughter behind me.

"So, you considered running? I thought you were smarter than that, seeing as you're an American doctor."

The guard re-tied my hands and yanked me by my arm.

"Ouch! You don't have to be such a brute. Is this how you treat women in your country?"

"No, just unwanted foreigners in our country!" he sneered with a nasty laugh.

We walked back to the cave, and I was tossed inside.

"What happened to her?" said my perpetrator.

"She tried to run and fell."

"Clean her up and bandage her head for now."

"Dr. Stevens, I'm a patient person, but even my patience has limits."

*That voice sounds so familiar, and those eyes*, I thought.

I just can't seem to place it. The voice sounded like someone was trying to alter their pitch. I couldn't make out anyone's face in any detail. They were all dressed like Bedouin desert dwellers with their faces covered.

My head was throbbing now, and I felt like retching. I sat on the opposite side of the cave as my captors. I leaned against the cool wall and rested my head to gather my bearings. Then, I remembered the hijab. I pulled out the torn piece from my back pocket and placed it in a dark area against the cave wall. I proceeded to draw the symbol of the fish on the hard-packed dirt and slowly scooted away from the wall. Soon, I felt myself drifting off.

Suddenly, one of the guards came running into the cave.

He placed his hands on his knees and drew in a deep breath, "I saw two drones. They're close to finding us."

"We must leave now," interrupted the familiar voice. "We will move to our alternate location."

### ~ Kasim, The Rescue Attempt ~

The day moved painstakingly slowly. We all gathered back at the dig site on the Ma'an-Petra border. We reported our findings, but nothing was conclusive. I could see the worry in Sky's eyes. Fasar was comforting her. I made a mental note to speak with Fasar about his budding relationship with Sky. Miri kept pacing the floor. Akhab remained level-headed, and for that, I was grateful.

I had remained calm on the exterior but was beginning to unravel on the inside. I knew the longer we waited, the more danger Issa faced. I leaned my elbows on my knees and buried my face in my hands, trying to regain some semblance of composure.

Just then, the phone rang. One of my men was reporting in.

"Kasim, our people have noticed some unusual activity in the caves near the Siq. Our drones are over the area now."

"Send me the feed immediately, and send our Bedouin elite fighters to Siq. I'm dispatching Akhab there now. They're to work directly with him, and he will report directly to me. Are my instructions clear?"

"Yes."

Akhab walked over and gripped my shoulder, "Kasim, I will find her. I promise."

"Go with God, my friend," I replied.

"We received some video feed of a cave on the north side of the Siq!" yelled Fasar.

We all ran to the monitor.

"It's deserted," said Sky.

"Yes, but do you see what I see? Whoever was in this cave only recently abandoned it. The coals in that fire look like they were recently extinguished," replied Miri.

Fasar sighed, "All we can do now is wait for the team to get to the cave."

~ Akhab, Near Siq ~

I climbed the rugged mountainside through a well-worn path that led to the top. Any other passage would have been difficult, even for a native Bedouin. I finally reached the cave, and Kasim's distant cousin Salek was already there with the Bedouin elite fighters.

"As-Salaam-Alaikum, Salek."

"Wa-Alaikum-Salaam, Akhab."

"What have you found thus far?" I asked.

"The embers are still warm from the fire. My men also found a torn piece of hijab, purple in color. Dr. Stevens was here, alright. She left a note in the dirt over there."

I looked at the purple hijab. Then, I noticed an inscription etched into the dirt floor. It was the symbol of a fish—the ancient sign the Christians used in times of persecution.

"Any tracks?" I replied.

"Yes, they lead down the south side of the mountain. It's a dangerous trek. Mostly mountain goats tread there. Human foot traffic is rare," responded Salek.

"We need to take a few men and follow the lead. I will have Kasim redirect the drones to concentrate in that area."

"I will go with you, Akhab."

I called Kasim to update him on my findings. He immediately redirected the drones. Ten minutes later, he called and transmitted pictures and coordinates to my phone. There appeared to be three people in a small cave carved sharply off the south side of the mountain.

### ~ Kasim, Taking Charge ~

As soon as I received the pictures from the drones, I called Akhab.

"I'm sending you the coordinates now. I'm on my way to the base of the mountain. I'll meet you there."

"Salek's men are ready to move in, I will accompany them on your signal," replied Akhab.

After I finished the call, everyone was shouting at once. No one wanted to be left behind.

"Fasar, you stay with the women! Keep an eye on the drone feed at all times and keep radio contact. Let me know the minute you see anything that looks suspicious, no matter how insignificant."

"Yes, Kasim. You can trust me."

I wanted to take the helicopter to Siq, but it would only draw unwanted attention. Instead, I took two of my guards and hopped in the Escalade. We made it to the mountain base in record time. One of Salek's men was waiting for us. I would have to thank Akhab later. I desperately wanted to climb the mountain and join in the fray, but it was a forty-minute trek. I would never make it in time. I prayed for the strength to trust God and to trust my men.

I asked Salek's man, "Are you in radio contact with Salek?"

"Yes, I was instructed to radio him as soon as you arrived."

"Good, let me speak to him."

"As-Salaam-Alaikum, Salek."

"Wa-Alaikum-Salaam, Kasim. We've surrounded the cave. I'll leave the radio on so you can follow what is happening, but my end will be muted. I don't want to alert them of my coming."

### ~ Akhab, The Rescue Attempt ~

"Salek, my main concern is Dr. Stevens's safety. What is our plan?"

Salek used his finger to draw an imaginary map on the rock.

He said, "Akhab, we have surrounded the cave on both sides and on top. They will not be able to escape straight down the mountain, even if they had the proper equipment. Besides, they will not have enough time to prepare for a surprise attack."

"Let's do this without loss of life, if possible," I replied.

"My men will create a diversion on this side of the cave. You're assigned to Dr. Stevens's extraction. She's probably disguised like a Bedouin woman and most likely has on the torn purple hijab. Find her and bring her to safety. Kasim is waiting at the base of the mountain."

Salek's men stealthily incapacitated the two guards, who were at the perimeter of the cave. They were able to confirm the information received from the drone. According to the guards who were captured, there was a third man in the cave.

Salek then relayed the final orders, "I will dispatch a series of three taps on the radio. On my signal, flood the cave. No shooting until Dr. Stevens is safely extracted, and then only if absolutely necessary. One, two, three, go!"

### ~ Issa, My Extraction ~

Dread settled over me like a heavy shroud. All I could hear were loud noises and shouting. I prayed it was Kasim and his men.

"Surrender, surrender! You're surrounded, and there's no way to escape! Your two men outside have already been subdued."

Someone approached me, and I recoiled.

The voice spoke and hope surged. "Akhab, is that you?"

"Yes, Dr. Issa."

Akhab gently lifted me off the floor.

"Are you ok?"

"As good as can be expected," I replied.

"How many men were with you in the cave?"

"There were three, but the one in the cave left right before you arrived."

Then I heard someone say, "Akhab, do you have Dr. Stevens?"

Akhab replied, "Yes, Salek. I'm taking her to Kasim with a few of your men as rear guards. There was no one else in the cave. Issa confirmed that there was a third man, but he was outside when we stormed in. He must have escaped when he heard the commotion."

"I will have the remainder of my men search the surroundings," said Salek.

Akhab turned his attention to me. "Dr. Issa, are you sure you're alright? Can you walk?"

"Yes, yes, Akhab. Just a bit bedraggled."

"Kasim is below waiting for us. You can speak to him using my radio."

"Kasim, Kasim. It's me, Issa."

"Thank you, Jesus! Issa, your voice is the sweetest thing my ears have heard."

Akhab reached for the radio, "Kasim, I will have her to you shortly."

It seemed like it took forever to get down that mountain. I could make out Kasim's silhouette. His long, sleek, muscular frame with his broad shoulders, narrow hips, and slim waistline. I ran as fast as I could. I tripped over a rock but was able to steady myself. Kasim was at my side with lightning speed. I threw myself into his arms and buried my head in his neck.

"Kasim, I love you so much. I never want to spend another day without you!"

"Habibti, worrying about you had me on the brink of losing my mind. You won't have to spend another day without me. I love you with my life!"

Kasim twirled me around like we were in our youth without a care in the world. Then he lifted me in his arms and carried me to his car with Akhab in tow. I knew we needed to debrief, but I would savor this moment for as long as possible.

I lifted my head and whispered, "Is Miri safe?"

I held my breath, waiting for his reply.

"Yes, she's well and worried sick about you. Miri, Sky, and Fasar were all a part of this rescue mission. And Sky, well…suffice it to say she's like her mom in so many ways."

Kasim tapped me playfully on my nose and gently kissed me. I sighed and silently thanked God for his saving power.

When we reached the car, Kasim gently lowered me into the passenger seat, and we drove off as the sun was setting. The landscape unfolded in serene indifference, betraying no hint of the turmoil that just took place. The glow of the setting sun on the mountain was stunning. It cast a glow that made the colors dance off the mountainside. Relief washed over me, but the illusion of safety it granted was only temporary—a mere respite for the moment. As soon as the moment passed, I felt an ominous stirring in the pit of my stomach.

## Chapter 20

# Getting Ready

*~ Issa, Debrief & Prep ~*

As the car approached the excavation site at the Ma'an-Petra border, I saw Sky, Miri, and Fasar running. The car stopped, and I didn't wait for Kasim to exit. I ran to hug Sky, but the three of them converged on me and embraced me in a hug.

"Mom!" "Issa!" "Dr. Stevens!" They yelled, "We were so worried."

Kasim joined in on the love, and we all cried and laughed at the same time.

"We make a good team," I said. "We'll find those scrolls in no time."

"Issa, you must rest first," said Kasim.

"What about the excavation?"

"The excavation can wait."

"And the wedding?"

"You're going to take a few days off. The rest of us will help with the wedding plans. We wed in one week. I cannot wait any longer."

I blushed. Miri was teary-eyed. Sky gave me a wry smile and leaned on Fasar. *Did I just see what I thought I saw?*

Then, Fasar informed me in his most gentleman-like voice, "Miri,

Sky, and I will assist Kasim at the dig site while you recover. Sky and Miri will work half days. Then, they can help you prepare for the wedding."

Is this the same flirtatious man-boy I've come to know over these past few weeks?

*What a shift*, I thought.

Then it dawned on me. *He's probably trying to win my approval to get to know Sky.* I'll have to talk to Kasim about this.

We gathered back at the estate and took some refreshments.

I was sitting in the chair, sipping a hot cup of tea, staring out the window, and trying to make sense of all that transpired when Kasim interrupted my thoughts.

"Issa, now tell me what happened."

After recounting the story, I remembered, "There was a third person."

Can you describe him? Asked Kasim.

"From the sound of the voice, it was a male with a slightly higher pitch. His voice sounded so familiar. I think it's someone we know."

"What did he look like?"

"Everyone's face was covered with a shemagh, so I can't identify anyone. But his eyes were hazel. He was not in the cave when Akhab rescued me."

"We're still looking for him."

"I think your Uncle Fasim is behind all of this."

"Don't worry, Issa. You're safe here."

*~ Kasim, Confronting Fasim ~*

I dispatched a few men to keep an eye on Fasim to ensure he didn't try to leave the country. We waited to confront him until the morning meal to see if he would come. He showed as usual, with that perpetual scowl on his face. I had Issa's meal delivered to her room. I didn't want to traumatize her any further. Sky and Miri dined with Issa. Father and Fasar joined me at the table.

"Where's the infamous Dr. Stevens? I thought you two were inseparable," asked Fasim.

"She's feeling a little under the weather today, Uncle."

"Is she not taking well to our way of life?"

"On the contrary, she loves it."

"Kasim, Fakmad, do you really intend to go through with this wedding? Can you not see what the consequences will be, even if unintended?"

"Enough, Fasim!" yelled Fakmad. "Do you dare to tell us where you were all day yesterday?"

"What are you insinuating?"

"Issa was kidnapped!" I interjected. "Do you know anything about this?"

"No! Kasim, I may not be overly fond of Dr. Stevens, but I'm no monster! Fasar, tell them!"

"Uncle, I was there helping find Dr. Stevens. Whoever did this has a vendetta against her or our family," replied Fasar.

"You must know I had nothing to do with this! I respect Dr. Stevens and her work. I even find her quite fair and pleasant. I just have a strong opinion about what her role should be concerning our family. I don't think she should be grafted into this household. Tirsa is still the best choice!"

"Don't you see, Uncle, that gives you all the motive in the world to harm Issa," I replied.

"Wait a minute! Harm her? Fakmad, you don't agree with this nonsense, do you?"

Father responded, "You have been overly critical of Dr. Stevens. She has expressed being afraid of you, even before this incident."

"What happened? I wish her no ill will."

"We rescued her. But the perpetrator got away. The men were hired hands and didn't know who hired them."

"Very clever, Uncle," said Fasar.

Screaming, Fasim stood and claimed, "I had nothing to do with this. You must believe me!"

Fasim grabbed his chest and bent over in agony. I jumped up and caught him before he collapsed.

"Fasar, quickly, get Uncle some water and add a teaspoon of turmeric."

Fasar responded, "Yes, Kasim," as he was heading out the door.

"Uncle, you must calm yourself down. Please tell us, if you did not do this, then who?"

Fasim wiped the sweat from his brow with his napkin and responded, "There are many who oppose us for our wealth alone. And, if anyone outside this family knows about our excavations, they would oppose us too."

"Give me a name, Uncle!"

"Fakmad has had many attempts on his life, and we are none the wiser as to who is behind it all."

My uncle sounded sincere. I wanted to believe him. He was right about the assassination attempts on my father's life. I closed my eyes to say a quick prayer. *Holy Spirit, please give me wisdom and discernment to know the truth from the lie.*

"Ok Fasim," conceded Fakmad. "We will believe you until the evidence gives us reason not to. You're to stay in your residence until we are able to investigate this mystery. And you are not to come to the wedding. We still don't know who is the mastermind behind this diabolical plot."

"I'm sorely offended and shocked by my kin's reactions toward me. I love Kasim like a son. He is my deceased sister's only child. It's because of my love for him that I will hold my tongue. The Lord will avenge me. I serve him too, you know."

Uncle's last declaration left us all a bit unsettled. However, Issa's safety took precedence. If we were wrong, the Lord would have a work to do, to heal our family, to restore our trust in one another.

~ *Issa, To Rest, Or Not* ~

The week leading up to my wedding was a whirlwind of activity.

"Kasim, if this is your idea of rest, then I rested more while I was working at the dig site."

He chuckled and shook his head. I sighed and chastised myself. Although I didn't care much for the fanfare, I was enjoying every moment of the preparations. Every bone in my body still ached. Miri made sure I soaked in the baths every day, using medicinal herbs in hot and cold water. Then, Rajah massaged me with essential oils mixed with frankincense and myrrh.

Sky preferred to go with Kasim to the dig site. I was glad she was spending time with him, but it probably had more to do with Fasar.

That evening, I told Kasim, "Their relationship is moving too fast."

"Don't trouble yourself my love. I'll not allow this to get out of hand."

"Any new developments with Fasim?" I asked.

"No, he still maintains his innocence."

Kasim had told me he confronted his uncle, who vehemently denied any involvement in my kidnapping. Although Kasim wanted to believe him, Fakmad decided that Fasim would remain in his home under guard until the perpetrator was caught.

There have been no further incidents, probably because Fasim was placed under guard. This did not bode well for him. Although not conclusive, all the evidence pointed to his guilt. Thinking about Fasim was far too exhausting. I made a conscious decision to focus all my attention on my wedding preparations.

The day of my wedding was fast approaching. Miri was an enormous help.

She kept saying, "There's no way I could have done this without Sky."

Even Fasar helped out, running errands for Miri. And wherever Fasar went, Sky tagged along. Why that irritated me so much, I really couldn't tell you. Fasar was like a stubborn pebble that gets stuck in your shoe, continuously irritating you until it's removed.

Miri appeared at my door, carrying different sized bags up to her neck.

"Issa, would you like to review the itinerary for the wedding?" she asked.

I grabbed some of the bags and replied, "Yes. I wish I could do more, but I'm still sore all over."

"No worries. I'll start from the beginning, and you can tell me if you want anything changed."

"Thank you, Miri."

"First things first. Your dress is absolutely astonishing. It's just as you envisioned it on paper. The pearl white color is quite suitable. There are pearls strung throughout the gown. The flower-like designs are in an Arabic pattern and are made of lace with pearls in the center of each flower."

"That sounds more than stunning. I feel like I'm in a fairytale. Only, I'm no princess."

"You are a princess, and Papa is the prince who has found his bride."

I sighed. I was at a loss for words. Kasim was way out of my league, and I knew it. *This, indeed, is a fairytale.*

Miri continued describing my dress.

"The material is light and sheer, but not too sheer. The dress should be ready for fitting and alterations this evening."

## Getting Ready

"Is the veil made of the same material?"

"Somewhat. Our tradition requires that your face be covered, so the design you wanted remains, but I'm having a sheer, breathable material that feels and looks like silk sewn into it. No one can see your face, but you have partial visibility."

"That's ingenious. You've thought of everything."

"Next are the flowers," Miri replied. "Papa has made all the arrangements and has included the various colored roses you requested. Your bouquet has an assortment of flowers that match the arrangements in the garden."

"You are amazing! And the shoes?"

"I have them with me."

Miri pulled out a box from one of the bags, and what I saw did not disappoint. Of course, they were designer shoes. The material was the same color as the dress. They were made of satin with lace and pearls.

"Here, try them on."

"Oh, they are so beautiful and comfortable."

I twirled around and around until I got dizzy and landed on the bed. We both laughed. Then, there was a knock on the door.

"Issa, it's me Kasim."

Kasim opened the door and peeked his head in.

"Hello, Habibti."

"Hello, my love."

Kasim gave me a kiss on the lips that lingered far too long in Miri's presence. I blushed. Miri smiled. Kasim laughed, a deep, rich laugh.

"So, what brings you here?"

"Just checking on the most beautiful woman in the world."

"I'm marvelous! Thank you for checking. Miri and I are going over the itinerary for the wedding."

"Oh, then I better leave you to it. I'm headed back to the dig site."

"Have you made any progress?"

"No. I must admit, not having you there has slowed us down."

"Oh, no. Maybe we should postpone our honeymoon?"

"That won't be necessary. We've waited this long. A couple of weeks won't make much of a difference. My team will continue the dig. They know what they're doing. It's just that your keen eye and intuition is not something you learn, it's a gift."

"Whatever you think is best, my love. But I won't be disappointed if we have to postpone it."

Kasim kissed me on the forehead, "Everything will work out fine, Habibti. I'll see you later this evening."

Miri caught my attention as she went rumbling through another bag. "Here, this is the ring you commissioned for Papa. Do you like it?"

"It's beautiful. Will he like it?"

"Yes, it is elegant, yet simple, not gaudy. He'll love it. Wait until you see his tuxedo. It has a long coattail and is midnight black, silk, and slick."

I closed my eyes, leaned my head back, and smiled. "I can envision him now. I'm the luckiest woman alive. I hope I don't disappoint him, Miri."

"You must not say such things. My Papa loves you so much."

"Yes, I know. It's just sometimes, I don't feel like I fit in. Like I'm a disappointment to most of your family."

"Issa, you're a blessing. You're a gift from God to this family. Some may not know it yet, but they will see. They'll ask for your forgiveness when they finally do."

I threw myself into Miri's arms and wept.

## Getting Ready

"You must not cry. Your eyes will be puffy for tomorrow's wedding."

We looked at each other, and this time, I saw mist in Miri's eyes.

"Miri, what about the bridesmaid dresses for you and Sky?"

"Our dresses are ready, and Fasar has his tuxedo. Everything is set, so don't worry about anything."

I sighed in relief, stretching my neck and shoulders, willing them to relax.

"Oh, there's one more thing we have to go over," Miri shouted.

I jumped in response, my nerves jittery. "What else could there possibly be?"

"The festivities. I must teach you the dances."

A knock on the door interrupted us.

"Who is it?" I called out.

"It's Rajah. I've come to help with the wedding preparations."

"Rajah, come, I need you," replied Miri. "Let's show Issa the dances of our people. We are a festive bunch."

"Look Issa, cross your arms like this. Then move forward, to the side, then backward, to the side, and forward again, so you will make a complete circle around Papa. All while stomping your feet."

"This is fun, but I'm not coordinated. How do I move like this with my dress on?"

"I was hoping to surprise you, but seeing as nothing gets by your keen eye, I will tell you now!"

Miri clapped her hands in excitement as she described the dress I was to change into. It sounded so elegant.

Miri continued. "Before the dance, you will change into the Thoub. You're going to love it. The women are still working on it. It's the traditional Jordanian dress adorned with elaborate embroidery, beadwork, and gold accents representing my people's craftsmanship and heritage. I will help you change. We also had some bejeweled sandals made to match the dress so you can move with ease."

"This surpasses even my wildest imagination!"

Miri smiled broadly, "I'm glad you like it."

"Has the music been selected yet?" I asked. "I know it will be in the Arabic style. Perhaps, if you play it for me, I can become familiar with the beat and tempo for the dances."

"Yes, that's a great idea. I'll give you the playlist."

Miri and Rajah taught me the most popular dances. We danced and twirled for what seemed like hours. I had so much fun I forgot how much my body ached. I was so tired, and Miri knew it.

"Off to the baths you go," Miri sang.

"I will make sure you are ready for tomorrow, Dr. Stevens," said Rajah. "I promise."

Tomorrow! My smile spread ear to ear. Tomorrow, I will be Mrs. Issa Ma'an!

# CHAPTER 21

## WEEK OF CELEBRATION

*~ Issa, The Wedding ~*

I woke up feeling refreshed and full of energy. Lots of prayer coupled with Rajah's ministrations had me up and moving with little to no discomfort. Kasim had sternly ordered me to do no strenuous work. I told him it was therapeutic. It calmed both the wedding jitters and the post-traumatic stress I was experiencing. I bounced out of bed and twirled over to the mirror, upending the side table in the process.

"Ouch," I yelped. *Here comes another bruise*, I muttered.

I gazed in the mirror and sang out loud, "Today, I will be Mrs. Ma'an."

A knock on the door brought me to my senses.

"Mrs. Ma'an, I mean, Issa."

I heard giggling behind the door and instantly knew it was Miri and Sky.

"We're here to help you."

They entered, accompanied by Rajah. Miri carried the dress. Sky had the shoes and accessories in hand. Rajah had a cart laden with makeup and hair adornments. Soon after, the Maître d' arrived with brunch.

Miri immediately took charge, "We'll have brunch here on the balcony, then head to the baths."

I hadn't realized how long I had slept. As much as we all tried, it proved hard to sleep last night. Yesterday evening, I tried to help in the gardens to prepare for the wedding festivities, but Kasim kept distracting me with his charms. I think it was his way of keeping me from doing work. While I was admiring the display of roses, he snuck up from behind and wrapped his arms around my waist.

He whispered alluringly in my ear, "You know we can skip all of this and sneak away to my room right now."

"Kasim," I sputtered in horror.

"Issa, the wedding contract is already signed. We're already married, technically speaking."

I smiled at him.

Gesturing at the elaborate setup, I reminded him, "We must do this before God and for our families."

Kasim nibbled on my ear and chuckled, "If you say so."

Then he abruptly left. I haven't seen him since.

*What a tease*, I thought, shaking my head at the memory.

Our meal that morning was simple fare. I had yogurt parfait with an assortment of berries, granola, and some freshly-squeezed orange juice. Then we headed to the baths. We lingered there a bit longer than we should have.

"We must leave immediately if I'm to have Dr. Stevens ready in time," said Rajah.

We returned to the room, and I was feeling bereft. I hadn't seen Kasim since yesterday evening when he threatened to whisk me away. Now, I wish I would've let him. Miri discerned something was amiss and left the room. She returned with a smile on her face. The next thing I knew, I heard someone knocking on the door.

"It's Papa. He wants to talk to you through the door. According to

## Week of Celebration

our tradition, you can't see one another before the wedding." Then, Miri giggled, "But it doesn't say anything about not talking to one another through the door."

"Issa, it's me, Kasim."

"Kasim, I miss you so much!"

"I miss you too! Place your hand on the door midway up. I'm doing the same. Can you feel it?"

I leaned into the door and concentrated for a moment.

"Yes, I can feel it. It feels like electricity! My hairs are standing up on my arm. I feel the energy of your love radiating through the door."

"Good, Habibti. Now, put your cheek to the door. I'm going to give you a kiss."

I did as he asked and put my cheek to the door. I closed my eyes and imagined being in Kasim's arms. My insides were warmed by his gesture. Kasim must have known I was nervous and wanted to reassure me that he was nearby.

"Kasim, I love you."

"I love you too, Issa. I'll see you at the altar soon."

I heard my entourage sighing in the background. And to my surprise, Sky was sniffling with mist in her eyes. Rajah had a look of longing in hers. Miri was still smiling, eyes sparkling.

"Ok, everyone, let's do this before I do something I'll regret."

Rajah did most of the work, expertly applying makeup to my face. She placed the kohl to my eyes in the way of her people and adorned my hair so that I looked native to the land.

Miri announced, "Issa, you look like an Arabian princess."

"Mom, Miri is not exaggerating. You really do look quite exotic and beautiful."

My wedding was to be a small but elaborate affair with lots of singing and dancing the traditional dances of Arabian culture. Kasim had ordered so much food. There were more people invited than I had expected for such a small wedding.

I had asked Kasim the day before, "Are all these people your family?"

He had replied, "For the most part. Some are close, trusted, associates and believers. We had to keep the wedding contained, so mostly you'll see the chiefs of each tribe or heads of families. Our family is enormous, and many do not reside in Arabia. The family business is run mainly by family, and the businesses are strategically located world-wide."

Sky interrupted my reflection, "Mom it's time. Miri and I will go ahead and Rajah will help you to the garden entrance where you will meet Fakmad."

"I am as ready as I'm going to be."

When I arrived at the entrance to the garden, I took a moment to take it all in. It was a sight to behold. The beauty of it all took my breath away.

"I hope this is all you have dreamed of and more, Dr. Stevens," said Rajah, as she straightened my dress and veil. Sincerity and love resonated in every word she spoke.

"Thank you for always being there for me and for treating me like family."

I took one last look at the beauty of my surroundings. Thanks to Miri and Sky, the garden was elegantly adorned with traditional motifs and contemporary decorations, reflecting the blending of old and new. There were rich fabrics in vibrant colors adorning the couches. I saw deep reds, golden yellows, and royal blues creating an atmosphere of opulence and elegance. Intricate Arabic patterns were woven into carpets, drapes, and ornamental details honoring Kasim's cultural heritage.

There was a fusion of flowers including jasmine, roses of varying colors, and some exotic blooms I had never seen before. The air was perfumed, engaging my sense of smell.

The warm Jordanian sun danced off the walls encasing the estate.

## Week of Celebration

The sun was a glow of orange and yellow. Miri's final touch could be seen in the charming lanterns that were placed throughout the garden. They created a magical ambiance as the sun set on the western horizon, welcoming the evening's festivities.

The guests had arrived dressed in a mix of traditional attire and stylish Western clothing, creating a colorful tapestry of cultural variety. The joyful atmosphere was palpable. A few friends and heads of families gathered, exchanging warm embraces and well wishes.

As for Fasim, he was under house guard. And Tirsa was nowhere in sight. I looked toward heaven, closed my eyes, and gave God thanks for giving me Kasim.

Arabic music filled the air with the sound of traditional tones from the oud and darbuka, adding a rhythmic pulse to the celebration. Kasim stood at the altar in his tuxedo, and it took my breath away. Could he look any more handsome? This striking, unassuming, wealthy, influential man. A man who also happens to love the Lord as much as I do. Someone who enjoys my field of work. He will be mine till death do us part. I barely took note of anyone else around me. Most were strangers.

Sky, Miri, and Akhab were off to the side of Kasim. Fasar was Kasim's best man. Sky and Miri were my bridesmaids. I had come to care deeply for my makeshift family. The fact that Sky was here and enjoying herself was more than I could ask for. If only Mom and Dad could be here. I knew my father's health was declining. Kasim, always so thoughtful, was making it possible for them to watch the ceremony live. Kasim's father was taking my father's place, walking me down the aisle.

Fakmad looked at me with tenderness and eyes misting, "Issa, I'm honored to escort you to the altar. You're my daughter now. You're the wife of my only son, and you've made him the happiest man in the world."

"Thank you Fakmad, this is the Lord's doing."

I looked heavenward and thanked my heavenly Father for supplying all my needs. This was indeed the Lord's doing, and it was marvelous in his sight. I tried to prevent my eyes from watering, but it was too late. My expertly applied makeup was about to unravel. It didn't matter. All I cared about was making it down to that altar.

As we were walking down the aisle, I noticed my palms were sweating. My stomach was fluttering like the wings of a butterfly. I tried to take a deep breath to calm myself, but my chest felt tight. My eyes began to water again. I love this man so much! I knew tears of joy would flow freely once we exchanged our vows.

Fakmad could sense my distress and whispered, "You're everything we could've asked for and more. Forgive me, my daughter, for ever doubting you."

All I could do was nod, but I was grateful for his words.

### ~ Kasim, First Glance ~

Then, I saw her, my beautiful Issa, walking down the aisle with my father. I watched my beloved make her grand entrance. Her presence illuminated the room, and my heart swelled with overwhelming love. She looked captivatingly beautiful in her exquisite pearl-white gown, made with lace, pearls, and delicate Arabic embroidery.

I could hear the gasps and whispers from those around me. The men had smiles on their faces, and the women looked on with anticipation. I didn't see Tirsa, and I was glad. I didn't want Issa to be anxious about anything. This was her moment, her day.

### ~ Issa, Our Vows ~

I finally made it to the altar. Fakmad placed my hand in Kasim's and nodded his approval on behalf of my father. Our eyes met, filled with yearning, waiting to speak our vows. Kasim took the lead in this solemn exchange.

"My beloved Dr. Issa Stevens. Today, in the presence of our loved ones and in the witness of our Lord Jesus Christ, I stand before you. From the moment our paths crossed, my life took on new meaning. You are my strength, my purpose, my partner, and best friend. I promise to cherish and honor you, to support and encourage you in every endeavor. I vow to love you unconditionally, to stand by your side in times of joy and sorrow. With each passing day, I will strive to build a life filled with happiness and laughter. Together, we will face whatever challenges come our way. I know that the Lord and our love will guide us through each day. You have my heart and my unwavering commitment. Now, and forever."

"My beloved Kasim, today I stand before you, overwhelmed with love and gratitude. From the moment our eyes met, I knew that you were the one who would fill my life with love and light. You're my partner, my confidant, and my rock. I promise to honor and respect you and to support and uplift you in all that you do. I vow to stand by your side, celebrate your triumphs, and comfort you in times of hardship. With you, I have found a love that knows no bounds. A love that transcends time and distance. I promise to love you fiercely and unconditionally, to be your safe haven, and your constant source of love. Together, with the help of our Lord, we will create a home filled with warmth, compassion, and understanding. You have my heart and eternal devotion, today and always."

The minister proceeded with his declarations, and I enthusiastically replied, "I do."

Before the minister could complete his sentence, Kasim blurted out, "I do."

We donned the wedding rings and were pronounced man and wife. Kasim leaned in and kissed me with a lingering kiss that lasted well past normal etiquette. I didn't pull away. I leaned into his kiss and returned the passion. The only thing that stopped us were the whistles and hoots we heard from the crowd. We both laughed, unlocking our lips and smiling with unrestrained joy.

Following the ceremony, the festivities began with a lavish feast featuring an array of Jordanian and Middle-Eastern delicacies. The aroma of fragrant spices, succulent grilled meats, and delectable pastries filled the room, enticing my tastebuds.

Miri, Sky, and Fasar came to greet us with hugs and kisses.

Miri replied, "Papa, Issa, my heart is so full it feels like bursting."

Miri leaned into her father and just above a whisper said, "Mama would be happy."

Kasim smiled and nodded, "Thank you Miri, you are the daughter of my heart, and I love you."

I had a feeling Miri's comment was just as much for me as it was for her father.

Sky came forth and hugged me. She didn't care to whisper, "Mom, you once told me Dad would want us to move on, to be happy. You were right. I feel truly happy for the first time since Dad died."

Sky began to cry deeply, like years of pain were being let loose and washed away. I joined her, succumbing to the emotion. Kasim embraced both of us. Then, Sky fell into his arms and melted there. She looked so vulnerable and innocent. Her shoulders moved up and down with each inhale and exhale, in tune with her sobs.

Kasim stroked her hair and whispered, "You never have to be alone again. Your mother loves you. I love you. We are here for you. More importantly, the Lord our God goes before us, to clear our paths, and make the crooked things straight."

What Sky did next astounded me. She turned toward Miri, gesturing her forward. Then, holding them both in her embrace, she looked at Miri, then at Kasim, and spoke in such a vulnerable, child-like manner.

"Kasim, would it be alright if I call you my Papa, like Miri does?"

Sky looked tentatively at Miri, and before Kasim could reply, Miri answered with unbidden tears.

"Yes, Sky, you are the sister of my heart."

Kasim looked at Miri with eyes like a river that refused to spill over.

Turning to Sky he said, "I've considered you my daughter from the moment your mother agreed to marry me. You, too, are the daughter of my heart."

Fasar interrupted our intimate moment with a light-hearted gesture. He embraced Kasim and me, exchanging the formal greeting of a kiss to

## Week of Celebration

each cheek. For once, I was grateful for Fasar's interruption. I was about to unravel. I knew there was more work that needed to take place to complete the healing process for each of us. The emotions of the moment were deep and rich, and they were the catalyst that allowed the seeds of healing to take root for our newly formed family.

"Let's eat!" shouted Fasar. "My stomach is growling from the smell of this delicious food!"

Sky and Miri eagerly agreed.

Kasim and I concurred.

The traditional Middle Eastern cuisines seemed to best serve our guests. There was creamy hummus, smoky baba ganoush, tangy tabbouleh, and crispy falafel. We had grilled lamb kebabs, tender chicken shawarma, and juicy beef kofta with rice pilaf and buttery saffron-infused mansaf. The cooks used the traditional Jordanian spices of sumac, za'atar, and cardamom. Deserts included baklava, knafeh, and halva. The tables were adorned with fine china, crystal glassware, and sparkling silverware. This added a touch of sophistication to the overall décor.

There was so much love and laughter that I'd almost forgotten about the danger that still lurked in hidden places. While Kasim seemed relaxed and happy, I could sense that he was still on high alert. His keen eyes missed nothing. He surveyed the room every so often and honed in on every word that was spoken.

The speeches given were heartfelt, celebrating our journey and offering words of wisdom for the road ahead. Our loved ones shared their hopes and dreams for our future, their voices resonating with love and support. My parents were also able to give words of wisdom and blessing for our union.

Kasim even surprised me with a video-recorded greeting from my long-time friend Fatima and her father, Ibrahim. Ibrahim was like a second father to me. He was so instrumental in my educational pursuit as an archeologist. I owed much to him, for had I not followed in his footsteps, I would never have met Kasim.

After a while, the love and happiness in the air dissipated any paranoia from recent events. I began to think we were all just being overly anxious.

Miri approached me and whispered, "It's time to change into the Thoub."

I leaned over to inform Kasim, and he gestured to his guard to accompany us back to the room. We returned without incident, and just in time, as Fasar led the way for the night's merriment.

"Come, Kasim and Issa!" Fasar shouted over the din. "You must start us off with the first dance."

Kasim reached for my hand and whispered in my ear, "Are you trying to make me lose my mind before our obligation to our family is complete?"

Eying me eagerly, Kasim continued. "I see your beauty knows no bounds."

Kasim stomped around me and then pulled me close. He whispered, "You wear our traditional garments like a queen, my beauty."

"No darling, this is actually Miri's doing. I was unaware of this tradition, but I'm thoroughly impressed with the outcome, if I may say so myself."

Kasim and I performed the traditional dabke dance. Then, we were joined by Fasar, Sky, and Miri, who formed lively circles and began stomping their feet to the rhythm and clapping. Before long, everyone joined in the dancing. Excitement hung in the air, spreading like wildfire. Kasim and I were in the middle of the fray. I threw my head back and enjoyed the moment of laughter and fun with my new family and friends.

At the height of the festivities, while everyone was merry and distracted, we escaped to the roof of the estate. The view was staggering. We could see Petra in the glow of the moonlight in the far distance. The backdrop was a blend of ancient history and modern development. There were towering buildings, sleek architecture juxtaposed against glimpses of historical landmarks, and the rugged hills surrounding the city.

I looked down on the festivities and saw Sky laughing at something Fasar murmured in her ear.

## Week of Celebration

I turned to Kasim, "We'll have to watch those two."

"I declared Sky my daughter today. Fasar is very clear about what that means."

"Yes, but if they think themselves in love, the heart will often act before the head. Then reason goes out the door."

"No worries, I have eyes everywhere, my love."

From our perch on the roof, we saw Fakmad ambling around from person to person, such a proud father. All seemed well. Either those who were gathered were sincerely happy for Kasim, or they played the role all too well. I chose to believe the former. Even Kasim had relaxed. He was not his earlier guarded self. His face was lit, and his smile was relaxed and genuine. He obviously loved his family, and he loved his culture.

I glanced his way, "Thank you my love, for all of this. Everything is perfect. I wouldn't have had it any other way."

Kasim stared at me for a moment, perhaps gauging my sincerity.

"It was not too Arabic for you?"

I laughed, "What are you saying? I am Arabic. Miri told me I looked like an Arabian princess. And you are my Arabian prince."

We both laughed. In that moment, surrounded by the love and warmth of our family and friends, I knew that we were embarking on a lifelong adventure. It would be filled with boundless love, cherished traditions, and the promise of a beautiful future together.

We walked back to the festivities hand in hand, and enjoyed the food and all the well wishes. While Kasim was distracted by his uncles and cousins, I was whisked away by the women. Aunts, I presumed. They fussed over me, touching my gown, my face, my hair.

Miri glanced in my direction and offered a sympathetic look.

Kasim surreptitiously walked up from behind and kissed me on my neck.

"Excuse me, my dear aunts, but I need my sweet wife." They all gave shy smiles and giggles and left us to be alone.

"You look stunning, wife."

"And you are devastatingly handsome, husband."

"Are you ready to escape the celebration? You know they will not leave until we consummate our marriage."

"What!"

"It's our culture, Issa. Don't let it bother you. They won't be able to hear us."

My cheeks felt like they were on fire! Kasim tickled me, and unbridled laughter escaped, echoing in the air.

"Let's go, Issa!"

We intertwined our hands and ran straight to Kasim's room amidst the clapping, shouts, and whistles. When we arrived, Kasim gently picked me up and carried me over the threshold. I looked into his eyes and knew I had found my soulmate. He deposited me on the bed, and we sat in silence for a few moments, the air charged with electricity.

Then, without a word, he kissed me. It was like nothing I had ever experienced. A rush of warmth and desire flooded my body. In that moment, nothing else mattered. It was just the two of us lost in the magic of our love. And that night, my husband made love to me. And I felt alive. I felt like a woman again. In my soul, the Lord illuminated the beauty of what he created between a husband and wife. The act of making love with my husband was a show of God's love and care for us as the emotional beings he created.

~ *Kasim, Dream Come True* ~

*I can't believe this is really happening. Lord, you have answered my prayers and brought me the woman of my dreams.* I felt a trickle of sweat roll down my back, and my palms were sweaty. *Why am I sweating so much?* My stomach was in turmoil. You would've thought I'd never been with a woman before. True, it had been a long time since Abbie passed, and I hadn't known another woman, but I was by no means inexperienced.

Then it dawned on me. When I married Abbie, I was thrust into a marriage I didn't want to a woman I didn't know. I felt a tinge of regret for what Abbie had to endure because of our circumstances and my immaturity. I'd grown to love Abbie as she loved me. I thank God that in the end, before she died, she knew this to be true.

I swallowed my regret and focused on the woman in front of me. The woman whom I had loved since the first day we met at archeology camp when we were just seventeen. This time, I was marrying for all the right reasons. This time, I was marrying for love. The woman I loved passionately, with an unyielding intensity. In Issa, I had found my soul's perfect match. She was my life and my breath. Words could not express the intensity of emotions I was feeling in that moment.

I couldn't wait any longer. The drive of desire kicked in, and it required all my restraint to bring it into submission. This is Issa's night, and I want her to feel valued and protected. I slowed my breathing, leaned in, and kissed her.

Issa melted into my embrace, and I whispered in her ear, "You are mine, Habibti. You are finally mine."

That night, I made love to my wife. I felt loved in return. I felt safe in her arms. And I heard the Lord's whisper in my ear, *You will have a son.*

### ~ Issa, My Husband ~

I woke up before Kasim did. I took some time to examine him. This specimen of a man was my husband. He was sprawled out on the bed. In his sleep, I saw the boy I knew all those years ago. His face was relaxed, like he had not a care in the world. His angular jaw gave him a rugged, masculine look. The only thing that gave his age away was his salt-and-pepper beard set against his jet-black wavy hair.

I decided to get up and refresh myself when Kasim gently pulled me into his arms and whispered, "I'm not done with you yet, Mrs. Ma'an."

He made love to me again, and I knew I was meant to be with this man forever. I knew by his touch and his gentleness that he loved me as much as I loved him.

# Chapter 22

## Saul Preaches to the Gentiles

*~ Saul, The Confirmation ~*

"Simeon, I have given it much thought and prayer. I believe we should start meeting at the Inn. There are many Gentiles in the marketplace. They've been asking about what we preach and teach."

"Saul, I fear what King Aretas will do if he finds us preaching Jesus and not the gods of this land."

"I thought you said he'd leave us alone as long as we don't disrupt the worship and financial resources of his temple? Besides, I've only spoken to a few of the locals. I mainly speak with the traveling merchants. I'm eager for them to go abroad and spread the word about the Messiah to their countrymen on their journey."

"Let's speak with Youssef and Kasim and get their support. I wouldn't want any harm to come to the believers who live in this city."

"Yes, you are correct, Simeon. We'll do as you say."

The next Sabbath, Simeon and I went to the caves to worship. The Spirit of the Lord was present, and the people were giving thanks to God. Kasim rose from his seat and began to prophesy.

"Hear the Word of the Lord, servants of the Most High God. 'I, and I alone, can move mountains. I tell the seas when to stop so as to separate the great waters from the land. I tell the sun when to rise and when to set. I ask you, is there anything too hard for God? Can I not keep a city? Saul of Tarsus, you've been called and set apart to preach my Word to the Gentiles. Hasten and tarry no longer.'"

I turned to Simeon, "Did you hear what I heard, my friend? We just received the confirmation we needed."

"Yes. May God help us all."

The following morning, I went straight to the marketplace. I gathered all the merchants who had expressed a desire to know more about the Messiah. What I didn't expect was the sheer number of people who appeared at Simeon's Inn that evening. There was standing room only.

"Saul, why didn't you tell me there would be so many?"

"I only invited a handful. I suppose the word has spread about the risen Messiah."

"Simeon, Saul," called Anna, with hands on hips and a scowl on her face.

"How am I supposed to feed all these people?"

Simeon shouted over the chatter and replied, "Simple fare will do, flat bread with an olive spread."

As we walked toward Anna, I replied, "My apologies. My guess is that you'll have an increase in patronage after tonight's meeting."

"Humph," was all the response Anna could offer.

Simeon called for the crowd to settle down. "Tonight, Brother Saul will speak to you about the saving grace and power of our Messiah, Jesus Christ."

"My friends," I greeted everyone. "The One True God, the Creator of the Universe, the Holy One of Israel, has made a way for us to approach him in a personal way. He sent his Son Jesus to take our place as a sin offering that we might be made holy and acceptable before a holy God. We no longer have to sacrifice bulls and rams to atone for our sins. You Gentiles no longer have to sacrifice your children in the fire to appease a

## Saul Preaches to the Gentiles

god made of wood and stone."

Everyone began to talk at once.

A big, burly man with a thick beard and accent bellowed, "I believe! I will follow your Jesus. The gods have done nothing for me except exact my coins. They care nothing for me and mine. At least your Jesus cares what happens to me and my family."

A thin, pale-looking man cowered, "I fear the gods will take retribution, and the King will have our heads."

"I would rather die a martyr than bow down to gods made of wood and stone, gods who require my firstborn. My wife is with child even now, and we will not sacrifice another," proclaimed a short, stocky man in the back.

"Saul, what of the Jewish leaders? They will come after us," replied a fellow Jew.

I continued my speech, "Jesus's own people, the Jews, cast him away. They delivered him into the hands of Rome to be crucified as a common criminal. In this, Jesus fulfilled the Scripture, 'cursed is everyone that hangs on a tree.' Jesus became a curse that we might be redeemed from the curse of the Law. No one took his life. He laid it down. Our lives are hidden in Christ, and he has become our righteousness."

"I, too, want this Jesus!" yelled someone.

"Saul, teach us more!" yelled another.

"My brothers, there is much to teach and so little time. We will meet again tomorrow. Be sure to bring coins and feast on a full meal. Simeon's wife Anna is the best cook in town."

The crowd lingered for some time, and Anna befriended the women and children who came with the men. On the next Sabbath, we joined Kasim at the caves. Simeon and I stood and reported all the wonderful things the Lord was doing among the new Gentile believers.

"Kasim, we're running out of space at the Inn. There are so many that want to learn of Jesus," I reported.

"What a wonderful problem, my friend."

"We need more cooks to help my poor Anna," said Simeon.

"How about we invite the local Gentile believers to worship here at the caves each Sabbath? Saul, you can continue to teach the traveling merchants at the Inn," replied Kasim.

Eyebrows tightly knit together, Youssef pleaded, "I fear the more people that know of our worship here in the caves, the more exposure we risk of being found out by the King."

"We'll have to trust the Lord on this matter," reminded Kasim.

"We must preach Jesus," I said.

"We must preach Jesus," we all agreed in unison.

Merchants from the Far East, Egypt, Africa, Hispania, and Armenia were present. Many had moved onward in their journey, and new merchants were coming to market. Youssef was becoming bolder in his faith, speaking about Jesus with his fellow merchants and patrons. He often invited them to the shop, and I expounded on the Scripture concerning Jesus the Messiah. Anna, too, spoke with the women in town. We only sent those believers who showed maturity in discipleship to the caves. Meanwhile, I continued to teach the traveling merchants at the Inn. Simeon and Anna were profiting nicely and contributing their funds towards the work of the Lord.

"Saul, there are whispers in the King's court concerning believers of the Way. It appears that some want to know more about Jesus, but I am unsure if this is a genuine request. It might be a setup by the King," cautioned Youssef.

"If they're sincere in their desire to learn about Jesus, I will meet with them in small groups in their homes. That way, we'll not place the other believers in harm's way."

That night, I fell on my knees and petitioned the God of my salvation. I prayed fervently that all the believers in Arabia would remain safe.

"Lord, I'm willing to sacrifice my life for you. But, I pray, please protect the believers from the King."

That night, I tossed and turned in bed. I woke up at the first hour drenched in sweat. The dream was so vivid, but what could it mean? I found myself before King Aretas preaching Jesus. The next thing I knew, I was back in Damascus.

I lowered my head in my hands and sought the Lord, "Jesus, please keep us safe and grant us the wisdom of Solomon."

### ~ Saul, The Wisdom ~

Sabbath had come, and I was glad. Kasim bade me to rest from teaching and to receive from the Lord. I started to argue against this wisdom but thought better of it. I worshiped from the depths of my soul and found my strength in the joy of the Lord.

"Saul, come quickly," said Youssef.

I was rushed down the rugged mountainside, and what I encountered soured my spirit. Two Gentile merchants were arguing over a failed business transaction. I hastened my steps to intervene.

"Brothers in the Lord, let's resolve our differences amicably, as Jesus would have us do. Youssef, please take the others to break bread. And send me Kasim, so that we may resolve this matter in a holy manner, acceptable unto our Lord."

"Yes, Saul." Youssef nodded and left straight away.

Kasim appeared out of nowhere and immediately directed us in a word of prayer. I was grateful.

We sat on some rocks, and Kasim started a fire to ward off the morning chill.

"Now, let us hear your story, one at a time," I said.

The merchant seated closest to Kasim erupted in anger, pointing at the other merchant, "He uses dishonest scales!"

"I have done no such thing!" spat the other. "The cost of sand has almost doubled since our last transaction because the Romans buy it all for their arenas, as does the King. Sand of that kind is harder to come by. Therefore, the price has gone up."

"You lie in order to extort me!"

I raised my hand to halt the vitriol that spewed from their mouths.

"Brothers, how do you intend to settle this? Should we not verify the price among the other merchants to prove the facts?"

"I will do no such thing! I refuse to sell to him anymore."

Stomping away and waving his hands toward the caves, the merchant yelled over his shoulder, "I no longer will be a part of this subterfuge against the King!"

My heart thumped like a horse at the races. My stomach felt like a boulder lay at its pit.

"I'm so sorry, I've brought this trouble upon the believers. I should not have entreated him. I should have gone elsewhere to buy my sand," said the merchant who remained.

Kasim comforted and prayed with the man.

I left immediately to meet with Artemis, one of the officials in the King's court who had become a believer. It was a joyous day when Artemis gave his life to Christ. I had to admit, I was afraid at first. When I met with a group of the King's officials at Artemis's house, I was sure they would drag me before the King and have my head on a platter, like John the Baptizer. Of the four officials, I had not expected Artemis to give his life to Christ. The whole time I was speaking, his face remained hardened, unflinching. The officials were intrigued by my preaching about Jesus and informed me that they would consider my words. Artemis didn't comment at first. When his comrades left, he asked me to be seated.

"Saul," he remarked, with a thick accent in the Aramaic Nabatean language I had become so familiar with. "Tell me more about Jesus and how he was raised from the dead."

Tears rolled down this dignified man's face as he dropped to his knees and gave his allegiance to Jesus, declaring him Savior.

## Saul Preaches to the Gentiles

*Four Weeks Later*
*~ Saul, Audience with the King ~*

I was working in Youssef's shop when the King's guard came pounding on the door.

"Saul of Tarsus, by order of King Aretas IV, you must come with us and appear before the court."

I passed word to Youssef to have the believers pray for me.

"Don't be consumed with fear over me, my brother," I whispered to him.

The guards grew impatient, but the one who was in charge looked familiar. He may have been one of many who had come to Artemis's house to hear me preach Jesus.

"Please, allow me to get my cloak."

He nodded, and the other guards backed away.

My cloak was hanging on a pole. As I passed by to retrieve it, I leaned in once more and whispered to Youssef, "We live to live again my brother, be of good cheer."

Little did I know that would be the last time I saw Youssef.

The guards herald me away to the King's palace, none too gently.

I had never been inside the walls of the palace. The palace itself was carved into the rose-red cliffs. The structure was highly intricate, a skillful blending of Hellenistic, Roman, and indigenous Arabian influences. There was an open courtyard and a garden adorned with plants and flowers of various colors. Many were vibrant and pleasing to the eyes. Some were native to the region, and others must have been obtained from traveling merchants and carefully cared for.

In the center of the garden, there was a water fountain, much like the Romans in design. I guessed that the stone nymph, holding a jug from which the water flowed, must have been one of their gods. We then entered a large hall, and my eye caught Artemis standing off to the right. Artemis walked up to the guard, the one who looked familiar, and whispered something in his ear.

Artemis then approached me and spoke for my ears only, "Saul, my friend, please be terse with your words and agree to go back to Damascus."

"Artemis, I will tell the King about Jesus in very few words. As for Damascus, the Lord revealed to me in a dream everything that is playing out before our eyes. Please take care of the believers in my absence."

Artemis nodded and bade the guards to take me to have an audience with the King. The audience chamber was huge, with vaulted ceilings that made the chamber echo. No wonder Artemis spoke barely above a whisper. There were four columns designed to support the structure. There were complex carvings, along with pictures etched on the walls. The blend of cultures was evident in the carvings and statues of their gods.

In a deep, resounding voice that echoed off the walls, King Aretas demanded, "Saul of Tarsus, what is your business in my kingdom?"

I looked the King eye to eye, not as a show of disrespect, but to convey with all sincerity what the Lord would have me say. At the moment, I knew not what that was to be.

"Honorable King Aretas, I came here by way of Damascus to seek work as a tentmaker."

"Why Raqmu?"

"I'm looking to start over."

"Saul of Tarsus, do not mince words with me. I know of your reputation in Jerusalem. My emissaries are placed throughout the region. Do you think to find Christians here, and take them back to Jerusalem? I will not have you disrupting our economy. There is no synagogue here, and you have no authority in this region."

This was the moment. I felt the Spirit of the Lord bubbling up within my belly, springing forth like living water.

I replied, "To the contrary, King Aretas. This same Jesus, whose followers I persecuted, came to me on the road to Damascus. He appeared

## Saul Preaches to the Gentiles

to me from the Heavens in a light so bright that it blinded me for several days. He inquired of me, 'Saul, Saul, why are you persecuting me?' I replied, who are you, Lord? 'I am Jesus whom you are persecuting,' was the Lord's response."

"So, you think to hide from your religious leaders here in Raqmu?" The King's reply was more of a statement than a question.

"I was looking to start over and to learn more about my new faith in Jesus."

"So, I've heard. You are quite the orator and have gathered many followers. This concerns me."

"Your noble King, I do not seek to do harm to anyone or disrupt life here in Raqmu. I simply have relayed to others my experience and faith in Jesus Christ, the risen Lord."

"What do you mean by risen Lord?"

"The Romans crucified Jesus on a Roman cross at the behest of the Sanhedrin court in Jerusalem. He was innocent of any wrongdoing. He preached a message of love and salvation from the God of all creation. God loves us so much that he allowed his Son to die on a cross as a substitution. For he made Jesus, who knew no sin, to be sin for us, that we might become the righteousness of God in him."

"You speak pretty words, Saul of Tarsus, but the gods of Raqmu are enough for me. Those who worship other gods are welcome to worship alongside our own gods. Is your Jesus willing to be worshiped alongside our gods?"

I hung my head, "No, noble King. Jesus is the One and only true God. He is the God of my fathers, Abraham, Isaac, and Jacob. He is the Alpha and the Omega, the beginning and the end. There is no other besides him. He is the way, the truth, and the life, and no one comes to the Father but by Jesus."

"Nonsense, Saul. I know that you Jews only serve one God. So how are you different from them now?"

"Jesus is our long-awaited Messiah."

King Aretas's eyes smoldered and bore into me, "Then you seek revolt!"

"No, Jesus did not come to take life. He came to offer eternal life and life more abundantly. We live to live again because Jesus rose from the dead on the third day, conquering death, hell, and the grave."

"Saul, what you say is impossible. One God? A God who loves his people and died in their place? The gods have no use for us past this life, and we are here at their bidding."

"Then, what is the sense of living, noble King?"

"We are doing just fine here in Raqmu. And, to keep it this way, I must send you back to Damascus, lest you anger the gods, and they pour out their wrath on us."

"But, King."

"Enough Saul, I could have you killed! I have chosen not to anger any of the gods. So, I will allow you safe passage back to Damascus."

At that ruling, I was escorted out the door, followed by a small contingent of soldiers. They accompanied me about three-quarters of the way. I was left by an oasis, less than a day's journey to Damascus.

# Chapter 23

## Change of Plans

*~ Issa, So Much For a Honeymoon ~*

Kasim was relaxed, just as I remembered him from our youth. I treasured the time we spent together sequestered in residence. After three days, we emerged from our cocoon and joined the family for breakfast.

Fakmad greeted us with a smile, "Kasim, Issa, it appears that married life suits you well."

Fasim was invited as a gesture of reconciliation. He had not been allowed to attend the wedding. He made an attempt to be congenial after all that had transpired—though it was a paltry attempt.

"Hello Kasim. Hello Issa. You both look so…married," uttered Fasim.

"Good morning, Uncle."

"Kasim, you know you broke your cousin's heart."

"Uncle, you know I have loved Issa since I was a mere boy, growing into manhood."

"Ah yes," said Fakmad. "We had to snatch you out of that place so quickly, or I would have lost my only son."

I looked at Kasim with concern in my eyes. Kasim looked at me.

"My father ran the business in those days. Many of the artifacts I showed you were from his archeological finds. Unbeknownst to us at the time, he had found a rare jewel worth millions of dollars during an excavation in Turkey. Throughout the centuries, many raiders have been rumored to be in search of the lost treasures from the Ottoman dynasty."

"I read about some of those rumors. Which one are you speaking of?"

"What I speak of is not in the academic journals, or anywhere else for that matter. I speak of an early sixteenth-century legend that tells us the Sultan family during the reign of Suleiman I had stolen a rare jewel from the Sultan family during the reign of Selim I. The stories tell that they hid an exquisite jewel in an undisclosed location."

"I have no knowledge of this story. It reads like a movie script," I interjected.

Kasim continued. "Although my father received many threats, he was not easily scared and would not give up the claim to his find. The jewel was a rare beauty. The stone changed colors when it came in contact with various light sources. The stone was twenty carats in weight. It was set in a pendant carved into the shape of a genie in a bottle. The pendant was made of eighteen-karat gold. The stone was surrounded by diamonds and pink sapphires. The unnamed stone was a rare find. My father found it near the Anatolian Mountains. Father decided the best course of action was to return it to the heirs of the family—from whom it had been stolen."

"Naturally, I received a handsome reward and notoriety from the royals for my find," said Fakmad.

"The notoriety we could have done without," Kasim reminded him.

"We were all in agreement that such news was better kept a secret," replied Fakmad.

"That's when the assassination attempts started," he continued. "Then we received word of a plot to kidnap Kasim and hold him for ransom."

Fasim must have seen the horror in my eyes.

## Change of Plans

He said, "My dear Issa, this is the ugly side of what we do. Archeology is more than excavations and artifacts. It can get very messy."

Akhab entered the room, his face flushed and his breathing rapid. He looked at each of us, and his eyes finally settled on Kasim, "Come quickly, we've found something."

Little did we know those last three words would turn our world upside down. We had planned to take a few weeks off to have some semblance of a honeymoon. I inadvertently overheard the steward of the house talking with another servant. They spoke about the preparations Kasim was making. I learned that we were to go to an island somewhere off the coast of the Mediterranean Sea. What I didn't expect was that he was speaking about Kasim's family's island. They owned an island! It was to be a surprise, a ten-day honeymoon. All that changed when the plans for the excavation were escalated. While married life seemed to get off to a rough start, I had no regrets.

*~ Issa, Excavation Resumes ~*

At Akhab's pronouncement, we put in motion plans for a full-scale excavation at the headquarters site. Kasim's men had unearthed some first-century pottery and jewelry. Four weeks later, his men found what looked like a cave. With renewed determination, we prepared ourselves for the next phase. We were eager to uncover the hidden treasures that lay dormant beneath the surface. The artifacts we uncovered thus far merely whispered stories of a bygone era, hinting at the grandeur and turmoil that once graced these lands.

I asked Kasim to take pictures of the findings on hand and use his state-of-the-art software to recategorize them in several ways. First by age, then by location, then by possible matching sets, then by category. This process took almost two weeks. The findings had to be properly prepared, categorized, photographed, and cataloged. I worked from home during that time while Kasim and his men continued digging.

It was during week four that I joined Kasim at one of the dig sites.

"Issa, I think you may be on to something," called out Kasim.

"Come look, I have a working theory about the approximation of the property just west of the mountain base to this site. It has to do with how the layout of your ancestor's village may have been arranged."

"Which property do you speak of?"

"The property midway between here and the mountain base, which could have been the center of town where trade occurred."

"Ah, yes. This would have been the area where my ancestor Youssef had his shop. Currently, the land surrounding it is vacant and is owned by the government."

"If we believe this current location to be the dwelling site of your ancestors, as far back as the third century, which our findings suggest, then it makes sense to continue the dig downward."

"Yes, the likelihood of unearthing a first-century find is greater."

"Conversely, if the property East of here, close to the estate, is the geographic location of your ancestors from the first century, then the dig will need to be expanded out by at least a half-mile north and south from the property because the catacombs would not have been in such close proximity to the village. Remember, your ancestors were Christian Jews and, therefore, would have kept some or most of the purity laws."

Kasim motioned to garner Akhab's attention, then recited his orders.

"First, we must look for any evidence of a meeting place where the believers may have gathered. We must find supporting evidence that the boxed structure we found at the headquarters site is indeed a mikvah, where ritual cleansing or baptisms would have taken place. And there's one more thing, we need to rerun our tests on the stone work in the tombs. We need to get a more accurate dating to see what we are dealing with, a first to second-century site, or third century and later."

"Yes, I will personally rerun the tests," said Akhab.

"Maybe they hid them in close proximity to the tombs, assuming no one would search such a sacred place," replied Kasim.

"For our sake, I hope it is a later find. I don't think your ancestors would have hidden the scrolls in such close proximity to their possessions to be easily confiscated and destroyed. Plus, grave robbers care nothing about sacred grounds," I countered.

"That would mean they would have been hidden in the caves where your Bedouin ancestors lived," said Akhab.

"Or your ancestor Youssef's shop," I replied.

"Akhab, Issa is on to something. Let's run those tests now."

Kasim's face seemed pinched with concern.

"Is there something wrong?"

"Issa, your theory raises a major issue. If we expand our dig outside of our land, we run the risk of drawing attention to ourselves, and we must get the appropriate permits to dig on land owned by the government. Any archeological find would be considered the government's property."

I turned to Kasim and whispered in his ear, "Then we dig deeper, and then we dig laterally. We should not need to dig outside the half-mile boundary. We dig down to the level of a first-century find, then widen the search."

Kasim kept his voice low, "Akhab, is this possible to dig deeper and laterally?"

"Yes, but it's dangerous."

"Is there any way to purchase the additional land from the government?" I asked.

Kasim hesitated, "It's a risk, and it may draw too much attention. First, let's see how far laterally we have to dig before causing legal problems."

"We have the cover we need for an underground dig to accomplish this. My only concern is the stability of the tunnels that will have to be dug underground," said Akhab.

"Issa, this is why I need you here. Your knowledge of ancient landscapes and artifacts is quite impressive."

"Well, I am the right man, I mean woman, for the job. So much of the research I collected while doing my dissertation was in the time period of your ancestors."

"Yes, I know. I obtained the video lecture you gave on the probability that the Apostle Paul wrote letters to the church in Arabia."

"Paul, or Saul, I should say, spent quite a bit of time with the believers in Arabia, and he would have left them instructions. He would have written to them after he left by way of greetings, encouragement, or instructions. I'm sure Saul, after he returned to Damascus and was almost murdered by the governor under King Aretas IV, would have written to warn the Arab believers of his circumstances."

Miri meandered our way and interrupted our conversation, "This is such a huge task, and there is so much land to cover. Where should I prioritize my focus?"

"The missing piece of the puzzle is tied to whether your late ancestors had enough time to take the scrolls with them when they escaped to Egypt—during their exile in the first century. Or, if they left them behind and hid them?" I replied.

"Do you think they could have carried the scrolls in such haste? Or maybe they hid them with the intent of returning? What if they were confiscated by the rulers and destroyed?" asked Miri.

"My gut is telling me they hid them. And if they did, they would be close to the place where they worshiped," replied Kasim.

"Your ancestors were traders," I said. "They would've traveled to Egypt on more than one occasion. They would've known what life was like there. What if they carried the scrolls with them to Egypt to learn how to preserve them in the way of the Egyptians, to ensure their survival?"

Miri added, "Yes, and they would have brought them back stored in amphora or vases to preserve them from the elements and to disguise them as articles of trade."

"Now we have several working theories," said Kasim.

"Issa, please work on prioritizing the plausibility of each. We will not

## Change of Plans

need you onsite during the preliminary digs unless we find something of interest. I promise you will be the first to know."

"Kasim, there is one area that I would like to explore at this site. I believe the hollowness in the wall at the East end of the site may indicate another cave. Your men have already started preliminary work in that area."

"Akhab, please take Issa to the site and prepare to scan the rock to see its depth and stability. You may blast or drill if all the safety parameters are met."

"Yes, Kasim, right away."

### ~ Issa, Falling for It ~

Akhab and his men commenced with drilling after the appropriate tests came back with minimal safety concerns. The rock formation was thick in some areas. There was a small section that was thinner with a cylindrical tunnel carved into the rock. Surprisingly, the drilling only took three days to reach that particular area. The tests indicated there was a cave-like structure beyond the tunnel. However, to get to that point we needed either to traverse the space with special equipment in tow or blast the solid rock formations without causing the cave to crumble. I convinced Kasim to allow me to supervise the first few days of the project. Akhab sent a few men ahead of us to ensure our safety while I continued my work. A few hours later, he returned.

"Come, Dr. Issa. It appears that the cylindrical passageway is narrow in dimension but not impossible to traverse. We confirmed there is indeed an entrance to a cave at the far end. How would you like us to proceed?" asked Akhab.

I crossed over into the cavernous rock alcove, and it sounded like an echo chamber. I had the crew set up the lighting fixtures, and each of us focused on an area just east, west, north, and south of the cave. My curiosity got the better of me, and I assigned myself the area where the drilling had already commenced on the tunnel.

"Dr. Issa, this is too dangerous. Kasim will have my head if anything were to happen to you."

"But Akhab, I'm the smallest here, and no one else will fit through the narrowest section of this tunnel."

Akhab directed one of his men to bring Kasim to our location. When he returned, he informed us that Kasim had gone to the surface to take an important call.

"Akhab, I'm an archeologist. This is what I do. I'm not a novice. I'll be alright."

"Dr. Issa, I will only back this if you allow me to secure this rope around your waist so we have a means to pull you to safety."

"I feel like the Jewish High Priest on the Day of Atonement. Are you going to put bells on the hem of my garment as well?"

"That's not funny, Dr. Issa."

I climbed into the small tunnel and immediately regretted my decision. The space was smaller than I expected, and the air was thicker, with little to no oxygen. The sound was muted in the small space, and all I could hear was my heartbeat. On top of that, there were bugs crawling on me. This was the one part of my job I hated. Bugs! My headlamp lit the way, but I decided to light a small torch to keep the bugs at bay. Now, I was hot, and the heat was sucking up the little oxygen I had.

"Dr. Issa," I heard Akhab calling. The sound was so muted I couldn't make out what he was saying.

I thought I heard him say, "We're running out of rope."

I will have to gather what information I can and crawl backward to make my way out of this place.

"I'm okay, Akhab!" I yelled back.

I advanced through the small tunnel surrounded by rock. I moved like a snail, inch by inch, and noticed some broken pieces of clay that looked like shattered pottery. I gathered the pieces and secured them in a pouch around my neck. Then, something caught my eye. It looked like a piece of a rag. Could it be a scroll?

## Change of Plans

Suddenly, the walls began to move. My breathing accelerated, and I felt like I had no air. I tried to reach for the rag-like material, but the rope would not give way. I felt like I was stuck and realized the rope had come to its end. I began to pray fervently.

*Lord Jesus, is this the scroll? Please, help me to calm my breathing. Please stop this shaking.*

At that moment, I felt pieces of rock breaking off and pelting down on me.

*Oh Lord, no!*

"Issa, Issa! We're going to pull you out slowly."

I thought I heard Kasim's voice. Then, I felt a pulling. I extinguished the torch and buried my head in my hands. The pulling was agonizing. The rocks beneath me scraped my exposed skin. Thank the Lord Kasim had my gear made with durable yet breathable material.

The air seemed to be evaporating inside the tunnel. At the rate they were pulling me, I felt like I would run out of this precious, life-giving resource. I started to panic. All I could do was close my eyes and call on the name of Jesus. Then, everything went black.

*~ Kasim, Only Time Will Tell ~*

I thought I would never see Issa again. It was taking too long, and she was no longer responding when I called her name.

Finally, we could see her limp body. Her face and hands were smeared with blood, likely due to the multiple small cuts made by the rocks. My heart was beating fast, and I couldn't catch my breath. I threw up a quick prayer: *Lord, please let Issa be alive!*

We slowly pulled her out of the tunnel. I saw no movement. I removed her jacket and helmet and readied myself to perform CPR. I couldn't see the rise or fall of her chest. I put my face to her nose and felt air, barely perceptible. Then, I felt a pulse. The pulse was weak, but it was there!

I looked to Miri, "Hurry, get me an oxygen tank and mask, then quietly summon the family physician. No ambulance."

Miri's face had a look of terror on it. Her eyes were wide, and her face was white as a sheet. But she remained calm. I, too, vowed to remain calm for Issa's sake. Everyone around me was quiet. All I could hear was the remnant of rocks cascading down to the ground.

"Kasim, the tunnel has collapsed. We will seal it off," said Akhab.

"Thank you."

"How is Dr. Issa?"

"Why did she go in there?"

"All the testing showed the tunnel was safe. None of the men could fit in the narrowest section of the tunnel. Dr. Issa insisted that she go because of her size. I asked her to wait for your return, but she didn't want to disturb you."

"This stubborn woman is going to be the death of me."

Issa began to moan, and my eyes fixated on her face. Then she began to cough.

"Are you okay, Habibti?"

"Kasim?"

"Yes, sweetheart."

"I found something."

"Rest. We can talk later."

Miri came running back with Dr. Bashar. He performed a thorough examination and suggested we move her back to the estate, where he could monitor her for the next few hours before sending the nurse.

I walked over to Akhab to give him some additional instructions. Afterward, I pulled Dr. Bashar aside and asked for more details concerning Issa's condition.

"Kasim, I need to run additional tests to confirm my suspicions."

## Change of Plans

I rubbed the back of my neck and bit my bottom lip until I tasted blood. Then I demanded, "Dr. Bashar, do not spare me any details."

What he revealed next both frightened and delighted me.

"Kasim, I suspect your wife is pregnant."

My mouth stood agape. I felt disoriented for a moment. I finally managed to form my words in a high-pitched voice, "What?"

"Yes, she's early on. During my examination and questioning, she said she's been unusually tired and nauseated. She thought the nausea was due to her not being accustomed to our diet and the richness of some of the foods."

"But the accident. She seemed not to be breathing at first. Is she okay? What about our baby?"

"Issa will be fine. I will need to perform some additional tests as soon as she returns home and has rested."

Back at the estate, I was bombarded with requests from Sky and Miri to see Issa. I assured them she was doing fine but divulged nothing more. I didn't want to reveal that she was pregnant if she wasn't. I sat beside Issa most of the afternoon. She dozed in and out of sleep, speaking only a few sentences and drifting off again. Dr. Bashar stopped by several times to check on her and to complete his examination and testing. I heard a knock on the door and suspected Dr. Bashar had returned.

"Hello Kasim, it's Dr. Bashar." The voice behind the door sounded calm.

Instead of inviting him in, I stepped outside.

"Kasim, I've confirmed that your wife is indeed pregnant."

"Was the baby harmed in any way during the accident?"

"No, your wife is in the early stages, and no harm was done."

I sighed in relief. Then laughed a hearty laugh and smiled. I gave Dr. Bashar the customary greeting of a kiss on each cheek, which I should have done earlier. I half-skipped, half-ran to tell everyone the news. I abruptly stopped and thought better of the idea. I need to share this good news with Issa first. I ran back to the room, and before I could enter, I was greeted by the nurse—who had taken over for Dr. Bashar.

"How's my wife?"

"She's fine, Dr. Ma'an."

"Is she awake?"

"Yes, I just finished giving her some food."

I entered and saw my wife sitting up for the first time since the accident. I sat next to her and kissed her on the cheek.

"Habibti, how are you feeling?" I asked.

"Much better, my love."

Issa's voice was low but audible.

"Issa, I have some good news for you."

"What is it? Did you find the scrolls in the cave?"

"No, no. We're going to have a baby."

"But how?" replied Issa.

Winking, I reminded her, "Habibti, we have been inseparable since we married."

"You think? Do you really think so? Could it be?"

Issa found her voice and squealed with delight, a melodious sound echoing in the room. Suddenly, her face contorted in pain. She put her hand on her abdomen and questioned, her voice filled with emotion, "Is our baby okay?"

"Yes, Habibti, everything is fine. However, you cannot stress yourself anymore."

"But the scrolls, I found what looked like a fragment of parchment, or maybe a leather encasement in the cave, just beyond my reach. We have to go back!"

## Change of Plans

"Habibti, don't worry about that. My men and I will take care of it. The most important thing is you and our baby, so rest."

Issa buried her face in my chest, and I stroked her hair. I felt her body relax and the tension drain out of her. I cupped her face in my hands, and I kissed her once more gently on the lips.

Finally, I said, "I was on my way to tell everyone. Would you prefer I wait?"

Nodding, she replied, "Let's make sure our baby is safe first."

I nodded in return and lay next to my sweet Issa. We both fell asleep in each other's arms. I woke up first. Issa was still sound asleep. I decided to go for a walk in the gardens.

# Chapter 24

# The Gardens

*- Tirsa, One Last Effort -*

The gardens were lovely this time of year. I caressed the orchids and irises, inhaled the fragrance of the roses, and admired the crocuses and narcissus. The smell was stimulating. I leaned my head back, and the sun kissed my face. I smiled, then sighed, as my plans would not be complete until Kasim was mine.

Just then, I noticed him walking into the garden, and I called his name.

"Hello, Kasim."

"Hello Tirsa, what are you doing here?"

"I stopped by to speak with Uncle, but I thought I would talk to you first. I apologize, I couldn't attend your wedding. I wasn't feeling well."

"I see you are well now. You look lovely as ever. The yellow dress compliments you well, Cousin."

I knew I had to use the full arsenal of my charms, so I put on a coy smile. "Oh Kasim, you can still take me as your wife. We were meant to be together."

"Tirsa, what is done is done. I have always loved Issa, and I will only marry for love."

"You love me as your cousin. You could learn to love me as your wife."

"I'm already married."

"We would've been husband and wife now if Dr. Stevens was not sought after for this mission. We can find the scrolls without her. I have done some research, and there is a world-renowned archeologist in Egypt who can help us."

"Tirsa, my father, and Fasim should never have presumed to choose my life for me in this way. It has hurt you, for this, I'm very sorry."

At that moment, I noticed Issa standing by a bush behind Kasim. I didn't know how long she had been standing there. Instantly, a plan formulated in my mind. I grinned and thought to myself, *It's now or never*. I threw myself into Kasim's arms and began to sob.

"It's not too late, Kasim. You can get what the Americans call an annulment. You can make this right for our family, for our legacy."

*~ Kasim, The Temptation ~*

Tirsa's perfume was tantalizing. She looked more lovely than all the exotic flowers in the garden, which were in full bloom. She melded her body into mine, and time froze. I stiffened. My first reaction was to push her away. But my body wanted to respond to her nearness. I had a strong urge to pull her closer and kiss her, to see if I could silence my conscience once and for all. To ensure myself that I had made the right choice. Then, I heard the Holy Spirit whisper the words I needed to hear.

*Issa is the gift I have given you.*

*~ Tirsa's Retort ~*

Kasim gently pushed me away and said, "Tirsa, I must obey God and follow what the Spirit is saying to my heart."

I felt defeated. Why did he have to bring God into it? I believe, but I'm not fanatical like the rest. This is not going as planned. It's time to change my strategy.

## The Gardens

"Kasim, I want to know why Uncle Fasim is still being held under guard. I have been told there is no evidence of any wrongdoing on his part. There have been no more attempts on your wife's life. You must believe that he wouldn't do such a thing."

"My investigations are not yet complete. I will continue to search until I find out who was behind this diabolical scheme. And when I find the culprit, they will wish they had never set foot in Jordan."

Kasim's face showed several emotions, none that were endearing. Then, a stone mask descended over his handsome features.

I, too, set my face like a flint. "Perhaps there are those who do not agree with a Westerner usurping what rightfully belongs to an Arab."

"Watch your tongue Tirsa. You sound as if you are disappointed that nothing happened to my wife."

At that moment, I became enraged and did the unthinkable. I slapped Kasim.

### ~ Kasim's Anger ~

No matter how angry and bitter Tirsa was, I didn't expect her to slap me. I involuntarily put my hand to my face and said, "You forget your place."

"Kasim, can't you see? You're destroying everything our families have worked so hard for. You're letting your feelings for that interloper come between our family! She's not a Ma'an. She will destroy us all. You've allowed a boyhood fantasy to tarnish our bloodline."

"Tirsa, I would be very careful if I were you. You know not what you speak of."

"I don't know what I'm talking about. It is you who does not know. You have allowed your manhood to act over reason."

At that venomous remark, I became angrier than I had ever been before. I've never shown disrespect to a woman, not once in my life. I've always granted women the same respect that Jesus did. But this woman acted neither like a true believer in Christ nor a woman raised in the culture of Arabia.

### ~ Tirsa's Reaction ~

Kasim's voice raised ever so slightly with an authority that brokered no argument. It was then that I knew I had overstepped my boundaries.

He replied, "Tirsa, you had better choose your next words carefully if you want to remain a member of the Ma'an family."

At that directive, I lost my senses and blurted out, "You insolent man!"

I raised my hand to slap him again.

### ~ Kasim's Realization ~

Tirsa raised her hand to strike me again, but this time, I caught her wrist. Her face contorted and transformed into a grotesque mask. The presence of evil descended on her pretty face.

She yanked her wrist free from my grasp with unnatural strength and announced in a voice that didn't sound like her own, "This is only the beginning."

In the background, I heard a gasp and then a whimper. I turned and saw Issa take flight from behind the bushes.

Furious, I turned back to Tirsa. "You will leave this property at once and never return."

### ~ Tirsa's Realization ~

When Kasim spoke, it was as if I awakened from a trance. By the look on his face, I knew I had gone too far. What was I thinking? I ran and hid behind the wall. My whole body trembled. I was shaking my head as if waking out of a dream. *What have I done?*

### ~ Kasim's Turmoil ~

I found Issa stooped over the garden wall at the other end of the courtyard. She was heaving and holding her stomach, her face contorted as if in pain.

"Issa, sweetheart. Are you well?"

Issa slowly turned her head and looked at me. She had a grave tone to her voice, "The enemy has begun his attack."

When she raised her hand, I saw blood. My face paled, and my pupils dilated as fear gripped my heart.

I whispered, "The baby," and Issa fainted. Time stood still for that split second. I barely caught Issa in time before she hit the ground. I lifted her in my arms and ran toward the house, yelling for help. My steward heard me shouting and ran to assist.

"Call the physician at once! I think something is wrong with the baby. And have my guards escort Tirsa off the property. Now! She is no longer welcome here!"

Dr. Bashar found himself back in my home for the second time that day.

"Kasim, what has happened?"

"The stress of the day overtook her. How is she?"

"The baby is fine."

"And Issa?"

I watched as Dr. Bashar took a slow, deliberate breath, trying to find the right words to say to me.

"Your wife's health is fragile from carrying a child at her age. She will need to remain on bed rest for at least three to four weeks."

"What does that mean?"

"Carrying a baby at this age comes with many dangers. The stress and shock of all that has transpired have also taken a toll on her body. However, she is relatively healthy and should recover quickly if we take the proper precautions."

I was not completely convinced that all would be well. I asked Dr. Bashar to leave the nurse detailed instructions for Issa's care and a written copy for myself. After he left, I sat on the bed next to Issa and looked at her beautiful face. I smoothed her hair and stroked her cheek with my finger. She looked so peaceful. She had recovered since fainting and was now asleep.

I walked outside and gestured for the nurse to take watch. I gently closed the door, leaned against the wall, and slid to the floor. I put my face in my hands and wept. When the heaviness of my emotions lifted, I began to pray. Then, my countenance was lifted. Why did I not think of this before? This is exactly what Issa would have done if it were me lying in that sick bed.

"Dear Lord, Issa means the world to me. I love her and cannot bear to lose her or our child. Please watch over her and restore her to full health. Please watch over the child in her womb. We vow to set him apart for your glory. Amen."

I returned to the room and sat on the bed. Issa was still asleep. I laid my right hand over her heart and continued my prayer. "Lord, let your virtue flow through your daughter and bring healing to her body, and keep our child safe for your glory. I know you love us. You have a plan and a future for us, as you have declared in your Word. Do it for your Name's sake."

Issa's eyes fluttered open, and she whispered, "Kasim."

"Shh Habibti, you need your rest."

Issa lifted a fluttering hand and touched my face. I leaned into her touch and closed my eyes. The next words she spoke shook me to the core.

"That voice, I knew it sounded familiar. I just couldn't place it at the time."

Her words trailed off. It seemed like she was drifting back to sleep.

"What voice? Who are you speaking of? What are you trying to tell me?"

## The Gardens

She did not open her eyes. She simply spoke.

"Tirsa is the one who took me captive."

"What? Are you sure?"

"Yes."

"How do you know, my love? That would be a huge accusation, and I'll need proof. Can you give me anything that would help point to her involvement?"

"Her voice changed. When she became angry with you. It deepened and matched the voice of the person in the cave."

I was too shocked to respond. My thoughts were racing at all the possibilities. I knew that Tirsa and Fasim were pushing for marriage within our family. Tirsa would have been the perfect choice. Her actions today certainly could point to her involvement in some way.

"Issa, the nurse will stay with you. Our room will remain under guard. I need to speak with my father and settle this matter once and for all."

I went straight to my father's study.

"Hello, Son, what brings you here?"

"Father, I'm sorry to disturb you, but I must speak to you at once. I have news."

With concern in his eyes, father spoke, "Is Issa okay?"

"Yes. I have news about the kidnapping."

"Speak, boy, speak!"

"The encounter I had in the garden with Tirsa earlier today was not so strange after all. When I went to check on Issa, she told me that Tirsa's voice was the same as the kidnapper in the cave."

"How can this be?"

"When Tirsa became enraged, her voice deepened and took on another tone. At that moment, Issa recognized the voice."

"Where is Tirsa now, Son?"

"I had my guards escort her off the property shortly after the incident. I will dispatch some men to go look for her. In the meantime, I will have Uncle Fasim brought here for further questioning."

"Yes, yes! Go now. Tirsa must not escape, and we must ascertain Fasim's involvement in this."

An hour later, Fasim was brought to the estate. Tirsa was nowhere to be found. We met in father's study. Father had a small fare of pita bread, hummus, olives, goat cheese, and a variety of fruits and coffee waiting for us.

Without preamble, Father spoke in a calm voice, "Fasim, have you heard from Tirsa? We are unable to locate her."

"No. I last saw her yesterday evening. She visited with me for a short time and asked how I was doing. You know the poor girl is mourning over your marriage, Kasim. She loves you. It was never about the legacy for her."

"What is done is done, Uncle, and it will not be undone. As I have indicated before, I love my wife, and I know the Lord sent her to me."

"I know, Kasim, you will not hear from me on this matter again. I will submit to God's will concerning this. I'm just concerned for my dear Tirsa. Before she abruptly left last night, she was mumbling incoherently about something. I have not seen her since."

"Uncle, try and remember what she said."

"Why is something wrong? Did something happen to her?"

"We're not sure. If you can remember anything that would be helpful, it might aid in finding her."

"Well, she was crying, talking in half sentences, saying Dr. Stevens was not supposed to be here. Everything is ruined. Then she just stared out the window and mumbled under her breath saying, 'I must go and fix this.'"

"Uncle, what do you think she is capable of doing? That sounds like a threat."

"I don't know. She's distraught, and it's partially my fault for pushing the idea that she could be with you. I was only thinking about our legacy. I didn't consider her feelings, her heart, her motives, or her desires. But I can't see her being a threat or capable of doing harm to anyone."

"Uncle, Tirsa was the kidnapper."

I saw Fasim's face fall, his eyes teared, and he lowered his head in his hands, grief overtaking him. My heart was conflicted. I wanted to believe him.

With his face in his hands and shoulders jerking, Fasim voiced his anguish, "I'm so sorry, Fakmad, nephew. I never meant for any of this to happen. I never imagined Tirsa would be capable of any of this."

Silence ensued. I finally said, "Uncle, we are sorry for accusing you of this crime. We will work together to find Tirsa. We will not turn her over to the authorities, but she is no longer considered part of this family. She will be exiled and put under continued watch."

I contemplated for a moment, allowing the weight of my thoughts to settle. *I'll give my uncle the benefit of the doubt. For now.*

# CHAPTER 25

# TROUBLE IN ARABIA

*~ Youssef, The Tent Shop ~*

Breathless, Artemis entered the tent shop, eyes wide open and hands planted on his knees. He looked undignified in his dignified robe.

"Youssef," he said, "The King has taken Saul back to Damascus under escort."

"What? Come, my friend, sit down and let me get you some water."

"You should have seen him; he boldly proclaimed Jesus to the King, and the glory of God was upon him. His eyes shone bright, and his words enlightened as he spoke about our Lord."

"Was he harmed in any way?"

"No. I assigned one of the guards who came to hear Saul preach to lead his escort to Damascus."

"What did the King say?"

"After Saul was taken away, all the magistrates and religious leaders were arguing over Saul's words. King Aretas was in awe of Saul and was afraid to anger our God. So instead of killing him, he sent him to Damascus."

"Why Damascus?"

"Damascus is annexed to Nabatean land, and he has emissaries there to watch Saul."

"I need to go tell Kasim. Can you inform Simeon of all that has happened?"

"Yes, but we must be careful. No decree has been made forbidding us to worship—yet. However, the King will change his mind if he thinks it will compromise his kingdom. Also, he will not be tolerant if he receives complaints from his subjects. I fear the latter. I have already heard grumblings among the idol makers. They complain that the people are not patronizing their establishments like before."

"Artemis, I trust that you will inform us if anything changes? I must go tell the others."

"I will notify you immediately."

I arrived at Kasim's encampment on a camel. He took one look at me and knew something was wrong.

"Youssef, since when do you approach me in such haste? What has happened? Your hair is out of sorts, your face is drained of its color, and you're holding on to the camel like your life depends on it."

"Brother, I have awful news. Saul was called before the King, and he was exiled to Damascus."

"Are you sure?"

"Yes, Artemis came to the shop right after Saul was taken away by the guards."

"We must gather the others. They have a right to know the danger that exists," replied Kasim.

~ *Saul Returns to Damascus* ~

The sun was soon to set. I was determined to make it to Damascus before the city gates closed and the wild animals began their search for an evening meal. The city should come into view at any moment now. I rounded a bend in the road and there she was. The city I left because my life was endangered. Here I find myself leaving yet another city, my life endangered, only to return to the previous danger.

Shaking my head, I pulled my tallit across my face and entered the city without harm. I immediately went to Ezra's house and knocked.

"Shalom to this house. It is I, Saul."

"Saul, what are you doing here?"

"I was hoping for a more endearing greeting."

"Yes, yes, shalom. I've missed you, my friend. Come in, come in!"

"How are you, Ezra?"

"Things are just now settling down. The Sanhedrin sent people to investigate. The leaders threatened to expel me from the synagogue for good this time."

"And, the believers of the Way?" I asked.

"We are all fine. We no longer worship at the synagogue. I believe we are constantly being watched, but there have been no arrests."

"Good, good, my friend. I have prayed continually for the brethren here. I have prayed for your safety and for your growth. Are there any new believers?"

"Not many. Some have left Damascus. Others are afraid to gather with us. More and more, I find myself teaching Gentiles rather than our own people."

"Yes, Ezra. Jesus came to his own, and his own did not receive him."

"Why are you here, Saul? I thought the Lord commissioned you to the Gentiles in Arabia."

"Yes, the work there is growing, and it's marvelous in the Lord's sight. I met a group of Arab believers who were present on the Day of Pentecost when Peter preached. Our Lord had told them to tarry in Jerusalem to receive the promise of the Holy Spirit. The Arab believers received the promise!"

"Then why are you here? Is your work done there?"

"Our work is never done. I angered the King, and he sent me here with an escort of guards. The work continues there. But I'm concerned that the tide may soon turn, and it will not be safe for any of us."

"Come and sup with me. You must be hungry and tired."

"Yes, I am, indeed."

The next day, Ezra sent for Ananias and a few of the other believers. I recounted the story of my time in Arabia. Then they ministered to me, and we worshiped the One true God. I was refreshed. I prayed for the Lord's guidance. I knew I could not go to the synagogue. Instead, we met in the homes of believers. One day in prayer, I felt the prompting of the Spirit to pen a letter to Kasim and to address the believers in Arabia.

My salutation began as such, "Greetings Kasim, in the name of our Lord Jesus Christ. I pray all is well. Please give my regards to Simeon, Youssef, and Artemis. A day has not passed without a thought of you. I pray continually for the believers in Arabia. I made it to Damascus without incident. I'm unable to teach or preach in the synagogue. I meet with fellow believers here but have not been able to preach Jesus to the Gentiles like I would like. I'm beginning to believe the Lord would have me rest for my next assignment. I take comfort in knowing that I have a family of believers who care for me. And you, Kasim Ma'an, are like blood to me. We are blood-bought brothers in Jesus Christ, which is an even stronger bond than flesh. Your love for the Lord and care for fellow believers has not gone unnoticed by our Lord. May the God of our salvation continue to bless you and continue your legacy until his return."

A stray tear trailed down my face and into my beard. I truly missed my friends in Arabia. *Lord, keep them safe.*

I finished the letter with words of encouragement to the believers.

"I was blessed by the believers in Damascus and taught some of the words Jesus spoke to his disciples. I leave you with the words of our Lord to encourage you in your journey. 'Let not your heart be troubled. You believe in God, believe also in me.' Let us believe in the promise of our

Lord's return, so we will ever be ready to meet him."

I prayed for the opportune time to send the letters. The next Sabbath, God answered my prayer. A traveling merchant named Joseph, also a believer of the Way, stopped in Damascus for trade and for rest on his way to Arabia. I met and supped with him.

Joseph said, "The Lord came to me in a dream and told me that I was to take something of value to Arabia by way of Damascus."

"Praise be to our Lord Jesus! You were sent by our Lord to carry these words of encouragement to the believers in Arabia."

Joseph spent a Sabbath with us and then headed off to Arabia.

I gave him the customary kiss on each cheek and urged him, "Go with God, my brother, and ask for the merchant Kasim Ma'an. Someone will direct you from there."

"Thank you, Saul, for entrusting me with such a precious treasure. I will complete my assignment with the help of the Lord."

## ~ Kasim, Trouble on the Horizon ~

I was sitting by the sheep gate when Youssef came running toward the encampment.

"Kasim, Kasim!" he yelled. "We received word from Saul. Hurry, the letter is addressed to you."

"I will send a runner to get Simeon and Artemis. I believe Saul would want us all to be present," I replied.

Youssef and I sat and waited, each minute feeling like an unending stretch of time. We were about to break bread for supper when we saw two camels striding at high speed directly toward us.

"Simeon, Artemis, we thought you would never get here."

"It was nearly impossible for Artemis to break free from the court," Simeon explained.

Artemis interrupted, "I have some sad news, my brothers. There have been a number of complaints brought before the King from idol merchants and from those who are in competition with businesses owned by believers. They seek to have them banished from the market as a way of increasing their profits by extinguishing the competition. Some are lies. Some are not. The idol makers are truly losing business because many of the Gentile believers no longer patronize them."

"What does this all mean, Artemis?" asked Youssef.

"Has the King made any decrees yet?" I asked.

"No, but if temple offerings decline any further, the King will act swiftly."

"Let's read the letter, then we will pray," I said.

After reading Saul's letter, we sat in silence, each one navigating through the depth of shared emotions.

Finally, I said, "We will share this with the believers on the next Sabbath."

Sabbath had arrived, and Youssef and Artemis were the first to show.

With urgency, Artemis spoke. "Kasim, the King is holding court tomorrow to discuss the growing discontentment among the merchants concerning the believers. The merchants are saying they cannot afford to give the generous donations they once gave to the temple. I'm afraid of what this might mean for us."

"We must stop speaking the message of Jesus to new people for the time being," warned Youssef.

"Let's speak with the other believers and see what the consensus is concerning this matter," I replied.

We spread the word to as many of the believers as possible, on short notice. To my surprise, very few were missing. First order of business was to share the letter I received from Saul.

"Fellow believers, we have heard from Saul in a letter, and he is well."

Cheers erupted.

I continued, "He sends his greetings and encourages all believers with words spoken by our Lord Jesus, saying, 'Let not your heart be troubled. You believe in God, believe also in me.'"

The believers were smiling, patting each other on the back, and speaking words of encouragement.

I cleared my throat, "Second order of business: the King has taken notice of us. We must discuss what course of action to take."

The fear was palpable. I could feel it in the air. Everyone began speaking at once. I stood and raised my hand for silence, "Remember Saul's words from our Lord; do not let this trouble your heart. Our God will make a way of escape."

"What are you recommending we do, Kasim?" asked Youssef.

"We will continue to meet on the Sabbath, but we will not preach Jesus to any new people at this time unless they ask you a reason for the hope that is in you."

Everyone bowed their heads in agreement.

"Artemis will keep us updated on any new developments concerning the King."

### Kasim, The Persecution Begins

The time had drawn near, Artemis came to me by night to warn of the King's new decree, banning the worship of Jesus in his jurisdiction.

"The King was angered because the idol makers banded together to seek an audience at court today. I knew this would mean nothing but trouble for the believers," said Artemis.

*The persecution will now begin,* I thought.

Artemis continued, "They threatened to take their businesses elsewhere due to the steep decline in coinage and the low demand for the idols of their gods. The merchants instilled fear in the King's heart. They pronounced the gods are angry."

They told the King, "The gods will see justice served on all who do not seek retribution against those who oppose them."

I ran my hands through my gray-streaked hair and began to pray silently.

*Lord, what would you have us to do?*

*Go to Egypt.*

"Artemis, did you just say something?"

"No Kasim. When I saw you praying, I too began to pray."

"I believe the Lord just spoke to me, and I must obey, but it will be hard on the others."

"What did the Lord say?"

"Go to Egypt."

"Egypt?"

"Yes, it's the most logical course of action. I have many contacts there from my merchant trips. I even have a few distant relatives."

"This will be hard on those whose livelihood and families dwell here."

"Yes, but we will move in stages by clan. I'm sure some will stay, and those who do can watch over the encampment."

"Kasim, those who stay will have to silence their faith until something changes."

"We will call all the heads of the clans, as well as the leaders of the Jewish and Gentile believers, and decide how to proceed."

When everyone had gathered at the caves, I told them about all that had transpired.

"Brother Kasim, we cannot leave our livelihood," voiced one merchant.

"Do you not fear persecution?" I asked.

"I fear no man," responded another. "As long as I do not openly speak of my faith, I believe it will be safe enough."

"For some, this may be true, but for others, the idol makers have pointed you out to the King because they want to sabotage your businesses. Would it not be wiser to set up trade in Egypt for now?" I asked.

The meeting went on for hours. We prayed, we reasoned, we argued, and then prayed some more. Some were adamant about staying, while others were plagued with indecision. So we cast lots.

"Those who are staying, you must continue to meet undercover and care for one another. It is the way of Jesus. Some will continue to prosper, but others will fall into hard times, and we must support one another," I said.

Simeon spoke up and pledged, "We will do as you say, Kasim."

Simeon had decided to stay. He and Artemis had developed a bond, a kinship. Artemis would protect him to the best of his ability. Besides, all the locals loved Ann's food, and most knew them as Jews from Jerusalem, not believers of the Way. At least not yet.

Once again, Artemis arrived by camel to the camp, brows furrowed. He spoke without preamble, "Kasim, you must leave at once! The King is now talking about jailing some of the believers who are merchants. Who knows what will happen next? He may even begin to confiscate property."

"Why the change in policy?"

"Now that some of the believers have departed, the city's economy is being affected. Whoever else is to leave must leave now."

"There are only four families left. They can leave with me. I will lead them to Egypt by the end of the week."

"Kasim, what will you do with Saul's letters?"

"I will take them to Egypt. The letters must be preserved for future generations, so their faith will remain strong, so our faith will remain an unbroken legacy for centuries to come."

"How will you preserve them?"

"The Egyptians are knowledgeable in the way of preservation. Not only mummification but also parchments and papyrus. I have merchant friends in Egypt who will know where to direct me. For a good price, that is."

"That is the way of business, Kasim."

"Yes, and Saul taught us that the laborer is worthy of his hire."

"I miss our brother Saul."

"Me too, Artemis, me too."

### ~ Kasim, Flight to Egypt ~

I thought we would never make it to Egypt. At the last minute, we had three Gentile families and two families of Bedouin chiefs join us. The chiefs had packed up their families and entrusted them into my care. The burden was wearing on me. Then, I thought about the burdens of those who had been left behind, and shame washed over me. I was glad Youssef decided to journey with me to help care for the believers in Egypt. He said he would return to Arabia once we settled. I prayed it would not be anytime soon.

Youssef came alongside my camel and pointed into the horizon.

"We are almost there, Kasim. The city is now within our range of vision."

As the sun beat down hard on our caravan, we were ready to settle into whatever life the Lord had prepared for us. The day before we left Arabia, I had received word from one of the Bedouin chiefs that all was well in Egypt. He informed me that he had found an old merchant friend of mine who agreed to prepare Saul's letters for preservation. Saul wrote on parchments, and we had received several more letters before leaving. In return, I wrote to Saul about the persecution and our sudden flight to Egypt.

We arrived without incident. Our only foe was the iron fist of the sun and the desert sand that made its home in our personal possessions.

## Trouble in Arabia

As soon as we settled with our kin, I went straight to see Jabari.

"Jabari, my friend, it's been a long time. All is well?"

"Yes, Kasim. I heard of your plight and prayed to the gods for your safe arrival."

"Jabari, you know I serve the One true God, Jesus the Christ."

"Yes, yes, my friend. At least here, you don't have to worry about being run out of town."

"Can you help me preserve these letters?"

Jabari inspected the parchment and nodded knowingly.

"Yes, of course. I have learned some new techniques, the ones they use for the documents at the Great Alexandrian Library. I will preserve them using beeswax and combine the letters into scrolls."

"Excellent! When can you get started?"

"For you Kasim, I'll begin tomorrow."

"And the cost?"

"That, my friend, is our dilemma. It is costly."

"I understand. I'm prepared to trade and barter."

"I'm sure you are. You've always been a shrewd merchant but fair in all your dealings. You will have your letters completed within the week."

# Chapter 26

# Tirsa's Truth

*~ Tirsa, The Set Up ~*

I ran home and began to pack my bags. I had already purchased a ticket to the States—leaving the next evening. I have connections there and can start over. I will create a new identity. The Ma'an family may have disowned me, but I've gained enough wealth from the family business to sustain me for quite some time. They forget how much I know. They forget how dangerous I can be.

*How dare they scorn me,* I thought.

I could wreak havoc. I could sell their trade secrets. Worse yet, I could report them to the King of Jordan.

*I'm not looking to do too much damage,* I sighed inwardly—feeling a pang of regret.

I might need their help somewhere down the line. Instead, I'll be like a hornet. I'll leave a sting that'll cause them to think twice before crossing me again.

The next morning, I went to the embassy to see my old flame, Samir, to ask a favor. Samir had been my lover for a season. No one knew. It was not the proper thing to do for a young Christian or Muslim woman. But we all have our vices. As I grabbed my keys, I looked up and saw my mother's picture hanging on the wall, her eyes peering into my soul.

A single tear trailed down my cheek. I couldn't help but think how disappointed she would be.

I collapsed in the chair, and the tears came unbidden, "Mama, I'm so sorry. Why did you have to die and leave me all alone?"

When I finally arrived at the embassy, I sat in the car for a moment to gather my wits and think over my plan. Then it hit me. I slipped on my hijab and walked into the embassy with renewed resolve.

"I'm here to see Samir. Please tell him it's Tirsa. He will know who I am."

The woman nodded and went behind a partition and through a large door. Within five minutes, the debonair Samir walked out. He was tall, dark, and handsome, with a short beard cropped to his jawline. He had the looks of a professional model, with his silk suit and designer shoes. A fire rekindled in me, and I thought back to our six-month tryst. As handsome as Samir was, he was not Kasim. Kasim outshone him in every way, from his handsome features to his charm to his intelligence and his respect for women, which Samir seemed to lack.

I sighed because I had lost something of great value.

*No, he was stolen from me by that American woman, Issa Stevens!* I raged inwardly.

I composed myself in time to greet my former lover.

"Samir," I purred in my most alluring voice as I trailed my index finger down his face.

"It's been quite some time, Tirsa. What brings you here?"

"I've missed you, dearest."

"Remember, it was you who walked away from me."

"Yes, and I regret every minute of it. I was pressured by my family to hold fast to our traditions."

"I respect that. I even applauded you for it. I would've taken you as my wife."

"You mean second wife? Anyway, my family had intended to betroth me to a distant cousin."

"And how did that turn out for you?"

"He married another woman."

"I'm sorry to hear this. It's truly his loss."

"I need you to go along with a story I've fabricated to bring a little humility to my cousin, Kasim. He was my intended betrothed."

"Oh, I had not heard this news."

"No, you would not have. The Ma'an family are very private people."

"Well, Tirsa, I'm not in the business of ruffling the feathers of the elite businessmen of Jordan."

"I know, but even you will get a kick out of watching Kasim squirm."

"What is it that you want me to do?"

"Tousle the peacock's plumage a bit. Tell him you've heard rumors that he is an infidel. And that you will need to investigate reports that he has conspired with Christians to draw our people away from the faith."

Samir drew in a sharp breath. For a moment, I thought I had gone too far. Then, a smile crept across his handsome face.

"I would be delighted to see a Ma'an squirm a little. But I will only allow this ruse to go so far. I'm sure you're aware that our neighboring countries are considering forbidding Christian worship in public places. This could prove dangerous."

"Let's just keep this little ruse between you and me. No one else has to know."

Samir's eyebrows knit tightly together. I didn't want him to second-guess his decision, so I leaned in and kissed him on the cheek, close to his lips.

He smiled. I hugged him and whispered, "Thank you, Samir. Thank you so much!"

### ~ Kasim, What is Tirsa Up to? ~

My phone rang. The caller ID showed the number of one of my personal guards.

"Kasim, Tirsa was seen entering the embassy, and she asked to meet with Samir. I arrived within ten minutes of the call. I waited until she left and followed her home. I've posted a guard there, and instructed him to follow her if she leaves again."

"Thank you. You've done well. Let me know immediately if she leaves."

*What is Tirsa up to?* I wondered.

### ~ Tirsa, I'm Being Followed ~

I noticed a familiar-looking man following me from the embassy. I made a right turn, then a left, and walked faster, but I couldn't shake him. *I wonder if this is one of Kasim's men?* I decided to go straight home. I'll have to think of a way to shake him so I won't be followed to the airport.

I arrived home and finished packing.

"Darn!"

I realized there were some items I needed to pick up for my trip.

A smile spread across my face. *Tirsa, you are smarter than you give yourself credit for.*

I devised a plan to shake the spy while shopping for the items I needed. I stuffed a change of clothes in a bag containing a hat, sunglasses, t-shirt, and jeans with holes in the pant legs.

*No one will think it is me in this attire.*

As planned, at the last stop, I changed clothes and slipped out unnoticed. Or, so I thought. I looked over my shoulder and saw the same man who was at the embassy spying on me. I immediately diverted my course and headed toward the mountains.

*This guy just won't give up.*

I found myself at the same mountain where I held Issa hostage. I knew these mountains. I ran up an embankment and disappeared around a bend in the passageway. I could hear footsteps behind me, but I saw no one. My bag dropped, and I didn't think it wise to retrieve it at the moment. The footsteps were getting closer. My heart rate accelerated, and I was running out of breath. The terrain was getting more difficult to maneuver, and I found myself slipping. Next, I heard a man call my name.

"Tirsa, stop. It's too dangerous on this mountain. You're going to injure yourself."

I turned around briefly and was caught off guard by the endearing nature of the voice. Suddenly, my foot gave way, and I slipped. I rolled down the rocky mountainside into the embankment. I screamed as I felt a searing pain shoot through my body. I hit my head on a large rock, then there was…nothingness.

*~ Kasim, Tirsa's Demise ~*

Over coffee, I was talking with Father and Fasim when my guard returned with a grave look on his face.

"What has happened?" I asked.

"Kasim, when I called Tirsa's name, I saw her falter as she looked back. She slipped and struggled to balance herself. I lurched forward to take hold of her arm when suddenly the rocks gave way, and she fell down the embankment. I went looking for her to see if she was injured. I searched but couldn't find the body. There's no way she could've survived the fall. I'm sorry."

Fasim fell to his knees, wailing, and tore his upper garment in two.

"I'm sorry, Uncle. I will have my men go and search the mountains again."

"It's no one's fault but my own. I should've done a better job guiding her after her mother passed."

Father comforted Fasim. "If we're unable to find her alive or recover the body, we will do the customary mourning and give our family the closure they need. She was one of our own."

I left to tell Issa what happened.

"Habibti, we didn't find the body. We looked for hours until the sunset. We found a bag of clothes she dropped while trying to escape, but there was no body. Perhaps the wild dogs dragged her away."

Issa wept in my arms.

"I didn't want any harm to come to the poor girl," she said.

"It's an unfortunate thing that happened, but she was up to no good. She was seen at the embassy visiting with Samir, the emissary. That could only mean one thing: she's revealed the secret of our heritage."

"Kasim, that means we must work even harder to find the scrolls. I need to get back to work."

"I don't want to jump to conclusions, but I fear you may be right."

# CHAPTER 27

## RETURN TO ARABIA

*- Kasim, The Lord's Leading -*

I had been in Egypt for nine months when I received word from Artemis to return to Arabia. While the danger had diminished in Petra, King Aretas still harassed Saul. Artemis received a letter from Saul recounting the story of his narrow escape from Damascus. The governor of the city had received orders from the King to kill Saul.

"Kasim, are you sure it's safe enough to return?" Youssef's voice sounded strained. "If they are still harassing Saul, what makes you think they won't do the same to us?"

"If that were the case, they would've done the same to our Bedouin kin, who remained in Petra. Neither Simeon nor Anna have encountered any problems."

"I suppose the merchants were happy when their competition left. But what did Saul do to awaken the King's ire in Damascus?"

"Oh, I'm quite sure it had something to do with preaching Jesus."

"I can see him now," Youssef chuckled.

"Saul is one of a kind. I sure do miss him."

"I miss him too, Kasim, and I miss home."

I was glad to be going home. The Bedouin families who left with us for Egypt were also returning. The Gentile believers remained, and my heart was glad. It brought strength to the believers there. Already, many Gentiles had been added to their number since our arrival. As I pondered this, I wondered how the believers in Petra were faring.

"Kasim, we're almost home. We should see the city as soon as we round this gorge," said Youssef.

"These narrow sandstone walls show the strength and magnificence of our God. The colors alone are majestic," I said.

Youssef replied, with a sense of awe in his voice, "These magnificent stones are the Lord's handiwork—the very fingerprint of our God."

I interrupted our wonderment as we exited the Siq and headed toward camp. "There, look, our village is ahead. I see someone at the edge of camp."

"Artemis!"

"Kasim, my brother!"

We embraced and exchanged the customary greeting.

"I received your letter and had anticipated your arrival," said Artemis.

"So the King's attention has been diverted elsewhere?" I asked.

"For the time being. He's been preoccupied, brooding as of late, over his daughter Phasaelis's divorce from Herod Antipas. He's deciding what course of action to take if Rome interferes," replied Artemis.

"And what of Saul?"

"The believers helped him escape through a window in the city wall. Once again, they lowered him down in a basket to flee death's grip. He's now in Jerusalem, meeting with the Lord's disciples. He will send another letter to inform us of his journey. There's so much to tell you, Kasim."

"Let's have a meal, and you can tell me all about it."

The women cleansed the dust from our feet and served us refreshments before preparing the meal.

"Artemis, I have brought the letters back to Petra. I think they should remain here with our people," I said.

"They are preserved?"

"Yes, preserved like the parchments in Alexandria's Great Library. I have hidden them in an amphora I brought back from Egypt."

"Do you think it's wise to keep them here?"

"You told me the King's attention was diverted."

"Yes, but for how long, I don't know."

"We will keep them in the amphora and bury them deep in the earth in one of the caves near my business in the city."

"Why there?"

"Because if the King were to look for the letters, the first place he would look is my home, then my shop in the marketplace. No one knows that several of the caves are annexed to my land. My Bedouin ancestors rightfully owned the land and used the caves as burial tombs before King Aretas came to power. It's recorded in the King's records, but I doubt he troubles himself about those minute details."

"He'll know when he decides to build some new majestic structure where those caves are," said Artemis.

"We will not borrow tomorrow's troubles today, my friend."

Youssef and Artemis exchanged weary glances and then looked at me with arched eyebrows.

"Well, do either of you have a better idea?"

"No," Youssef and Artemis shrugged their shoulders.

"Our King is superstitious. I don't think he will want to touch that area once he knows they are burial grounds," I said.

We all agreed that I would be the one to bury the letters. I didn't want Youssef or Artemis to have to lie to the King if interrogated about their whereabouts. How the King knew Saul had written to us, I do not know. Perhaps his network of spies? Well, it didn't matter. If the King were to torture anyone, I'd rather it be me. I'll never give up the location of the scrolls. These are precious letters that hold the penned words of Saul and tell of our faith in Jesus Christ.

The following day, I inspected the caves and found one carved deep into the rock face, just a short distance from the shop. I walked along the rock and caressed it with my hand. The rock structures were like God smiling at his creation in a colorful array of visual splendor. When I entered the cave, I was astounded by what I saw. There were intricate tunnel-like spaces. Natural light beamed in during the day. Deeper in the structure, there were dry places.

I said to myself, *These enclosures make good shelter. No wonder my Bedouin kin prefer the caves.*

A dark, dry area in the far corner caught my eye. I opened the cloth that held the tools I would need to dig a deep enough ditch to bury the amphora. The dirt appeared to be hard soil. I prayed that it was not rock. I hit the ground several times, but it would not give way. I repeated the process throughout the cave, but the whole surface appeared to be rock.

I fell on my face in frustration and began to pray.

"My Lord and my God, you are the Creator of this mountain. Please lead me to the place where the words of your servant Saul can safely reside—within the belly of your creation."

Immediately, I noticed another tunnel-like structure that I had not seen before. I ran toward it with tools in hand and began to strike the ground.

"Thank you, Jesus, thank you!" The dirt was soft.

I raised my head and caught a ray of sunlight beaming through a crevice in the rock. It caressed my face, and I felt the kiss of God on my cheek. I smiled, and the joy of the Lord filled me—renewing my strength.

I advanced farther back into the tunnel to find a dry area and began to dig. It was almost sundown before I finished, but the work was completed. The Lord had accomplished his purpose and allowed his creation to protect the scrolls that contained words of life and the legacy of my family. One day, when the time was right, the Lord would allow the earth to surrender its treasures once again to accomplish his purposes.

I walked back to the encampment in awestruck wonder. I allowed my feet to direct my path.

Simeon had deep lines of concern etched onto his brow. "There you are, Kasim. We were all beginning to worry about you."

"You have an ethereal glow upon your face," said Youssef.

I held my cheek with great reverence. "I've been kissed by God."

I looked around at all the believers who had gathered. They made this day a sacred day. We sat and broke bread together. We recounted the stories of Pentecost and of our time with Saul. The Holy Spirit prompted me to start an oral tradition that is to be told throughout the generations. They would include the stories of Jesus, our time with Saul, and how we lived out our faith during trials and times of celebration.

# CHAPTER 28

## EXCAVATION PARADOX

*- Issa, The Dreaded Tunnel -*

I was finally feeling well enough to resume the evening meals with my family. My strength and energy had returned, and I was ready to get back to work. Dr. Bashar gave me a good bill of health, but Kasim wasn't so sure.

"Issa," he said. "You need to get your rest and focus on taking care of yourself and our baby."

*Well, when he put it that way, how was I to argue?*

Akhab had joined us for the meal, and Kasim was recounting the gravity of our situation.

"I received disturbing news from the emissary Samir. The report stated that we're being investigated for possible illegal activity. Samir did not elaborate exactly what he meant by that statement."

I leaned over and whispered to Akhab. "Have you sealed the tunnel yet?"

"No, we decided to wait. We didn't want to cause any more movement or shifting of the rocks."

"How safe do you think it is to return?" I asked.

"It's hard to tell, Dr. Issa."

"Can you at least see if it's safe to remove the debris?"

"I'm not sure if that's a good idea."

"Akhab, I saw what looked like a piece of cloth, or leather scroll, and fragments of pottery that could be the amphorae used to hide and help preserve the scrolls. The pouch carrying a few of the pottery pieces dislodged from around my neck when I was pulled from the tunnel. We must recover the evidence before the Department of Antiquities comes to shut our work down. You know it's only a matter of time."

"Dr. Issa, I will be at the site tomorrow and will perform a safety check. I will inform you of my findings."

For now, I had to be satisfied with that answer.

Akhab returned early the next evening. During our meal, he reported, "The shifted rocks have finally stabilized. It should be safe enough to send a special team to retrieve the items Dr. Issa saw in the tunnel."

"Akhab, it's still too dangerous."

"Kasim, we are out of options. We must find something of value to show the government when they come knocking on our door."

"None of our men can fit through the tunnel," replied Kasim.

Raising my hand, I volunteered, "I can!"

"No, you cannot, under any circumstances!"

"Kasim, be reasonable."

"Issa, this discussion is closed! Think of our baby."

I dropped my head in my hands. *But there's no other way.*

At that moment, we were interrupted by the steward of the house who uttered the dreaded words.

"The chief emissary Samir is here to speak with you, Kasim."

Kasim and his father immediately rose and left the room.

I whispered to Akhab, "You must get me to the cave and allow me to excavate the tunnel. This is a matter of life or death either way."

Akhab scrubbed his face, and his forehead wrinkled in deep thought.

"I cannot do what you ask. Kasim will never forgive me if something were to happen to you. I would never forgive myself."

I pleaded with Akhab. "Without the scrolls, we're all doomed anyway."

Akhab considered my words, "What I can do is give you the resources you need to accomplish your goal. I will appear at the site as normal and ensure all goes well. But Fasar will be the one to navigate the tunnels, Dr. Issa. He's small enough. If Fasar encounters problems, then I might consider allowing you near the tunnel."

"Yes, thank you Akhab. All will be well! I've been praying, and all will be well."

"I hope you are right. For all of our sake."

Kasim and Fakmad returned from speaking with Samir.

"Kasim, what did the emissary say?" I asked.

He raked his fingers through his hair.

"They are calling us infidels and want to charge us with fraudulent business practices."

"They have no proof for any of it!" yelled Fakmad.

"Someone has told him we are conspiring with Christians to bring shame upon our nation. They were told we are trying to cause an uprising and overthrow the government." Kasim rubbed his forehead in exasperation.

"Tirsa!" We all exclaimed.

"My guard followed her to the embassy, and he saw her conversing with Samir."

Fasim issued a guttural scream.

"No, Tirsa, what have you done?"

I thought I saw a smirk cross Fasim's face.

"Papa, what are you going to do?" asked Miri.

"I will try to stall them as long as I can. I think Samir is going too far with his accusations."

"What do you mean, Son?" asked Fakmad.

"If there was any evidence that we were trying to overthrow our government, we would all be in the torture chambers right now."

"You have a good point," Fakmad agreed.

"Nonetheless, we must proceed with caution."

*What a nightmare*, I thought.

Kasim called for a meeting of the Bedouin clans and the leaders among the Jewish and Gentile believers. The meeting was to take place at first light.

I informed Akhab. "We will restart the excavation immediately after Kasim leaves for his meeting in the morning."

It proved difficult to keep anything from Sky and Miri. Akhab had already filled Fasar in on the upcoming adventure, and he was finding it difficult to contain his exuberance. No one wanted to be left out.

The next morning, I rendezvoused with my rogue band of family members.

"I would prefer that none of you be involved in this scheme of ours. Kasim is going to be hurt by the deception, and I don't want his wrath to fall on any of you," I said.

"Mom, I'm in. I won't allow you to do this by yourself."

"Me too, Issa. I know Papa will be hurt, but that's only because he doesn't want any harm to come to you."

"That's where I come in," said Fasar. "I'll be the one to go through the tunnels."

Akhab interrupted, "This time, we will add extra length to the rope.

Fasar will also have a camera on his helmet so we can see everything that is going on. I will take full responsibility. But Dr. Issa, you must remain away from the tunnel. You can view everything from the screen in the observation room. Fasar will have a mic so you can instruct him."

"Thank you Akhab, now let's go do this. We have some scrolls to find!"

As we were leaving for the excavation site, Kasim's car pulled up. I expected him to be furious at us.

Instead, he looked at Akhab, "We need to push our timetable forward."

"I'm on it! I've enlisted Fasar's help."

"Uncle, I will not let our family down," Fasar promised.

"Miri and Sky are my runners and recorders," said Akhab. "Dr. Issa can watch from the observation room via our live stream feed and assist when needed if that's acceptable?"

Kasim looked at me with such intensity that it felt like he was boring into the depths of my soul.

"Issa," he said.

His phone rang. He listened intently, then hung up without saying a word. He looked at Akhab and me, his face pinched, and said, "I will meet you at the dig site within the hour." Then, he turned on his heels and left.

"Akhab, did you tell Kasim?"

"No, Dr. Issa."

"Well, he reads us like a book. He acted as if he knew what we were up to."

"I would prefer that, anyway." Akhab's face showed a hint of relief.

We arrived at the excavation headquarters site in Petra in record time—the one located at the base of the mountain. Once underground, we gathered at the mouth of the tunnel and joined hands. I volunteered to lead us in prayer.

"Lord, you are the Creator of Heaven and Earth. You are the God of this mountain. Still, it is on our behalf. Cause it to open its jaws and spew forth the treasures it holds. Lord Jesus, you are the God of the Ma'an family. They have continued steadfast in their faith for nearly two millennia—creating an unbroken legacy. A legacy that has caused many to come to faith. Go before us on this day and prepare our hearts and minds to receive wisdom and instruction. Help us find the lost letters of Saul as a testimony of who you are and find the proof we need to exonerate our family. In Jesus's name, Amen!"

Akhab and his crew readied Fasar for the crawl. Fasar was thin and limber and moved dexterously, making him perfect for the job. He was eager to help and to prove his worth to his family. Fasar was deep in the tunnel when we started to experience interference with the camera that was attached to his helmet.

"Fasar, can you adjust your camera? All we can see are rocks, and the feed is going in and out," I said.

"Dr. Stevens, this is going to take longer than we anticipated. What you are seeing are rocks that have blocked the path. I think I can clear them, but it will take some time."

"Okay, Fasar, be careful."

One hour later, Fasar came back on the radio. "Dr. Stevens, I have cleared the rocks and adjusted the camera. Can you see ahead?"

"Yes, proceed with caution."

Thank God Kasim recommended that we attach a small oxygen container to Fasar's gear. This was taking too long, and I feared he would lose oxygen. Despite my fears, Fasar had made considerable progress. The rope attached to his waist would've given way by now if we had not lengthened it, which meant he was close to the artifacts.

"Fasar, you should be approaching the location where I saw the cloth," I said.

"Dr. Stevens, I don't see anything that resembles a cloth."

"Do you see any pottery shards or my pouch?"

"Wait a second. I'm going to add another light source."

"Dr. Stevens…"

"Fasar, can you hear me, repeat your last words."

There was no answer, and the video feed appeared like snow on the monitor. I ran from the office to the tunnel with Sky on my heels.

"What's going on, Akhab?"

"There must be some kind of natural electromagnetic radiation interference."

"Issa!" I turned around and stared into the angry eyes of my husband.

"What are you doing here? You're supposed to be in the observation room."

"I was there the whole time until we lost contact with Fasar."

"Is Fasar going to be okay?" asked Sky.

Akhab interrupted, "We need to get Fasar out of the tunnel. If his communication disruptions are due to electromagnetic radiation interference, there may be significant stress in the rocks, and the tunnel could collapse entirely."

"Issa, Miri, Sky, get to the surface immediately!" yelled Kasim.

Then he turned to Akhab frantically. "We need to get Fasar out of there, now!"

As the elevator door opened, I heard static coming from the radio. I looked over my shoulder.

Kasim glanced in my direction. He gave me a warning look that said, "I dare you to come this way."

"Dr. Stevens, K…"

Fasar's voice trailed off, and the ground began to rumble. Miri and Sky pulled me into the elevator, and we made it to the surface in time as the elevator swayed and the electricity flickered on and off. Bolting through the door, we felt the ground swaying beneath our feet—a telltale sign of an earthquake. There was a sudden jolt that sent ripples of movement through the ground, knocking us off our feet.

Sky was shaking her head on the verge of tears. "Mom, what's going to happen to Fasar?"

"Kasim!" I yelled before attempting to grasp for Sky—my hands trembling uncontrollably. I clasped my hands instead and said, "I have to go back and help them."

Miri crawled to where I had been knocked down and embraced me.

"Issa, we cannot go after them. We must pray instead."

Then her eyes roamed to my stomach, where I was instinctively cradling the baby that lay within my womb.

Miri was right, "Yes, let's pray!"

### ~ Kasim, Race for Time ~

"We have little time. Akhab, help me pull the rope! We've got to get Fasar out of there!"

The rocks were tumbling in every direction.

"Kasim, this is more than rock stress. This is an earthquake!"

"Pull, pull! I think Fasar may have lost consciousness. It feels like we're pulling dead weight."

"We don't have much time," shouted Akhab.

"Keep pulling!" I bellowed.

"Kasim, the tunnel is collapsing!"

I threw up a quick prayer, "Lord, save us all."

"One more pull, Kasim."

"Akhab he's stuck, I have to crawl in there and free him. You leave now!"

"I will not leave you!"

I crawled in the tunnel with painstakingly slow movements due to my size. When I finally reached Fasar, I noticed his jumper was caught on a jagged rock. I tried reaching for my pocket knife, but the space was too restrictive. I tried rolling to the side to extend my arm downward, but there wasn't enough room. I heard Akhab yelling my name.

"Kasim, we've gotta get out of here, or we'll all be buried alive!"

An idea came to me. I grabbed a rock and used its jagged edge like a knife and sawed at the fabric until it cut in half. The earth rumbled again, sending a landslide of rocks.

"Akhab, pull now!" I yelled.

I crawled out backwards as Akhab pulled Fasar forward.

"There, Kasim, we've got him! I'll carry him. You go ahead and clear the way."

I ran, and Akhab followed.

"The stairs are cut off!" I yelled. "We have to go through the back tunnels. They should exit on the other side of the mountain."

"Won't the rocks cut us off there too?"

"No, those rocks are sturdy and have passed the test of time."

Running and pointing, I called out, "There, over there, I see light."

"Do you hear that Kasim? I hear voices."

"Kasim, Akhab!"

"Papa!" yelled Miri.

"Fasar!" yelled Sky.

"Follow the voices. I think it's Issa, Miri, and Sky."

We ran toward the cacophony of voices and the light, which now peeked through the rocks.

"Issa, here we are!"

"Kasim, over here. Are you okay? I'm sending your men to help you."

Climbing the rocks, I responded, "Issa, we need the doctor for Fasar. Send one of my guards quickly."

Akhab exited with Fasar and gently laid him on the ground.

Sky knelt next to him. She put her forehead on his chest and wept. Fasar's hand began to flutter.

"Look, he's moving his hand," Sky said.

Then Fasar turned his head and, with a dry, parched voice, mumbled, "Water, I need water."

Sky gently held his head and poured water into the side of his mouth. Fasar choked, then said, "More, please."

"I thought I lost you." Sky reprimanded him with tears in her eyes.

"Never. I had an assignment to complete. Where's Dr. Stevens?"

"I'm right here."

Fasar reached into his vest, pulled out a large crumpled leather-like cloth, and handed it to me. I noticed he also had my pouch around his neck.

"Fasar, is this what I think it is?"

He nodded.

### - Issa, The Discovery -

I carefully peeked at the contents inside the leather-like cloth and found what looked like scrolls.

Leaning back on my heels in complete awe, I called out, "Kasim."

"I'm looking at it, Issa. It's a miracle."

Everyone cheered and hugged each other with excitement. Kasim went around personally thanking everyone. Then he sat on a rock with his head buried in his hands. The sheer joy of finding a piece of history, the words penned by the Apostle Paul to Kasim's ancestors, was overwhelming.

Kasim finally stood. He grabbed me by the waist, swept me into his arms, and kissed me fervently. His men found it entertaining, for they all cheered and whistled. Kasim smiled broadly. I felt the heat rise in my cheeks and sought refuge by burying my face in the curve of his neck.

"You smell good."

"And you, my love, taste like the dust of the earth," Kasim chuckled. "I must get you home and to the baths."

"I could take offense to that, my dear husband."

"Well, I thought it would be rather romantic if I joined you to remove said dirt."

At that declaration, I blushed deeply. I imagined my face must have turned three shades of red. Kasim tapped me on the nose and quickly amended his statement.

"It'll be like summer camp. Remember after the dig when we found the dinosaur bones? We were so dusty and dirty we didn't even bother to change into our swimsuits. We dived headlong into the river, trousers and all."

"How could I forget? We had latrine duties for the remainder of the week!"

## CHAPTER 29

# EPILOGUE

*~ Issa, The Scroll & The Legacy ~*

The earthquake had subsided, but my inward parts were still shaking. I was a tangled ball of yarn, equally horrified at the events that had taken place and in awe of the treasure we found beneath the earth. Kasim caught my attention as he carefully held up the scroll, admiring it.

"Habibti, you know we must do all the appropriate testing before we commence with a full-on celebration," he said.

"Yes, I know. We also must follow the necessary protocols to preserve each of the artifacts we found."

Kasim gently placed the document in my hand. The outer covering was a leather-like cloth, probably used to protect its inner contents. I slowly removed a small portion of the outer covering and peeked inside. What I saw left me mesmerized. I quickly sealed it to avoid exposure to light and moisture.

Later, we met for dinner. Everyone was present except for Fasar. He was still recovering from the accident. Akhab joined us as usual. We recounted the events of the day and gave thanks to God for his abundant grace and mercy. Fakmad turned to me and asked about the details of the scroll.

"It's a letter written on parchment, and it's written in Hebrew."

"What does it say?" asked Fasim.

"There are two areas on the document that have faded. I will read what I can."

Kasim excused himself to retrieve the scroll. I informed everyone that we should not handle the document much until it has been properly preserved.

When Kasim returned, he nodded in my direction. I followed him to a corner of the room, and he handed me a special fluorescent light with ultraviolet filters. I smiled knowingly and went to dim the lights. I began to read from the scroll.

"Greetings Kasim, in the name of our Lord Jesus Christ. I pray all is well. Please give my regards to Simeon, Youssef, and Artemis. A day has not passed without a thought of you and prayer for the believers in Arabia. I made it to Damascus without incident. I am unable to teach or preach in the synagogue...I am beginning to believe the Lord would have me to rest...And you, Kasim Ma'an, are like blood to me. We are blood-bought brothers in Jesus Christ, which is an even stronger bond than flesh. Your love for the Lord and care for fellow believers has not gone unnoticed by our Lord. May the God of our salvation continue to bless you and continue your legacy until his return."

"What a glorious day!" Fakmad shouted as he chewed on a piece of succulent beef.

Miri and I had tears rolling down our cheeks.

Sky interrupted the moment. "Does anyone know how Fasar is doing?"

"He's recovering nicely," replied Kasim.

Miri was shaking her head as she reassured Sky. "If it were up to him, he would be at the dinner table right now—sitting across from you."

We all laughed. We owed so much to Fasar. Maybe I underestimated him. Kasim and I looked at each other and smiled.

I looked at Akhab and asked, "How is the testing going?"

# Epilogue

He looked at Kasim, and Kasim nodded.

"Dr. Issa, we are ninety percent sure the letters are from the Apostle Paul. We await your and Dr. Ibrahim's inspection and testing. He has signed all the necessary non-disclosures."

"Issa, I know Dr. Ibrahim is a family friend from childhood and a renowned archeologist in his own right. But he is Muslim." Kasim looked genuinely concerned. "Are you sure you want to proceed?"

"Yes, I trust him with my life. Besides, his endorsement will strengthen our findings among scholars in the Arab world."

Akhab interrupted the awkward moment.

"Kasim, the letters, along with the pottery shards, should be enough to confirm your unbroken legacy."

"And exonerate our family from the fake charges filed against us," said Fakmad.

Miri chimed in. "I pray so."

"Fasar has done much for our family today. As the rocks were cascading down and he was being dragged out of the tunnel, Fasar managed to grab Issa's lost pouch, which contained the pottery shards," said Kasim.

"The critics will have a harder time disputing our findings with the shards from the amphora to corroborate the scrolls," I added.

The steward entered the dining room and whispered in Kasim's ear. Kasim nodded and promptly rose to leave.

"Kasim, is everything okay?" My heart skipped a beat.

"Yes, Issa, do not be overly concerned. I will return shortly."

We were all left with a perplexed look on our faces.

Kasim returned fifteen minutes later with a blank look. He left us sitting on the edge of our seats, waiting for an explanation. Finally, he blew out his breath, and a slow smile crept on his face.

"It appears we do not have to reveal our heritage quite yet."

Everyone began talking at once. Kasim held up his hand and spoke again.

"Samir, the emissary from the embassy, came to apologize. After his thorough investigation, he concluded the information given was false. He thought someone might be seeking to gain a business advantage over our family by smearing our good name."

Fakmad waved his hands and thanked God. "That's excellent news!"

"God be praised!" Miri shouted.

"When do we go public with our findings?" I asked.

Kasim took a deep breath and exhaled. "Since Samir's investigation is now closed, we no longer have to act in haste. For now, we will preserve the scrolls and the pottery shards. I intend to have them secured with the other artifacts here at the estate until the time comes to reveal them. I'm sure the Lord will give us the wisdom we need to make the right decision."

We all nodded in agreement.

At that precise moment, I said, "I think the baby agrees with us too. I just felt him kick."

~ *Issa, Continuing the Legacy* ~

Kasim and I returned to our room and fell onto the bed.

"How do you know it's a boy, Issa?"

"I just know. I believe the Spirit has revealed it to me."

Kasim leaned in, kissed me on the neck, and comforted me with his next words.

"I will accept whatever the Lord blesses me with."

"Kasim, I think it's time to name the baby. I thought he should have your namesake. That is, if he's a boy?"

## Epilogue

"Well, Issa, I used the data you provided me from your maternal family tree, along with the DNA sample we provided to Dr. Bashar, and was able to trace your lineage back to ancient Israel."

I shot up straight, "You used the same DNA testing method we use in the field?"

"Yes, with an accuracy rate of ninety-nine percent, when performed by a reputable geneticist. I thought to name our baby after one of your ancestors to honor your Jewish heritage."

I teared up at the thoughtfulness of my husband. I wondered to whom I could possibly be related to in ancient Israel.

"And who might that be, Kasim?"

"Issa, you are a descendant of King David from the tribe of Judah."

My mouth dropped open, and it took me a moment to recover.

"What did you say?"

"The Lord revealed to me in a dream that the baby will be a boy. I would like to name our son David, after his ancestor King David."

I was at a loss for words, and could only wonder what the Lord was up to, and what adventure he had in store for us next.

# Acknowledgments

First and foremost, I give thanks to my Lord and Savior Jesus Christ. "And whatever you do in word or deed, do all in the name of the Lord Jesus, giving thanks to God the Father through Him." Colossians 3:17

Thank you to my husband Charles, you are my gift from God. Thank you to my children, Charles Jr, Daniel, Leah, Chelsea, and Dee for encouraging me to pursue my passion. Thank you to my grandchildren Isabella, Aria, Charles III, and Zina, you light up my life. A special thanks to Isabella, the eldest of my grands. She helped me choose my book cover and inspired the name of my female protagonist Issa, which is the nickname I called my baby girl from early childhood.

Thank you to Lifeline Fellowship, my faith community, for your prayers and excitement for this project, you kept me revved up when my tank was empty. Thank you to Brian Dixon, T.J. Ray, Krissy Nelson, and the hope*books staff for coming alongside me in this publishing journey and believing in me and my story. Thank you, Amber, for your editorial prowess. A special thank you to my cohort of fellow authors for friendships forged, tears cried, for grace, and prayers prayed.

Finally, a special thank you to my beta readers Rebecca, Elaine, and Leigh Ann whose keen eyes and attention to detail were invaluable. A heartfelt thank you to my endorsers Naomi, Krissy, Kim, and Dr. Gwen for your time, and expertise, and for trailblazing the way for others. Thank you to Mesu and Carol for your invaluable insights and the gift of your time. And, to my launch team for all your enthusiasm and support. You are each a God-send.

# Author's Note

Thank you for reading *Petra: An Unbroken Legacy*. The greatest gift an author can receive is the gift of a review. It would warm my heart to hear about your reading experience. Your review will help me continue to bring faith in Jesus to the pages of every book I write. You, the reader, can globalize a work of faith through your reviews. They can help an author reach people worldwide, igniting faith in Jesus, and bringing words of hope alive. If you enjoyed this book, write a review at online retailers and websites, on social media, and recommend it to family and friends.

For more information about my work and my ministry, please visit my website: www.drlisadorsey.com

For the latest news about new releases, cover reveals, and more, please sign up for my newsletter:

info@drlisadorsey.com

Many blessings,

Lisa L. Dorsey

# About the Author

Dr. Lisa Dorsey has a combined experience of fifty years in business and ministry. Her expertise includes health care and business administration, consulting, writing, speaking, educating, and mentoring. She currently resides in Southern California with her husband, Charles, and has four adult children, one daughter-in-law, and four adorable grandchildren.

Dr. Lisa's faith in God was established in her early teenage years, and she continues to passionately serve the Lord today. Growing up, she developed a passion for reading, writing, theater, and the arts. She now combines her expertise, experience, and passions to write compelling stories that reveal the saving grace of Jesus Christ, offer hope in God, and a spiritual legacy grounded in God's steadfast Love, timeless Word, and infinite Wisdom. She loves writing Biblical Fiction because she believes it speaks to the deepest parts of the human soul and offers hope in God.

Dr. Lisa maintains her license as a registered nurse and has an earned doctorate in Public Administration and a Ph.D. in Theology. She currently serves in ministry as a pastor alongside her husband Charles and has done so for over twenty years.

Milton Keynes UK
Ingram Content Group UK Ltd.
UKHW020314070624
443692UK00003B/54